Index

Introduction

Our intention in writing this Manual is to provide the reader with all the data and information required to maintain and repair the vehicle. However, it must be realised that special equipment and skills are required in some cases to carry out the work detailed in the text, and we do not recommend that such work be attempted unless the reader possesses the necessary skill and equipment. It would be better to have an **AUTHORISED DEALER** to carry out the work using the special tools and equipment available to his trained staff. He will also be in possession of the genuine spare parts which may be needed for replacement.

The information in the Manual has been checked against that provided by the vehicle manufacturer, and any peculiarities have been mentioned if they depart from usual workshop practice. We have tried to cover the wide range of models on the market for this particular car and cross-references can normally, be made. Where in some instances this cannot be done, references are included in the Technical Data sections.

A fault finding and trouble shooting chart has been inserted at the end of the Manual to enable the reader to pin point faults and so save time. As it is impossible to include every malfunction, only the more usual ones have been included.

A composite conversion table has also been included at the end of the Manual and we would recommend that wherever possible, for greater accuracy, the metric system-units are used.

Brevity and simplicity have been our aim in compiling this Manual, relying on the numerous illustrations and clear text to inform and instruct the reader. At the request of the many users of our Manuals, we have slanted the book towards repair and overhaul rather than maintenance.

Although every care has been taken to ensure that the information and data are correct we cannot accept any liability for inaccuracies or omissions, or for damage or malfunctions arising from the use of this book, no matter how caused.

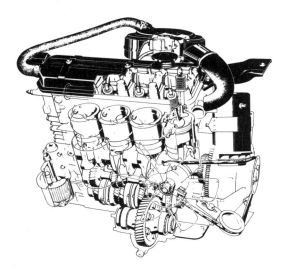

Cross-section through 204 engine

Exterior view of 304 engine

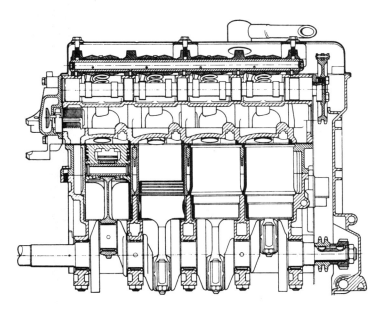

Longitudinal section through engine

Exploded detail of oil filter

GENERAL DETAILS OF ENGINE

12

P84675

WORKSHOP MANUAL

COMPILED AND WRITTEN
BY

intereurope

PUBLISHED BY
INTEREUROPE LIMITED
NICHOLSON HOUSE
MAIDENHEAD
BERKSHIRE
ENGLAND

SBN 0-85666-060-4

Technical Data

	204 Saloon	204 Estate	304 Saloon	304 Coupe	304 Estate
Engine type		4 - cyl. 1,130 c.c. O.H.C.		4 - cyl. 1,288 c.c. O.H.C.	
Overall length	3,990 (157.09)	3,970 (156.3)	4,140 (162.99)	3,740 (147.24)	3,990 (157.09)
Overall width		1,570 (61.81)		1,570 (61.81)	
Overall height		1,400 (55.12)	1,410 (55.51)	1,320 (51.97)	1,430 (56.30)
Turning circle dia. metres (feet)		10.3 (33.8)	10.5 (34.4)	9.4 (30.8)	10.5 (34.4)
Track - front		1,320 (51.97)		1,320 (51.97)	
- rear		1,290 (50.79)		1,290 (50.79)	
Wheelbase		2,595 (102.7)	2,590 (101.97)	2,305 (90.75)	2,590 (101.97)
Ground clearance		140 (5.51)		120 (4.72)	
Weight (dry)	835 (1,841)	890 (1,962)	870 (1,918)	875 (1,929)	905 (1,996)
Fuel tank capacity	9.2 (11.1)			9.2 (11.1)	
Fuel consumption	30.7 (25.6)	30.0 (25.0)	28.0 (23.3)		27.8 (23.1)
Maximum speed		140 (87)	150 (93)	152 (94)	150 (93)

NOTE: mm. (inches), kg. (lbs.), km./h. (m.p.h.), cubic metres (cu.feet), imp. galls (U.S. galls.), imp. gal. (U.S. gal.).

Engine

GENERAL

There are two types of XK engine fitted to the 204 vehicles, namely, engines with a one piece cylinder block, and engines with a cylinder block comprising two pieces, which are machined after assembly. It is important to ascertain the type of engine fitted to the vehicle since the two types of cylinder head gaskets are not interchangeable. Two piece cylinder blocks are fitted to engines up to serial number J44016G, and one piece blocks are fitted to engines with serial numbers from J44017G. Vehicles manufactured in a first pre-series, and having serial numbers from 6000001 to 6000400, and from 6002921 to 6003175, have a one piece cylinder block which is special having the cylinder head centered with two pins as on the engines with a two piece block. The cylinder head gasket for this special is a CURTY part number 0203.28 and cylinder liner protrusion should be between (0.0018 and 0.0047 in.) 0.045 and 0.12mm. The cylinder head gasket for the standard one piece block is a REINZ part number 0203.34, and the cylinder liner protrusion should be between (0.0075 and 0.0102 in.) 0.19 and 0.26 mm.

ENGINE - Removal

Place vehicle over a pit or on a car lift. Remove the bonnet, and drain the cooling system. Disconnect and remove the battery. Disconnect the hoses from the radiator, heater hoses from the engine, carburettor and inlet manifold heater hoses, and the fan thermo-switch. Remove the radiator. Disconnect the generator and regulator earth lead, starter motor, thermo-switch on cylinder head, distributor and oil pressure switch. Unclip HT lead support. Remove air filter cover, filter element and its support. Disconnect accelerator and choke controls. Remove clutch slave cylinder without disconnecting it, and place it on clutch master cylinder. Disconnect gear change links from mechanism cover, and speedometer drive cable. On engines with a three point mounting, remove the left and right engine tie links.

Drain oil from engine. Separate exhaust pipe from manifold, and remove bolt securing pipe collar to gearbox. Remove anti-roll bar link nuts. Disconnect arms of triangles, and recover cups and rubber bushes. Raise front of vehicle by upper frame crossmember special hoist bar 8.1501 (see Fig.A.2.). Chock vehicle under lower frame crossmember. Remove pivots from the two front triangles. Disengage drive shafts by spreading left and right suspension units until the drive shafts disengage, and then securing the shafts in position using special clamp 8.0407 pressed against the engine cradle (see Fig.A.3.) Avoid damaging the drive shaft oil seal bearing faces. On engines with four point mounting, remove the two nuts securing the lower left and right hand rubber blocks, and the bolts securing the steering box to the cradle.

Hook special hoist arm 8.0121, secured to a block and tackle, onto the engine (see Fig.A.4.). On engine with three point mounting, raise the engine slightly to release the engine blocks. Remove engine block securing nuts. Raise the engine, using the block and tackle, and rocking it slightly to clear the steering box.

NOTE: *If the vehicle is moved with the engine removed, it must be supported on a trolley jack to avoid damaging the drive shafts.*

ENGINE - Refitting

Check, and if necessary replace, drive shaft oil seals in differential housing. Smear oil seal lips with tallow or grease. Reposition engine on its support in vehicle.

Engines with three point mounting (204): Tighten nuts securing the three rubber blocks to the supports to 3.5 mkg. (26 lb.ft.). torque, while holding the engine slightly raised using the block and tackle. Slacken the hoist, and remove hoist bar. Refit left and right hand tie links, and fit new NYLOC nuts tightened to 1.75 mkg. (13 lb.ft.) torque.

Engines with four point mounting (204-304): Slacken hoist, and remove hoist bar. Fit upper rubber block securing nuts, and tighten to 3.25 mkg. (23.5 lb.ft.) torque. Fit lower rubber block securing nuts, and tighten to 3.25 mkg. (23.5 lb.ft.) torque after fitting heat dissipation plate between block and engine on right hand side. Fit and tighten steering box securing bolts to 3 mkg. (22 lb.ft.) torque.

All engines: Remove special clamps 8.0407 holding drive shafts in position, and clean oil seal bearing faces. Insert drive shafts into differential. Position triangles for assembly, fitting new VULKOLLAN washers between the rubber bushes and the triangle yokes. Tallow and insert the pivots. Fit new NYLOC nuts but do not tighten. Reconnect anti-roll bar links to the triangle fitting the cups and spacer (Ref. a.Fig.A.5.) as shown. Do not tighten the nuts. Manoeuvre the vehicle to re-establish its correct riding position. Tighten the NYLOC nuts on triangle pivots to 3.5 mkg. (25 lb.ft.) torque, and anti-roll bar link nuts to 1.75 mkg. (13 lb.ft.) torque. Refit components and reconnect hoses and unions in reverse order of removal. Refill cooling system. Refill engine with 4 litres (7 pints) of approved Motor Oil 20W/30/40. Refit bonnet and reset clock.

GENERATOR REMOVAL AND REFITTING

Remove belt tensioner and belt. Disconnect generator leads. Unbolt generator attaching collar, and remove generator. To refit generator, insert generator support centering dowel into corresponding hole in generator body, and tighten collar nut to 1 mkg. (7.25 lb.ft.). torque max. Refit belt and tensioner. Tighten belt by 2 to 2.5% for a dynamo or 1.5 to 2% for an alternator, and reconnect leads.

THERMOSTAT - Removal

Drain radiator and disconnect battery. Remove generator. Remove the five generator support attachment screws. Remove generator support and thermostat. The thermostat is equipped with a gasket, located around the valve seat, which should be replaced at each dismantling.

THERMOSTAT - Refitting

Thoroughly clean generator support to cylinder head mating surfaces. Position the new gasket on the thermostat using tallow, and insert thermostat into generator support.

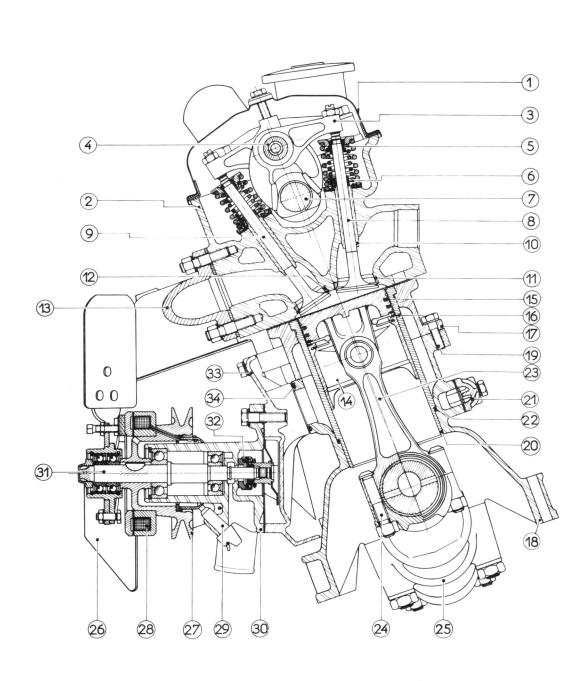

Fig.A.1. Cross-section of engine.

Fig.A.2. Raising vehicle using special hoist bar.

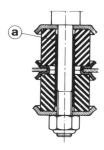

Fig.A.5. Spacer and cup positions when reconnecting anti-roll bar links to suspension triangles.

Fig.A.3. Securing drive shafts after disengagement.

Fig.A.6. Engine with dynamo removed.

Fig.A.4. Removing engine from vehicle.

Fig.A.7. Removing generator support to reveal thermostat.

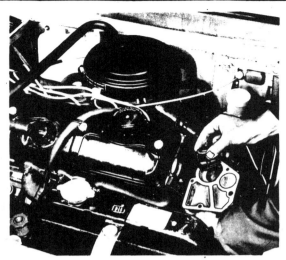

Fig.A.8. Replacing thermostat.

Fig.A.11. Withdrawing clutch.

Fig.A.9. Power unit assembly.

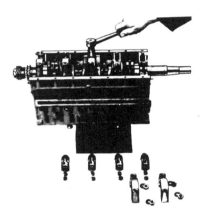

Fig.A.14. Removing big end and main bearings.

Fig.A.12. Unloading chain tensioner.

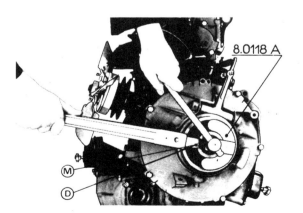

Fig.A.10. Unlocking crankshaft pulley bolt

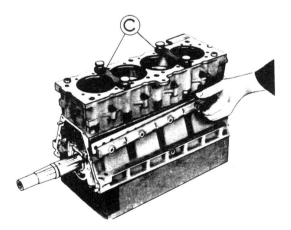

Fig.A13. Retaining cylinder liners.

Fit the generator support on cylinder head using a new seal smeared with Hermetic compound. Tighten screws 1.25 - 1.75 mkg. (9 - 12 lb.ft.) torque. Re-install generator, and tighten collar to 1 mkg. (7.25 lb.ft.) torque max. Reconnect leads to generator. Refit belt and belt tensioner, and tighten as appro - priate. Reconnect left-hand tie-link using a new NYLOC nut. Refit radiator upper hose, and refill radiator. Reconnect battery.

ENGINE - Dismantling

Remove power unit from vehicle, and clean thoroughly. Place engine on support base 8.0306Z or similar. Remove carburettor/inlet manifold assembly, timing gear housing, fan belt tensioner, and belt, generator, and starter motor. Unlock crankshaft pulley bolt by holding pulley with special jaw 8.0118A and unlocking bolt using 38mm. bolt spanner head 8.0118D or 24mm. bolt spanner head 8.0118M and the Facom extension SJ 214 or similar (see Fig.A.10.). Remove crankshaft pulley, thrust bearing spring (if fitted), clutch cover, and thrust bearing. Withdraw clutch using special puller 8.0203A for the 180DP clutch, or special puller 8.0206A for 200DE or TS190 clutches (See Fig.A.11.). Remove clutch housing. Withdraw drive pinion and thrust washer on the No.1. main bearing. Remove water pump and separate gearbox from engine. Place engine on special support base 8.0122 or similar. Unload chain tensioner as follows: Remove plug from body, and engage a 3mm. Allen key, through the hole, in the end of the plunger. Turn key clockwise to free pad from action of spring (See Fig.A.12.).

Unlock and remove bolts securing chain wheel to camshaft. Remove chain wheel and timing chain. Remove chain tensioner and filter. Remove cylinder head, and retain cylinder liners with special clamps 8.0118C (See Fig.A.13.). Remove oil passage cover plate and gasket.

Turn cylinder block over, and remove big end and main bearing cap nuts. Remove bearing caps and shells, and place them in a tray in the order of removal. Withdraw the crankshaft. Recover the two half thrust washers and main bearing shells. Place block sideways on support (See Fig.A.15), and remove piston connecting rod assemblies. Refit big end caps on corresponding connecting rods. Remove liner retaining clamps. Turn block over on its support, and remove cylinder liners using special extractor plate 8.0118B if necessary (See Fig.A.16.). Thoroughly clean the block and all removed parts.

Important: Since machining of 204 engines with two piece blocks is effected after assembly of parts (a) and (b) (see Fig.A.16.) the ten bolts (ref: 1 Fig.A.16.) must never be slackened.

Clamp crankshaft in a vice equipped with soft jaws. Punch sludge trap plugs using special key 0.0131 and a hammer (see Fig.A.17), and remove plugs. Slacken the nut, and remove oil pump pinion and timing chain wheel.

ENGINE - Reassembly

The reassembly of the engine should be performed in a dust free workshop. The parts to be reassembled should be laid out on a tray close to the work bench, after having been cleaned and dried. All parts which show signs of damage or wear should be replaced. All replacement parts should be degreased and dried. All parts should be lightly oiled during assembly.

Fit the four sludge trap plugs to the crankshaft, and tighten them to 4 mkg. (29 lb.ft.) torque. (See Fig.A.18.) Lock them with a punch mark. Fit a new locking washer, and tighten nut to 9 mkg. (65 lb.ft.) torque. Lock the nut. Position the main bearing half shells in the cylinder block. Oil the bearing faces, and place the crankshaft in position. Fit the half thrust washers on both sides of No.2 bearing (See Fig.A.19.), bronze face outwards. Fit bearing caps with the mark 'DIST' facing the timing end. The bearing caps are numbered 1 to 5 starting from the clutch end. Fit new flat washers, and tighten nuts to 5.25 mkg. (38 lb.ft.) torque. Rotate crankshaft in direction of normal rotation to ensure that no hard spots are present.

Check the end float in crankshaft using a dial indicator (See Fig.A.20) attached to block with the feeler in contact with the first crankshaft counterweight. By moving the crankshaft longitudinally, the amount of play will be shown on the dial indicator. The end float should be between 0.7 - 0.23mm. (0.0027 - 0.009 in.). The end float is adjusted by using half thrust washers of different thicknesses. The thicknesses available are 2.30mm. (part No. 0118.40), 2.40mm. (part no. 0118.41), 2.45mm. (part no. 0118.42), and 2.50mm. (part no. 0118.27). Fit No.2 bearing cap and proceed with final assembly.

When replacing liners/pistons, the cylinder liner protrusion should be set as described later in the section titled 'Setting Cylinder Protrusion'. Remove gudgeon pins from the new pistons, oil them and assemble the piston-connecting rods. Bear in mind the position of the rods in relation to the crankshaft, and the position of the liners in the block, determined when obtaining the protrusion, in order not to alter the piston-liner pairing. Check relative piston-connecting rod position. When looking at the connecting rod with the oil thrower on the right, the reference 'DIST' and arrow should be facing you. Never alter the gudgeon pin-piston pairing. Place gudgeon pin retaining snap rings in their grooves in the pistons. Fit oil scraper ring, and position the gap in the expander (Ref.1 Fig.A21) in line with the gudgeon pin. Fit the two flexible rings, and position gaps (Ref.2 and 3) offset by 20 - 50mm (0.75 - 2in.) in relation to the gap in expander. Fit the compression rings, and position gaps in a 'Y' in relation to the 'Perfect Circle' scraper ring gap. Oil pistons and piston rings.

Clamp pistons connecting rod assembly in a vice fitted with soft jaws, with reference on piston (arrow) facing you. Fit a piston ring clamp over piston, with the key facing down-wards. For engines with one piece cylinder blocks, remove cylinder liners, taking care not to tear the paper gaskets, and mark their relative position in the block (1-2-3-4). Oil bore of liner, and place chamfered edge lower part of liner on piston (see Fig.A.22.). Position liner reference on opposite side of rod to the oil thrower (to the left when facing the arrow) and push liner down over piston without turning it. Remove assembly from vice. Remove piston ring clamp, and place piston at mid stroke. Remove big-end cap. For two piece blocks, fit a new rubber seal on liners.

Insert liner-piston assemblies in block respecting the order of connecting rods (1-2-3-4), references on liners which should be oil passage side, and piston references (the arrow should face timing end). While fitting liner-piston assemblies, position big ends on crankshaft journals. Lock cylinder liners with special retaining clamps 8.0118C. Assemble each big end bearing, taking care not to scratch the shells. The casting marks on the rods and caps (a letter followed by a figure), should be on the same side. Use new bolts and nuts tightened to 4mkg. (29 lb.ft.) torque. *NOTE:* Do not fit washers between the big end caps and nuts.

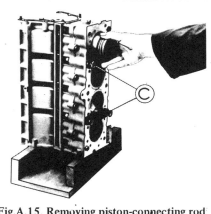

Fig.A.15. Removing piston-connecting rod assemblies.

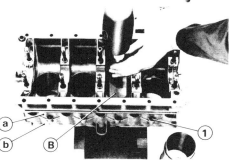

Fig.A.16. Removing cylinder liners.

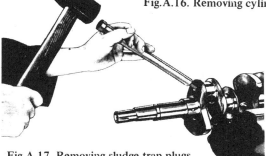

Fig.A.17. Removing sludge trap plugs.

Fig.A.18. Fitting sludge trap plugs.

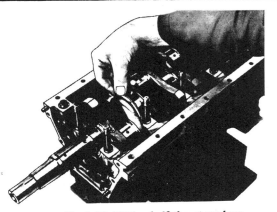

Fig.A.19. Fitting half thrust washers.

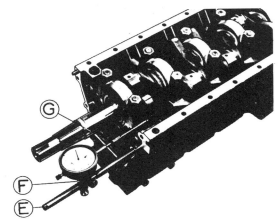

Fig.A.20. Measuring crankshaft end float.

Fig.A.21. Piston connecting rod assembly.

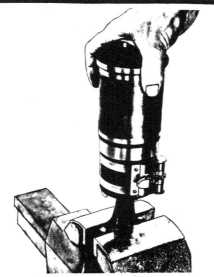

Fig.A.22. Fitting cylinder liner over piston.

Fig.A.25. Fitting drive pinion outer thrust bearing.

Fig.A.23. Fitting liner-piston assemblies into block.

Fig.A.26. Checking drive pinion end float.

Fig.A.27. Clutch housing, oil seal, shims and thrust washer.

Fig.A.24. Fitting thrust washer.

Fig.A.28. Assembling engine and gearbox.

Fig.A.29. Inserting drive pinion inner thrust washer.

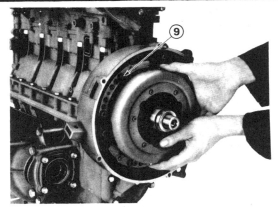

Fig.A.32 Mounting 180 DP clutch on crankshaft.

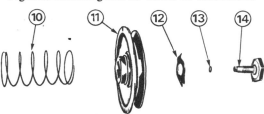

Fig.A.33. Crankshaft pulley and parts.

Fig.A.30. Replacing clutch housing.

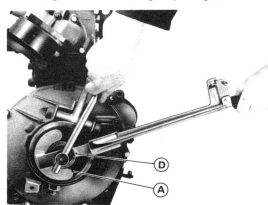

Fig.A.34. Tightening crankshaft pulley securing bolt.

Fig.A.31. Spraying Polygon with Molykote 321.

Fig.A.35. Crankshaft reference mark 200 DE and TS 190 clutches.

Place engine in its normal position on the support, and refit cylinder head (see separate section). Set the timing (see separate section). Place engine on the support on its side with No.1 bearing facing upwards. Position thrust washer (ref:4 Fig. A24.) on No.1 bearing. Place a new clutch housing gasket on the block. Place drive pinion outer thrust bearing (ref. 5, Fig.A.25) in clutch housing. Place pinion on outer thrust bearing in clutch housing. Press thrust washer against housing using drive pinion. Turn clutch housing over and fit it on cylinder block, ensuring that the thrust washer (ref.5) does not become disengaged. Tighten securing bolts to 1.25 mkg. (9 lb.ft.) torque to compress gasket.

Fit special rod 8.0118E, equipped with support 8.0118F on which the dial indicator and extension feeler 8.0118G are fitted, to avoid contact between dial indicator and crankshaft end (see Fig.A.26). Place feeler on edge of drive pinion, and check amount of end float in pinion. Determine the shims (ref.6, Fig.A.27) to be used to obtain an ideal end play of approximately 0.33mm. The end play extremes of tolerance are 0.25mm. and 0.40 mm. Shims are available in thicknesses of 0.07, 0.15, 0.20, 0.25 and 0.50 mm. Remove dial indicator and support. Remove clutch housing and gasket. Fit oil seal (ref. 7 Fig.A.27) in clutch using a drift. Fit shims (ref.6) between housing and thrust washer (ref.5). Lock with three centre punch marks while holding firmly in place. Retain drive pinion and inner thrust washer for later assembly.

Assemble gearbox and engine after fitting new 'O'-ring (ref.8 Fig.A.28) on the oil passage on clutch side of engine, and coating mating surfaces with 'Perfect Seal'. Using a drift insert oil seal in drive pinion, with circular groove against drift. Place oiled inner thrust washer (ref.4. Fig.A.29) against No.1 bearing. Insert oil seal protector 8.0203C for 180DP clutch, or 8.0206C for 200DE and TS190 clutches in drive pinion oil seal. Engage pinion on crankshaft and hold it firmly against thrust washer (ref.4). Remove protector. Fit special protector cone 8.0203E or 8.0206E as applicable (slightly oiled) over drive pinion. Fit clutch housing gasket, clutch housing taking care not to move drive pinion. Tighten securing bolts to 1.25 mkg. (9 lb.ft.) torque. Remove protector cone. Perform final check of drive pinion end play.

Prior to fitting the clutch, thoroughly clean the Polygon. Using a 'Molykote' 321 aerosol spray, apply a thin coat over the whole surface of the Polygon (see Fig.A.31) and the splined sleeve of the drive pinion. Take great care not to spray the drive pinion oil seal bearing surface.

180DP CLUTCH

Mount clutch on crankshaft, moving it around slightly to engage clutch plate on drive pinion, and tighten bolts (ref. 9. Fig.A.32.) to 1 mkg. (7.25 lb.ft.) torque when clutch plate is in position. *Note:* To enable the clutch plate to be centered, the six bolts (ref.9) should not be tightened before fitting. Lubricate clutch hub extractor groove with Multipurpose Grease. Fit clutch cover, taking care to position plain face of fork thrust washer on bearing side, and tighten cover bolts to 1 mkg. (7.25 lb.ft.) torque. Fit thrust bearing spring (ref. 10, Fig.A.33), crankshaft pulley (ref.11) and securing bolt. (ref.14) with new tab washer (ref.12) and 0-ring (ref.13). Tighten securing bolt to 6.5 mkg. (47 lb.ft.) torque using spanner head 8.0118D and torque wrench, while holding pulley with special jaw 8.0118A (see Fig.A.34). Bend tab washer up round bolt head.

200DE or TS190 CLUTCHES

Check that crankshaft reference mark (ref.15, Fig. A35) is facing top of engine. This reference mark indicates T.D.C. of pistons 1 and 4 when in this position. To enable clutch plate to be centered, the six bolts of the mechanism must be slackened off. Position clutch on crankshaft with notch in cover plate (ref.16, Fig.A.36) more or less opposite hole (ref.17) in clutch housing, Move clutch around slightly to engage clutch plate on drive pinion. Fit crankshaft pulley temporarily, and using spanner 8.0118M tighten securing bolt to fully engage clutch on crankshaft. Tighten the six mechanism bolts to 2.5 mkg. (18 lb.ft.) torque. Remove crankshaft pulley. Grease clutch hub extractor groove with Multi-purpose Grease. Fit ball thrust bearing. Fit clutch cover, taking care to position the plain face of the fork thrust washer on the thrust bearing side. Fit the thrust bearing spring (if fitted.). To fit a thrust bearing spring where it was not previously fitted necessitates replacing the thrust bearing and crankshaft pulley. Tighten clutch housing bolts to 1 mkg. (7.25 lb.ft.) torque. Fit crankshaft pulley, ensuring that it engages on drive pin solidly with the clutch hub. Fit the securing bolt, new tab washer, and tighten to 6.5 mkg. (47 lb.ft.) using spanner head 8.0118M and torque wrench, while holding pulley with special jaw 8.0118A (see fig.A.37). Bend tab washer up round bolt head.

After fitting clutch, fit clutch slave cylinder and clutch fork return spring. Adjust clutch fork free play by slackening lock nut (see Fig.A.38) and unscrew adjuster until fork touches. Screw adjuster two and a half turns to obtain a gap of 2mm. (0.079in.) at the thrust bearing, and tighten lock nut. *Note:* A gap at the push rod obtained by two and a half turns of the adjuster (between slave cylinder push rod and piston) must correspond to a free travel of 30-35mm. (1.181 - 1.380 in). at the pedal. If this is not so the clutch system needs bleeding. Refit oil passage cover after fitting new gasket. Replace copper washers under bolts and tighten bolts to 1.25 mkg. (9 lb.ft.) torque. Fit timing gear housing, distributor, generator, starter motor, water pump 'O'-ring (ref. 18, Fig.A.39), water pump, carburettor, and inlet manifold, and accessories. Fill engine with 7 pints (4 litres) of Engine oil 20W/30/40. Never fit fan belt by passing it over the pulleys, but proceed in the manner described. Fit belt on crankshaft, generator and water pump pulleys, taking care not to twist it through more than 90°. Engage tensioner pulley on fan belt, and secure tensioner to cylinder block. Using the adjuster, tension the fan belt. Make two reference marks on the fan belt 100mm. apart when slack (ref.A. Fig.A.40). When tensioned the two marks should be 102 to 102.5mm. apart for an engine fitted with a dynamo, and 101.5 to 102 mm. apart for an engine fitted with an alternator. Tighten tensioner pivot nut to 4 mkg. (29 lb.ft.) torque and the two support bolts to 1.75 mkg. (13 lb.ft.) torque. Tighten tensioner pulley nut.

CYLINDER HEAD - Removal with engine in vehicle

To prevent distortion of the cylinder head, remove it only when the engine is cold. Remove the jack (on 204 vehicles with the jack secured to the front frame and 304 vehicles). Drain oil sump and cooling system. Remove battery, and unclip starter motor supply cable. Remove air filter and rocker cover. Disconnect earth lead from cylinder head, HT leads and remove cable harness with distributor cover. Disconnect the coil and remove it. Disconnect the generator, thermoswitch and oil pressure switch. Disconnect the fuel lines from the pump.

Fig.A.36. Clutch plate in position.

Fig.A.39. Water pump 'O'-ring.

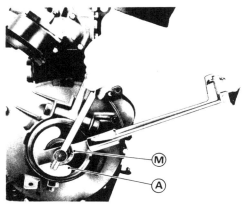

Fig.A.37. Tightening crankshaft pulley securing bolt.

Fig.A.40. Fan belt fitting.

Fig.A.38. Clutch fork adjuster.

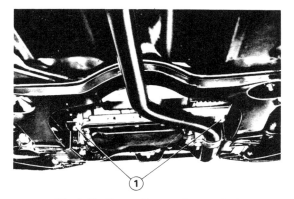

Fig.A.41. Supporting gearbox against frame.

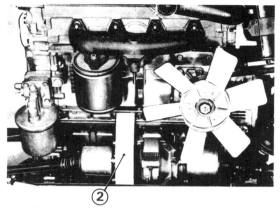

Fig.A.42. Supporting cylinder block against frame.

Fig.A.43. Retaining cylinder liners.

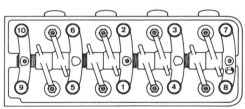

FRONT

Fig.A.44. Cylinder head bolt tightening sequence.

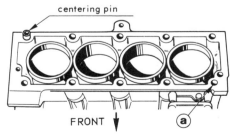

centering pin

FRONT

Fig.A.45. View on one-piece cylinder block (except 1st pre-series).

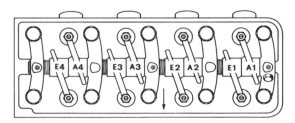

Front

Fig.A.46. Valve rocker identities.

Fig.A.47. Fitting adjustment plate calliper, and tensioner.

Fig.A.48. Dial indicator in position for measuring liner protrusion.

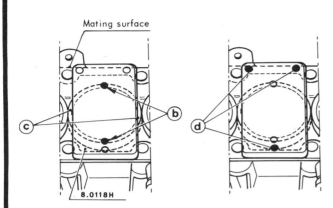

Fig.A.49. Details of measurements to be performed.

Fig.A.50. Liner fitted with gasket.

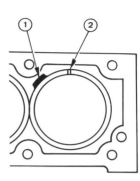

Fig.A.51. Position of gasket tab.

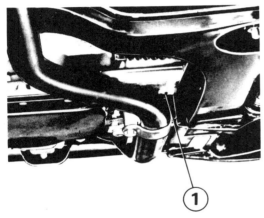

Fig.A.52. Supporting gearbox on four point mounted engines.

Fig.A.53. Removing timing gear housing.

Fig.A.54. Engine with timing gear housing removed.

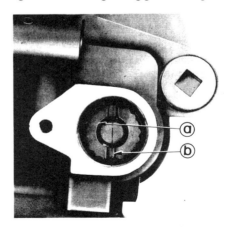

Fig.A.55. Positioning distributor drive shaft.

Disconnect the heater hoses from the cylinder head, carburettor and inlet manifold. Disconnect the choke and accélérator cables. Separate the upper radiator mounting lug, and remove the top hose. Separate the exhaust pipe, and remove damper. *Three point engines (204):* Disconnect right and left hand tie-links from their mountings on the cylinder head and timing cover.

Four point mounted engines (204 - 304): Place two steel blocks (ref. 1. Fig.A.41) measuring 10 x 25 x 75mm. (0.4 x 1 x 3 in.) between the gearbox and the frame. Position a wooden block (ref.2 Fig. A.42) 220 x 40 x 15mm. (8.66 x 1.57 x 0.59 in.) between the cylinder block and frame. Remove the two upper flexible blocks and the upper hand intermediate support.

All engines: Remove carburettor/inlet manifold assembly and generator. Clean parts close to mating surfaces, and remove timing gear housing. Unload chain tensioner as described previously. Remove camshaft sprocket and timing chain. Remove cylinder head bolts, and recover nuts. Hold the two front right hand nuts in position to prevent them falling down behind the water pump. Remove rocker shaft, cylinder head and head gasket. *Important:* On one piece cylinder block engines except the first pre-series engines, it is essential that the cylinder head be pivoted on the centring pin on the timing side without raising it, in order not to free the cylinder liners. Secure cylinder liners using retaining clamps 8.0118C (see Fig.A.43.).

CYLINDER HEAD - Refitting with engine in vehicle

Position reference on crankshaft sprocket horizontally to avoid contact between valves and piston crowns. Ensure that mating faces of cylinder block and head are perfectly clean. Remove liner retaining clamps. *Two piece cylinder blocks (204):* Coat both faces of gasket part No. 0203.30 with boiled linseed oil, and place it on cylinder block with tab on front right hand side. Fit sparking plugs into cylinder head, and tighten to 2.5 mkg. (18 lb.ft.). torque. Place cylinder head on block, making sure that the centring pins engage in the head. Tallow, and fit cylinder head bolts. Pre-tighten to 4 mkg. (29 lb.ft.) torque following the tightening order given in Fig.A.44. Finally tighten to 6 mkg. (43.5 lb.ft.) torque again following the tightening sequence.

One piece cylinder blocks (204-304) except first pre-series 204: Place dial indicator support rod 8.0118E fitted with guide sleeve 8.0118N in hole (ref'a' Fig.A45) . Place REINZ head gasket part No. 0203.34 dry on cylinder block. Fit spark plugs into cylinder head and tighten to 2.5 mkg. (18 lb.ft.). torque. Fit rocker shaft, engaging the centring pins in the head, in the end supports.

Fit the timing cover temporarily without gasket, and secure it to block using two bolts to facilitate positioning of head gasket. Place head in position. Tallow head bolts, and fit them. Pre-tighten to 4 mkg. (29 lb.ft.) torque following the tightening order given in Fig. A.44. Remove timing gear cover. Remove guide rod, and fit corresponding head bolt. Finally tighten head bolts to 5.5 mkg. (40 lb.ft.). torque again following the tightening sequence.

One piece cylinder block first pre-series (204): Place CURTY head gasket part No. 0203.28, with a thin film of boiled linseed oil, on the heat rings. Fit spark plugs to cylinder head, and tighten to 2.5 mkg (18 lb.ft.) torque. Fit rocker shaft, engaging centring pins in head, in end supports. Place head in position. Tallow head bolts, and fit them. Pre-tighten to 4 mkg (29 lb.ft.) torque

following the tightening order given in Fig.A44. Finally tighten head bolts to 5.5 mkg (40 lb.ft.) torque again following the tightening sequence.

Set the timing and fit timing gear cover.

Three point mounted engines (204): Refit left and right hand tie-links using new Nyloc nuts tightened to 1.75 mkg. (13 lb.ft.) torque.

Four point mounted engines (204-304): Refit upper left hand intermediate support and tighten to 2mkg. (14.5 lb.ft.) torque on generator support and 3.25 mkg. (23.5 lb.ft.) torque on the cylinder head and block. Refit the two upper flexible blocks and tighten flexible block support on wing valance reinforcement to 2 mkg. (14.5 lb.ft.) torque and flexible block nut to 3.25 mkg. (23.5 lb.ft.) torque. Remove the steel blocks and the wooden block. *All engines:* Adjust the valve clearances (refer to Fig.A.46).

Inlet	0.10 mm. (0.004 in.)
Exhaust	0.25 mm. (0.009 in.)

With E1 valve fully open adjust rockers I3, E4
With E3 valve fully open adjust rockers I4, E2
With E4 valve fully open adjust rockers I2, E1
With E2 valve fully open adjust rockers I1, E3

Refit rocker cover and generator. Re-connect all electrical leads. Tension fan belt as previously described. Tighten tensioner pivot nut to 4 mkg. (29 lb.ft.) torque. Tighten tensioner puller nut. Refit and re-connect battery. Refit and set the distributor. The initial advance point of 12⁰ is obtained on engines fitted with the 180DP clutch when the 8mm. diameter hole in the clutch cover is in line with the notch on the crankshaft pulley, and on engines fitted with the 200DE or TS190 clutch when the notch in the clutch plate is in line with the 8mm. diameter hole in the clutch housing. The engine may be turned over using special jaw 8.0118A. Refit carburettor/inlet assembly. Re-connect accelerator and choke cables. Refit all water hoses and remaining parts in reverse order of removal. Install jack on front frame of 204 vehicles where applicable and on 304 vehicles. Reset clock. Refill engine with approved engine oil 20W/30/40. Refill cooling system.

SETTING CYLINDER LINER PROTRUSION

This procedure applies only to one piece cylinder blocks. The liner protrusion must be as follows: 204 engine 1st pre-series between 0.045 and 0.12 mm. (0.0018 and 0.0047 in.) from 2nd pre-series onwards between 0.19 and 0.26mm. (0.0075 and 0.0102 in.) 304 engine from beginning of series: between 0.19 and 0.26mm. (0.0075 and 0.0102 in.)

Originally the liner is always below the mating face of the cylinder block 1st pre-series. Always above the mating face of the cylinder block 2nd pre-series onwards.

The protrusion is ensured by paper gaskets inserted between the liner lower collar and the shoulder in the cylinder block. The setting of the liner protrusion should be performed on all four liners to obtain a protrusion value in the accepted mean tolerance: 204 1st pre-series 0.08 mm. (0.0031 in.) 204, 2nd pre-series onwards 0.21mm. (0.0083 in.) and 304, 0.21mm. (0.0033 in.).

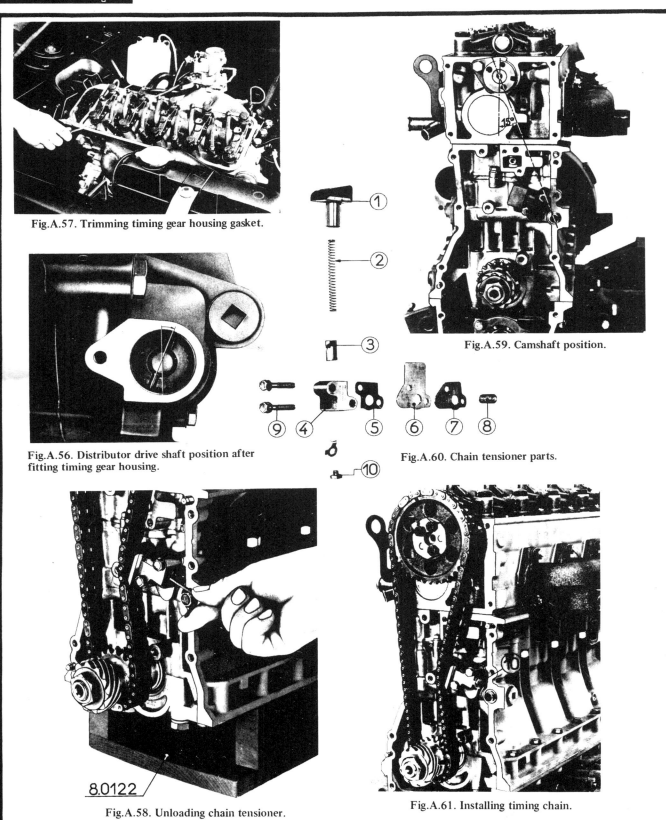

Fig.A.57. Trimming timing gear housing gasket.

Fig.A.59. Camshaft position.

Fig.A.56. Distributor drive shaft position after fitting timing gear housing.

Fig.A.60. Chain tensioner parts.

8.0122

Fig.A.58. Unloading chain tensioner.

Fig.A.61. Installing timing chain.

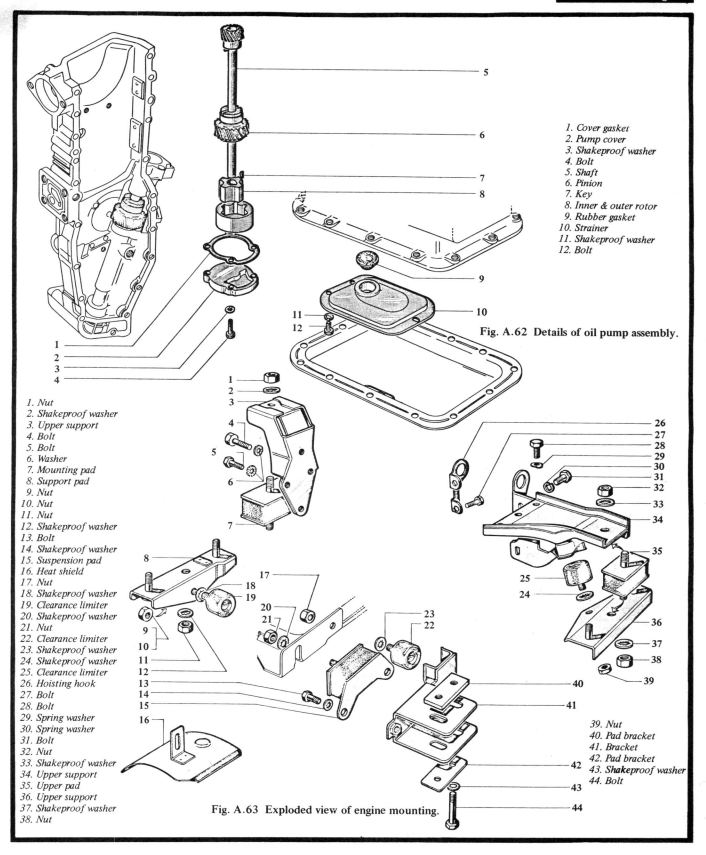

1. Cover gasket
2. Pump cover
3. Shakeproof washer
4. Bolt
5. Shaft
6. Pinion
7. Key
8. Inner & outer rotor
9. Rubber gasket
10. Strainer
11. Shakeproof washer
12. Bolt

Fig. A.62 Details of oil pump assembly.

1. Nut
2. Shakeproof washer
3. Upper support
4. Bolt
5. Bolt
6. Washer
7. Mounting pad
8. Support pad
9. Nut
10. Nut
11. Nut
12. Shakeproof washer
13. Bolt
14. Shakeproof washer
15. Suspension pad
16. Heat shield
17. Nut
18. Shakeproof washer
19. Clearance limiter
20. Shakeproof washer
21. Nut
22. Clearance limiter
23. Shakeproof washer
24. Shakeproof washer
25. Clearance limiter
26. Hoisting hook
27. Bolt
28. Bolt
29. Spring washer
30. Spring washer
31. Bolt
32. Nut
33. Shakeproof washer
34. Upper support
35. Upper pad
36. Upper support
37. Shakeproof washer
38. Nut

39. Nut
40. Pad bracket
41. Bracket
42. Pad bracket
43. Shakeproof washer
44. Bolt

Fig. A.63 Exploded view of engine mounting.

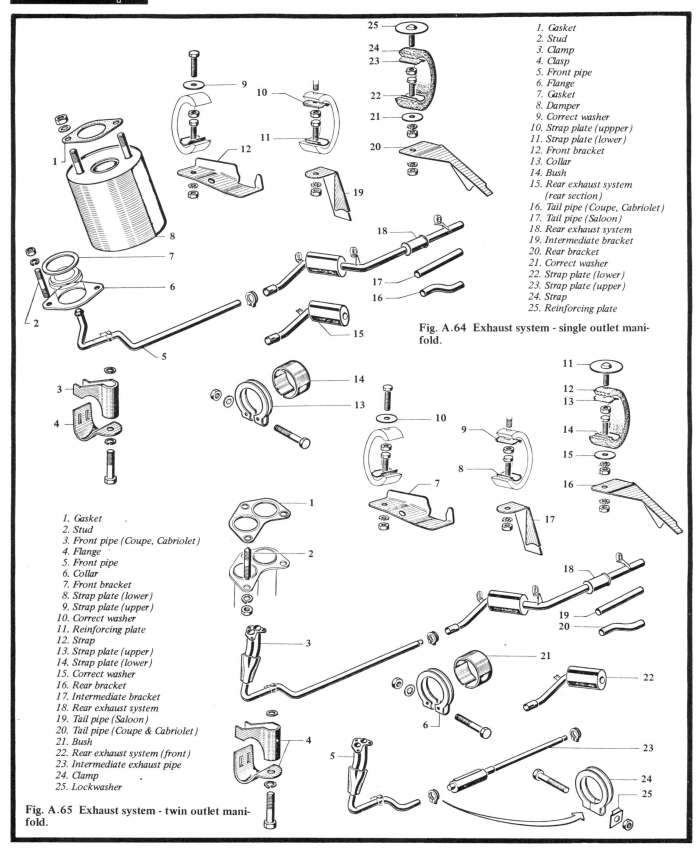

1. Gasket
2. Stud
3. Clamp
4. Clasp
5. Front pipe
6. Flange
7. Gasket
8. Damper
9. Correct washer
10. Strap plate (uppper)
11. Strap plate (lower)
12. Front bracket
13. Collar
14. Bush
15. Rear exhaust system (rear section)
16. Tail pipe (Coupe, Cabriolet)
17. Tail pipe (Saloon)
18. Rear exhaust system
19. Intermediate bracket
20. Rear bracket
21. Correct washer
22. Strap plate (lower)
23. Strap plate (upper)
24. Strap
25. Reinforcing plate

Fig. A.64 Exhaust system - single outlet manifold.

1. Gasket
2. Stud
3. Front pipe (Coupe, Cabriolet)
4. Flange
5. Front pipe
6. Collar
7. Front bracket
8. Strap plate (lower)
9. Strap plate (upper)
10. Correct washer
11. Reinforcing plate
12. Strap
13. Strap plate (upper)
14. Strap plate (lower)
15. Correct washer
16. Rear bracket
17. Intermediate bracket
18. Rear exhaust system
19. Tail pipe (Saloon)
20. Tail pipe (Coupe & Cabriolet)
21. Bush
22. Rear exhaust system (front)
23. Intermediate exhaust pipe
24. Clamp
25. Lockwasher

Fig. A.65 Exhaust system - twin outlet manifold.

In order to ensure accurate setting four gaskets of different thicknesses are available (all thicknesses given are under load). Part No. 0112.07, ref. mark blue 0.065 mm. thick; part No. 0112.08, ref. mark white 0.085 mm, thick; part No. 0112.09, ref. mark red, 0.102mm. thick; part no. 0112.10, ref. mark yellow 0.130mm. thick.

As the protrusion setting has to be precise it is vital to thoroughly clean the lower shoulders in the cylinder block, the lower collars and upper mating face of the cylinder liners, and the cylinder block mating face. Ensure that there are no burrs or scratches on the cylinder block and liner mating faces, the lower and upper bearing faces of adjustment plate 8.0118H and dial indicator support 8.0118 J.

The operations to be performed for each liner are:

1. Measurement of liner position in relation to cylinder block mating face.

2. Calculating gasket thickness to be installed to ensure an average protrusion.

3. Fitting gasket.

4. Checking liner protrusion.

Install liner in cylinder block with reference marks facing oil passage in cylinder block. Install adjustment plate 8.0118H on liner, machined face facing upwards. The plate should be positioned with the long side perpendicular to the engine axis. Engage calliper 8.0118K in two of the cylinder head bolt holes at the lower part of embossing. Pressing against the centring hole of the adjustment plate (end of threaded rod engaged in calliper) screw up adjustment bush of tensioner tool 8.0118L until slot (ref. 'a' Fig.A.47) is blocked by push rod guide. This corresponds to a pressure of 20kg. on the adjustment plate and therefore on the water jacket. This value is imperative for all measuring. Install a dial indicator in the support 8.0118J ensuring that the collar does not protrude from the lower face (see Fig.A.48).

Setting Dial Indicator on Liner

Insert dial indicator feeler in one of the two holes (ref. b Fig.A.49). of plate 8.0118H which line up with the liner. Set dial indicator to zero. Check on the four diametrically opposed points (Ref. b and c) the position of the dial indicator main needle. The difference should not exceed 0.01mm. (0.00039 in). either side of the zero point. If this tolerance is exceeded check that no burrs or foreign bodies exist between the liner and plate, or between plate and dial indicator support.

Measuring Liner Position in Relation to Cylinder Block Mating Face

Insert dial indicator feeler in one of the three holes (Ref.d, Fig.A.49) of plate 8.0118H which line up with the cylinder block mating face. Note the three measurements obtained. The difference between each measurement should not exceed 0.04mm (0.0016 in.). If this tolerance is exceeded, check that no burrs or foreign bodies exist between liner and shoulder, between plate and dial indicator support, or on cylinder block mating surface. Mark liner and corresponding shoulder. The average

dimensions obtained represent the depth value or protrusion value of the liner in relation to the upper mating face of cylinder block.

Calculating Gasket Thickness

1st. Pre-Series: Add 0.08mm. (corresponding to an average protrusion of the liner) to the average figure of the three dimensions obtained.

2nd Pre-Series onward: Deduct 0.21mm. (corresponding to an average protrusion of the water jacket) from the average figure of the three dimensions obtained.

The value obtained is the thickness of gasket to be used. Repeat for each liner. With the four different thicknesses of gasket available it is possible to obtain fairly equal protrusion for all four liners.

Installing Gasket on Liner

In order to facilitate fitting of the gasket on the liner, the inner circumference of the gasket is undulated. Place liner on its upper mating face. After having carefully cleaned the lower collar, install the gasket dry on the liner. Using both hands carefully slide the gasket down the liner until it rests against the lower collar. Insert undulated face of gasket in centring groove, taking care not to tear gasket. Position coloured tab(Ref.1 Fig. A.51) in relation to the marks (Ref.2) on the liner, as shown, to avoid cutting tab with neighbouring liner.

Checking Liner Protrusion

Insert liner in its corresponding housing, ensuring that it is correctly positioned. Re-install adjustment plate 8.0118H and its calliper. 8.0118K. After having tightened the adjustment bush 8.0118L to give a value of 20 kg. pressure on the liner, check the protrusion on the dial indicator. With the dial indicator on cylinder block, set it to zero in order to obtain the protrusion value by direct reading on the liner.

TIMING GEAR HOUSING - Removal

Disconnect and remove battery. Remove air filter. Drain oil sump. Thoroughly clean parts to be removed. Remove rocker cover, ignition coil and distributor. Disconnect oil pressure switch, and fuel lines from the pump.
Three point mounted engines (204): Remove right hand tie-link.
Four point mounted engines (204-304): Place a steel block 10 x 25 x 75mm. (0.4 x 1 x 3in.) (Ref.1, Fig.A.52) between gearbox and lower engine support. Remove upper right hand mounting block.

All engines: Remove timing gear housing bolts and earth cable. Remove timing gear housing (See Fig.A.53).

TIMING GEAR HOUSING - Refitting

Ensure that all mating faces are perfectly clean. Do not use cutting tools or emery cloth for cleaning. Prepare engine so as to obtain correct positioning of distributor drive shaft.

Rotate crankshaft to bring No.4 piston to T.D.C. end of exhaust, beginning of intake stroke. Fit a new gasket (Ref.2. Fig.A.54), dry, and a new oil passage 'O'-ring (Ref.3) smeared with tallow. Position the distributor drive shaft such that the smaller side (Ref.A: Fig.'a' 55) is towards the mating face, and the groove (Ref.b.) is parallel to the mating face. Re-install gear housing on cylinder block. The distributor drive shaft will rotate one tooth clockwise because the pinions are helically cut (see Fig. A56.). Refit the 17 timing gear housing bolts and the earth lead stud. Tighten to 1.5 mkg. (11 lb.ft.) torque. Cut off the timing gear housing gasket flush with upper mating face (see Fig.A.57). Re-connect earth lead. Refit and connect up ignition coil. Re-connect fuel lines to pump, and oil pressure switch.

Three point mounted engines (204): Refit right hand tie-link, and tighten the new Nyloc nut to 1.75 mkg. (13 lb.ft.). torque.
All engines: Refit and set distributor, turning engine using special jaw. 8.0118A. Refit rocker cover using a new gasket, and tighten bolts to 0.75 mkg. (5.5 lb.ft.) torque.

Four point mounted engines (204-304): Refit upper right hand mounting block and tighten support on wing valance to 2 mkg. (14.5 lb.ft.) torque and rubber block securing nut to 3.25 mkg. (23.5 lb.ft.) torque. Recover steel block from under gearbox.

Refit air filter. Refill engine with 7 pints (4 litres) of approved engine oil 20W/30 /40. Refit and reconnect battery. Reset clock.

TIMING GEAR - Dismantling

Position the timing mark on crankshaft sprocket horizontally to right. Unload chain tensioner by removing sealing screw from tensioner body and engaging a 3mm. Allen key, through the hole, into the tensioner piston hexagonal recess. Turn Allen key clockwise to free tensioner shoe from the spring action (see Fig.A.58). Unlock and remove camshaft sprocket bolts. Remove sprocket and timing chain. Remove tensioner and filter. When removing the oil pump pinion and timing sprocket from the crankshaft, hold the pulley using special jaw 8.0118A in order to avoid contact between pistons and valves.

TIMING GEAR - Re-assembly and Adjustment

Refit timing sprocket and oil pump pinion on crankshaft but fit a new lock washer. Tighten the nut to 9 mkg. (65 lb.ft.) torque and lock it. Position the camshaft, with the two threaded holes closer to each other upwards, as indicated in Fig.A.59 (approx. 15º from engine vertical axis).

Assemble the chain tensioner. Assemble the shoe (Ref.1 Fig.A.60.) spring (Ref.2) and piston (Ref.3), using a 3mm. Allen key. Turn key clockwise. Assemble tensioner body (Ref.4), body gasket (Ref.5.), backing plate (ref.6), plate gasket (Ref.7), and filter(Ref.8).Fit the assembly to the cylinder block, using bolts (Ref.9).Tighten to 0.75 mkg. (5.5 lb.ft.) torque. Insert tensioner shoe into its bore, making sure that it slides freely.

Position the timing chain on the camshaft sprocket, with the copper plated links on both sides of the reference mark (see. Fig.A.61). Hold it in position and install timing chain on crankshaft sprocket, with the copper plated link on the pinion reference mark. Fit and tighten the camshaft sprocket using a new lock washer. Tighten the bolts to 2mkg. (14.5 lb.ft.) torque. Lock the bolts. Load the tensioner using a 3mm. Allen key, turning it clockwise. Fit and lock the tensioner sealing bolt (Ref.10, Fig.A.61) by bending the tab over it.

Technical Data

ENGINE	204 (XK4)	304 (XL 3)
Designation	4 stroke, O.H.V. (inclined), single overhead camshaft	
Cylinders	4-wet liners	
Firing order	1 - 3 - 4 - 2	
Idling speed	750 r.p.m.	—
Bore	75 mm (2.953)	76 mm (2.992 in.)
Stroke	64 mm (2.520 in.)	71 mm (2.7953 in.)
Cubic capacity	1,130 cc.	1,288 cc.
Compression ratio	8.8 : 1	
Brake horse-power (DIN)	47.8 at 5,600 rpm.	65 at 6,000 rpm
Torque (DIN)	56.4 lb.ft. at 3,500rpm	69.4 lb.ft. at 3,750 rpm
Big-end diameter	45mm (1.7717 in.) nominal	
Main bearing dia.	47 mm (1.8505 in.) nominal	
Main bearings	5	
Crankshaft end-float	0.07/0.23 mm (0.0028/0.009 in.)	
Crankshaft end-thrust	at No.2 main bearing	at left intermediate main bearing
Camshaft bearings	5	
Camshaft drive type	Single chain	
Valve head diameter	Inlet 37mm (1.457 in.) Exhaust 29.5 (1.162 in.)	
Valve seat angle (included)	Inlet 120º, Exhaust 90º	

SET OF CRANKSHAFT BEARINGS: 204

Size	Standard	U/S: 0.30 mm	U/S: 0.50 mm.
Line of Shafting	0113.04	0115.68	0113.06
For Crankshaft Journal	47.000 to 46.984 mm	46.700 to 46.684 mm.	46.500 to 46.484 mm,
Front Intermediate:	0117.35	0117.36	0117.37
Centre and Rear			

SET OF MAIN BEARING SHELLS: 304

USED for:	Original Size	Oversize 0.30 mm
Line of Shafting	0113. 01	0113.02
Crankshaft Journal dia. (mm)	47.000 to 46.984	46.700 to 46.684
Main Bearing No. 1-3-5	0117.59	0117.60
Main Bearing No. 2-4	0117.62	0117.63

GUIDE valve:

	Original Size	1st Repair	2nd Repair
O.D.:(mm.)	14.02	14.29	14.59
Part Number	0220.28	0220.29	0220.30

SEAT, valve: 204

		Original Size	1st Repair	2nd. Repair
Intake	O.D.:	36.13 mm.	36.43 mm.	36.63 mm.
	Bore in Cyl. Head:	36.00 mm.	36.30 mm.	36.50 mm.
	Part Number.	0226.24	0226.25	0226.26
Exhaust	O.D.:	31.13 mm.	31.43 mm.	31.63 mm.
	Bore in Cyl.-Head	31.00 mm.	31.30 mm.	31.50 mm.
	Part Number	0227.25	0227.20	0227.21

SEAT valve: 304

		Original Size	1st Repair	2nd Repair
Intake XL 3	O.D.	38.13 mm	38.33 mm	38.63 mm
	Cyl. Head Bore	38.00 mm	38.18 mm	38.38 mm
	Part Number	0226.36	0226.37	0226.38
Intake XL 3 S	O.D.	40.13 mm	40.33 mm.	40.63 mm.
	Cyl-Head Bore	40.00 mm.	40.18 mm.	40.38 mm.
	Part Number	0226.45	0226.46	0226.47
Exhaust	O.D.	31.13 mm.	31.43 mm.	31.63 mm.
	Cyl-Head Bore	31.00 mm.	31.18 mm	31.38 mm.
	Part Number	0227.25	0227.26	0227.27

FUEL SYSTEM

	Normal	Emission control	Normal		Emission control
Petrol pump		AC (RA 2) or SEV (SP 127) mechanical			
Carburettor	Solex 32 PBISA - 3		Solex 32 PBISA - 4		Solex 35 EEISA
Choke tube	26	26	26	26	24
Main jet	137.5	130	140	132.5	122.5 ± 2.5
Compensating jet	180 E 2	150	180	150	120 ± 5
Slow-running jet	52	57.5	55	55	50 ± 3
Slow-running air jet	220	180	220	180	200
Accelerator pump jet	45	40	45	40	35
Needle valve	1.5 mm	1.5 mm	1.5 mm	1.5 mm	1.8 mm

Engine

Accessory Supplement

This self-explanatory Supplement has been added to identify the main components of the engine.

The exploded views provide the reader with a quick-reference facility when ordering spare parts and carrying out maintenance and reassembly work.

Figs A C 1 to A C 4 cover Cooling System

Figs A F 1 to A F 10 cover Fuel System

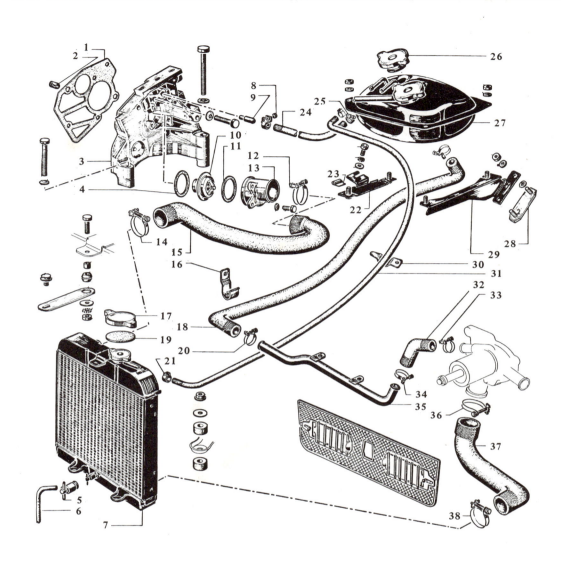

1. Water box gasket
2. Dowel
3. Water box
4. 'O' - ring
5. Drain tap
6. Plastic extension
7. Radiator
8. Clip
9. Discharge nozzle
10. Thermostat
11. 'O' - ring
12. Clip
13. Spout

14. Clip
15. Inlet hose
16. Clip
17. Radiator cap
18. Degassing tube
19. Rubber packing
20. Clip
21. Clip
22. Bracket
23. Rubber strip
24. Degassing tube
25. Clip
26. Degassing tank cap

27. Degassing tank
28. Fixing plate
29. Bracket
30. Strap
31. Degassing tube
32. Degassing tube
33. Clip
34. Clip
35. Intermediate pipe
36. Clip
37. Outlet hose
38. Clip

Fig. AC.1 General arrangement of cooling system.

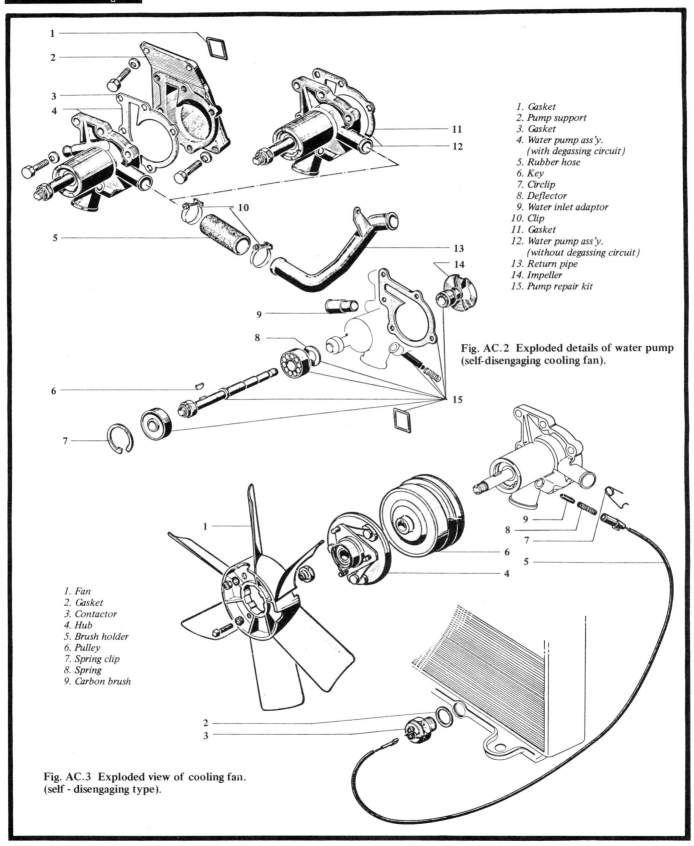

intereurope

1. Gasket
2. Pump support
3. Gasket
4. Water pump ass'y.
   (with degassing circuit)
5. Rubber hose
6. Key
7. Circlip
8. Deflector
9. Water inlet adaptor
10. Clip
11. Gasket
12. Water pump ass'y.
    (without degassing circuit)
13. Return pipe
14. Impeller
15. Pump repair kit

Fig. AC.2 Exploded details of water pump
(self-disengaging cooling fan).

1. Fan
2. Gasket
3. Contactor
4. Hub
5. Brush holder
6. Pulley
7. Spring clip
8. Spring
9. Carbon brush

Fig. AC.3 Exploded view of cooling fan.
(self - disengaging type).

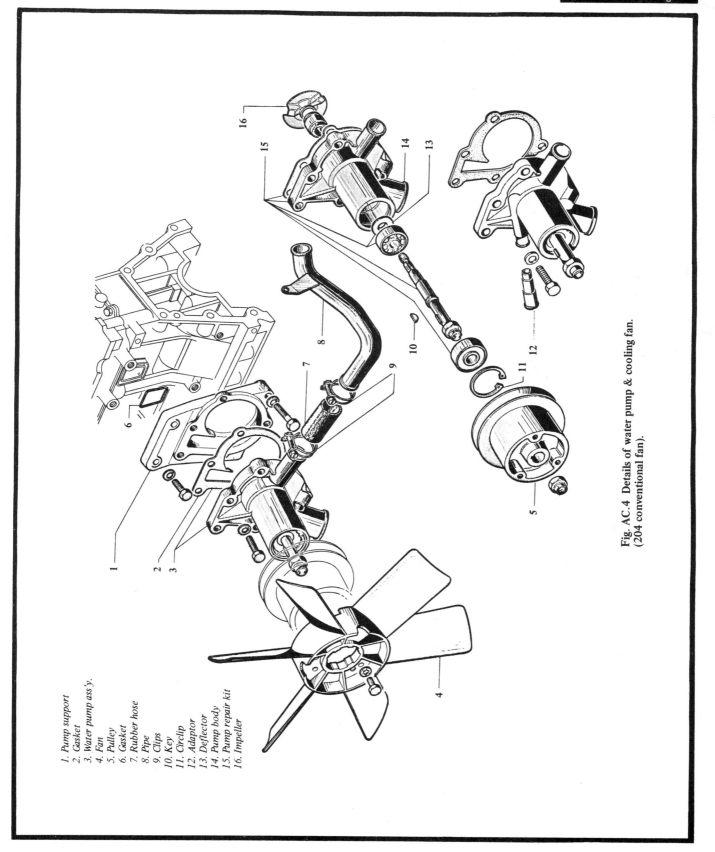

1. Pump support
2. Gasket
3. Water pump ass'y.
4. Fan
5. Pulley
6. Gasket
7. Rubber hose
8. Pipe
9. Clips
10. Key
11. Circlip
12. Adaptor
13. Deflector
14. Pump body
15. Pump repair kit
16. Impeller

Fig. AC.4 Details of water pump & cooling fan. (204 conventional fan).

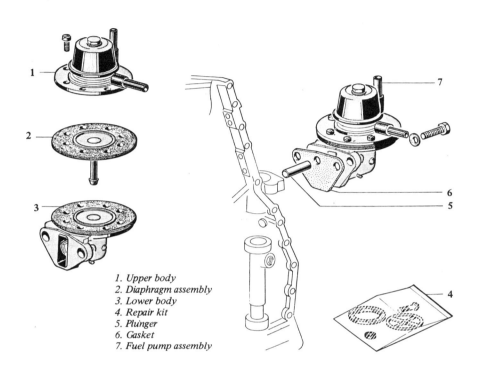

1. Upper body
2. Diaphragm assembly
3. Lower body
4. Repair kit
5. Plunger
6. Gasket
7. Fuel pump assembly

Fig. AF.1 Fuel pump - exploded view.

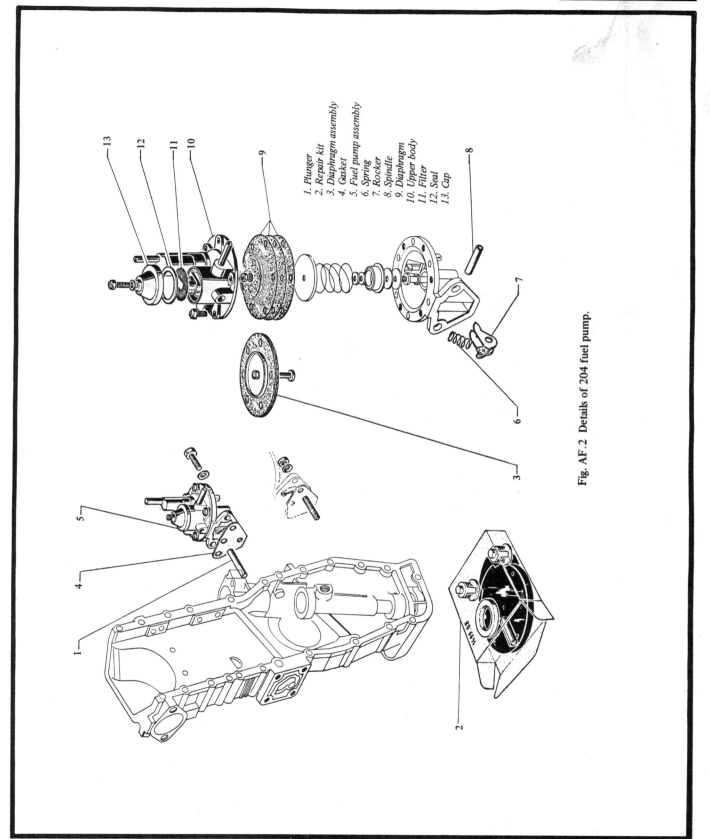

1. Plunger
2. Repair kit
3. Diaphragm assembly
4. Gasket
5. Fuel pump assembly
6. Spring
7. Rocker
8. Spindle
9. Diaphragm
10. Upper body
11. Filter
12. Seal
13. Cap

Fig. AF.2 Details of 204 fuel pump.

29

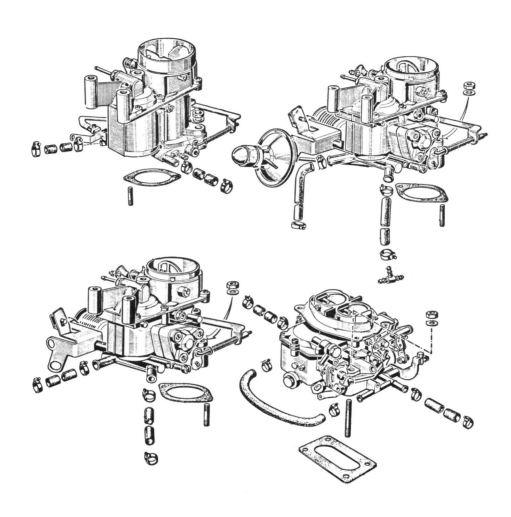

Fig. AF.3 Details of Solex carburettor 1

intereurope

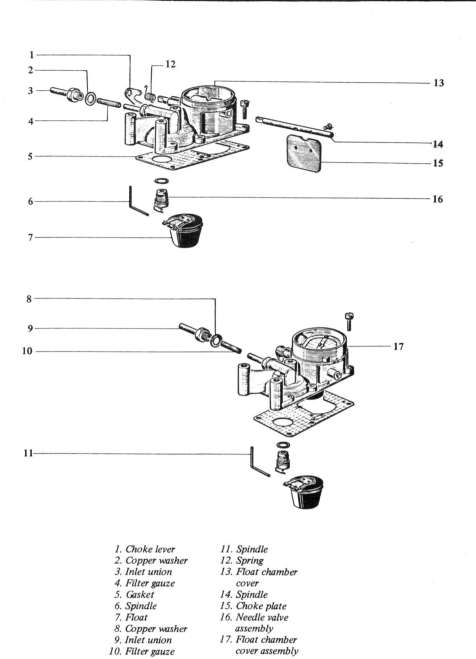

1. Choke lever
2. Copper washer
3. Inlet union
4. Filter gauze
5. Gasket
6. Spindle
7. Float
8. Copper washer
9. Inlet union
10. Filter gauze
11. Spindle
12. Spring
13. Float chamber
    cover
14. Spindle
15. Choke plate
16. Needle valve
    assembly
17. Float chamber
    cover assembly

Fig. AF.4 Details of Solex carburettor 2

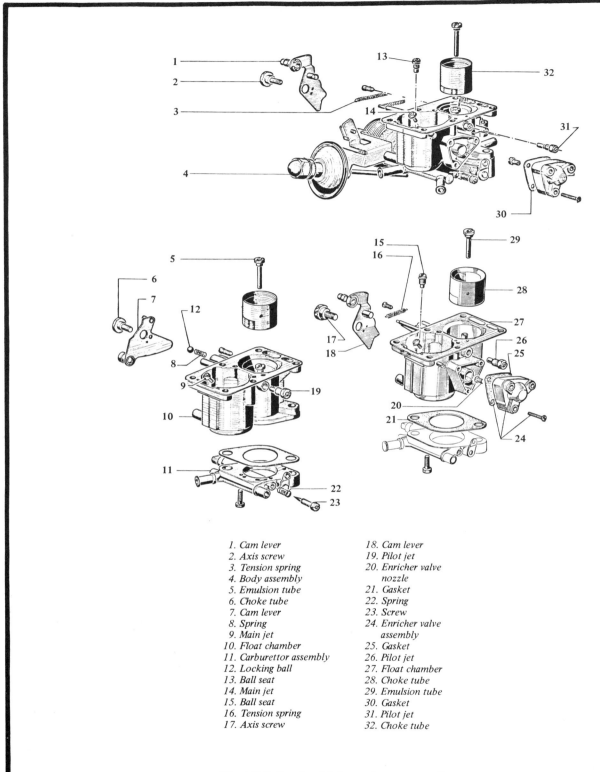

1. Cam lever
2. Axis screw
3. Tension spring
4. Body assembly
5. Emulsion tube
6. Choke tube
7. Cam lever
8. Spring
9. Main jet
10. Float chamber
11. Carburettor assembly
12. Locking ball
13. Ball seat
14. Main jet
15. Ball seat
16. Tension spring
17. Axis screw

18. Cam lever
19. Pilot jet
20. Enricher valve nozzle
21. Gasket
22. Spring
23. Screw
24. Enricher valve assembly
25. Gasket
26. Pilot jet
27. Float chamber
28. Choke tube
29. Emulsion tube
30. Gasket
31. Pilot jet
32. Choke tube

Fig. AF.5 Details of Solex carburettor 3

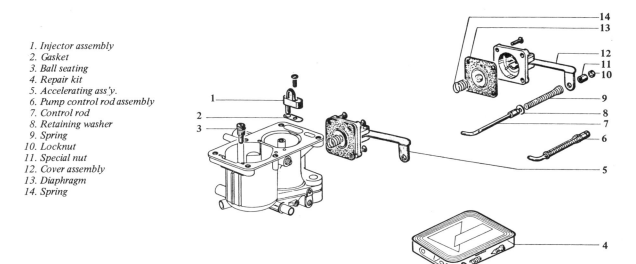

1. Injector assembly
2. Gasket
3. Ball seating
4. Repair kit
5. Accelerating ass'y.
6. Pump control rod assembly
7. Control rod
8. Retaining washer
9. Spring
10. Locknut
11. Special nut
12. Cover assembly
13. Diaphragm
14. Spring

Fig. AF.6 Details of Solex carburettor 4

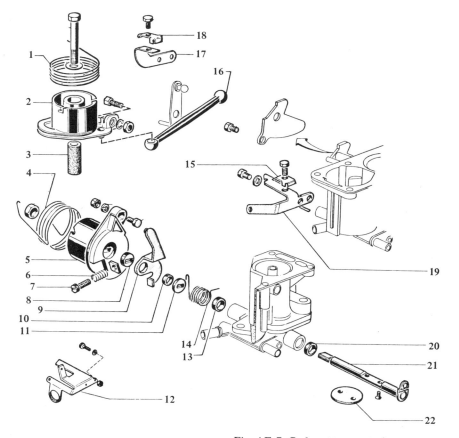

1. Return spring
2. Drum
3. Spacing tube
4. Return spring
5. Drum
6. Spring
7. Idle running screw
8. Washer
9. Lever
10. Bush
11. Washer
12. Cable support
13. Dust ring
14. Spring
15. Lug
16. Link
17. Retainer
18. Lug
19. Retainer
20. Dust ring
21. Spindle
22. Throttle

Fig. AF.7 Carburettor controls.

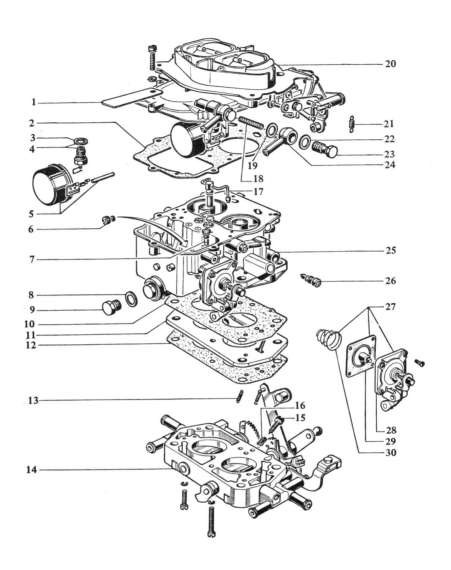

1. Ident plate	11. Flange	21. Spring
2. Washer (fibre)	12. Gasket	22. Washer (copper)
3. Seal	13. Spring	23. Union
4. Needle valve	14. Body assembly	24. Adjustable union
5. Float & spindle	15. Volume screw	25. Float chamber
6. Main jet	16. Spring	26. Pilot jet
7. Seat	17. Injector assembly	27. Accelerator pump assembly
8. Washer (fibre)	18. Gauze	28. Cover
9. Plug	19. Washer (copper)	29. Diaphragm ass'y.
10. Gasket	20. Cover	30. Spring

Fig. AF.8 Exploded view of 304 S carburettor.

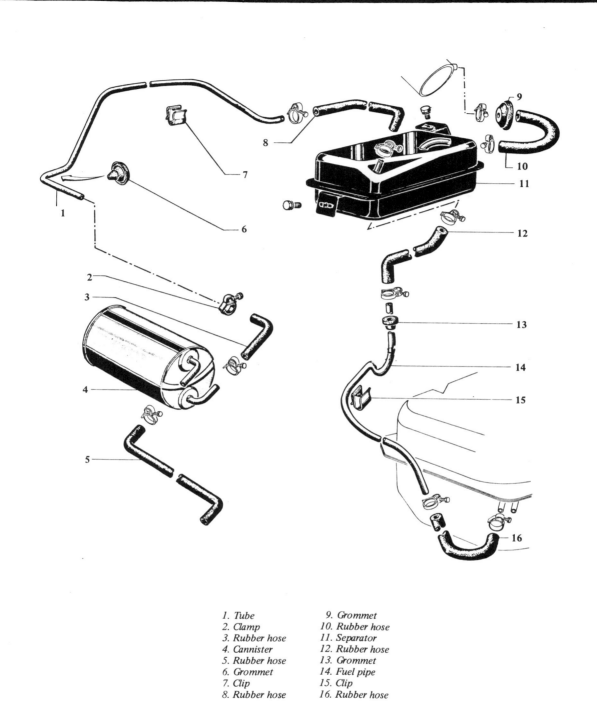

1. Tube
2. Clamp
3. Rubber hose
4. Cannister
5. Rubber hose
6. Grommet
7. Clip
8. Rubber hose
9. Grommet
10. Rubber hose
11. Separator
12. Rubber hose
13. Grommet
14. Fuel pipe
15. Clip
16. Rubber hose

Fig. AF.9 G.A. of fuel evaporation control system.

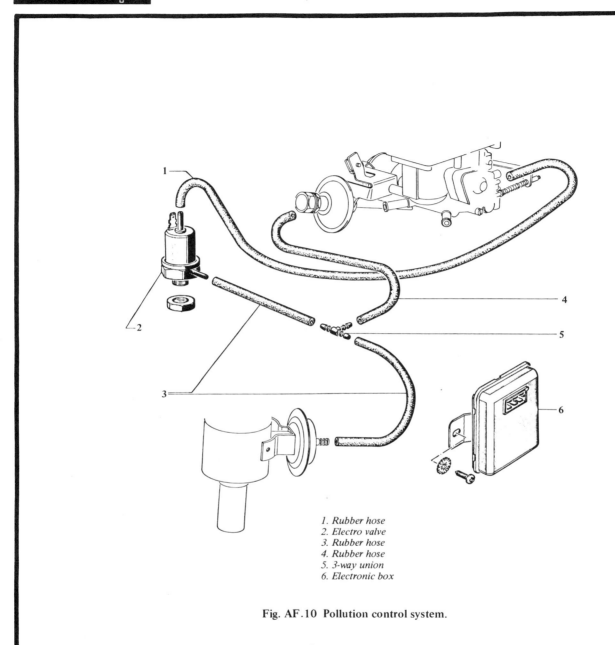

1. *Rubber hose*
2. *Electro valve*
3. *Rubber hose*
4. *Rubber hose*
5. *3-way union*
6. *Electronic box*

Fig. AF.10 Pollution control system.

Clutch

CHARACTERISTICS

1st installation: Ferodo 180DP, fitted to vehicles up to serial numbers 204 Luxe 6.063.800, 204GL 6.235.000 and 204B(Break) 6.655.400. The characteristics of the lined disc are: outside diameter 181.5mm. (7.1457in.), inside diameter 124mm (4.8819in.), thickness under load 8.1mm. (0.3189in). hub 13 splines.

2nd installation: Ferodo 200DE, fitted to vehicles as from serial numbers 204 Luxe 6.063.801, 204GL 6.235.001, 204B (Break) 6.655.401, 204C (Convertible & Coupe) 6.400.001, 204U4 (Van) 6.500.001. The characteristics of the lined disc are: outside diameter 200mm. (7.874 in.), inside diameter 130mm. (5.118 in.) thickness under load 8.1mm. (0.3189 in.) hub 14 splines.

2nd installation: LUK TS 190, fitted on all 204 types as from January 1967. Characteristics of the lined disc are: outside diameter 190mm. (7.4803 in.) inside diameter 127mm. (5in.) thickness under load 7.2mm. (0.2835 in.) hub 14 splines.

Second installation clutches, i.e. 200DE and TS190, cannot be installed to replace a 1st installation clutch (180DP). The lined discs used on the three types of clutch are not interchangeable. The complete 200DE clutch can be installed to replace a TS190 clutch, and vice versa.

CLUTCH THRUST BEARING - Removal

Disconnect battery, and drain cooling system. Remove jack where applicable (204 models with jack mounted on front frame and 304). Remove radiator. Slacken fan belt by loosening adjuster, and disengage belt from crankshaft pulley and tensioner. Remove bolt used for securing belt tensioner to clutch housing cover, and move belt tensioner aside. Remove the generator. Remove the regulator, after disconnecting battery wire, and place regulator on inlet manifold. Disconnect clutch release fork return spring. On three point mounted engines slacken, but do not remove, the two left hand front tie-link studs; remove both screws used for attaching the left hand front tie-link fork to the generator support, and position tie-link and fork assembly against wing valance. Disconnect heater hose from water pump. Rotate crankshaft, using special jaw 8.0118A, until tab lock for pulley attachment screw faces downwards. Unlock pulley attachment screw using special tool 0.0134 (see Fig.B.4).
180DP Clutch: Hold crankshaft pulley using special jaw 8.0118A, and slacken attachment screw using wrench 8.0118D with Facom SJ214 extension or similar. When removing screw ensure that the 'O'-ring Seal is not left on the crankshaft. Remove pulley and backing spring, clutch housing cover, and thrust ball bearing.

200DE and TS190 Clutches: Remove air intake silencer. Hold crankshaft pulley, using special jaw 8.0118A, and slacken attachment screw using wrench 8.0118M with Facom SJ 214 extension or similar. Remove crankshaft pulley and backing spring (if fitted), clutch housing cover, and thrust ball bearing.

CLUTCH THRUST BEARING - Refitting

Pack clutch hub extractor groove with Multi-purpose Grease. Install thrust ball bearing. Install clutch cover, ensuring that flat section of clutch release fork backing flange is facing thrust bearing. Tighten clutch cover attachment screws to 1mkg. (7.25 lb.ft.) torque.

180DP Clutch: Install bearing thrust spring, crankshaft pulley and attachment screw fitted with a new tablock, and 'O'-ring seal. Tighten screw to 6.5 mkg. (47 lb.ft.) torque by using torque wrench fitted with special socket 8.0118D, and holding pulley with special jaw 8.0118A. Bend tablock using special tool 0.0134 (see Fig.B5).

200DE and TS190 Clutches: Fit bearing thrust spring, if applicable. Re-install crankshaft pulley ensuring that it engages on clutch hub drive pin. Install attachment screw fitted with a new tablock, and tighten to 6.5 mkg. (47 lb.ft.) torque using torque wrench fitted with special socket 8.0118M, and holding pulley with special jaw 8.0118A. Bend tablock using special tool 0.0134 (see Fig.B5.).

All clutches: Install clutch release fork return spring (see Fig.B6). Adjust fork free travel by unscrewing adjusting screw locknut, and slacken adjusting screw until fork bears on its stop. Screw in two and a half turns to obtain 2mm. (0.08 in.) free travel at fork stop. Retighten adjusting screw locknut. *Note:* The clearance obtained with two and a half turns of the release fork adjusting screw (distance between adjusting screw and control cylinder piston) should correspond to 30-35mm. (1.18 - 1.38 in.) free travel at clutch pedal. If the clutch travel is incorrect, the hydraulic system should be bled. Re-connect heating system hose to water pump. Re-install generator and regulator. Never work belt over pulley grooves to bring it into position, but install belt on crankshaft, generator, and water pump pulleys, taking care not to twist the belt by more than 90º. Engage tensioner pulley on belt, and secure tensioner assembly to cylinder block. Using the adjuster tension the fan belt, make two reference marks on the fan belt 100mm. apart when slack. When tensioned the two marks should be 102 to 102.5 mm. apart for an engine fitted with a dynamo, and 101.5 to 102mm. apart for an engine fitted with an alternator. Tighten tensioner pivot nut to 4 mkg. (29 lb.ft.) torque and the two support bolts to 1.75 mkg. (13 lb.ft.) torque. Tighten tensioner pulley nut. On three point mounted engines, secure the left hand front engine tie-link to the generator support, and tighten both tie-link mounting studs to 1.75 mkg. (13 lb.ft.) torque. Re-install radiator and connect hoses. Refill cooling system. Refit intake silencer. Re-install jack, where applicable. Re-connect battery, and reset clock.

180DP CLUTCH - Removal

To remove the 180DP clutch the power unit must first be removed from the vehicle. Place power unit on support base. Unlock crankshaft pulley attachment screw. Hold pulley using special jaw 8.0118A, and unscrew attachment screw using special wrench 8.0118D with a Facom SJ214 extension, or similar (See Fig.B7). When removing the screw ensure that the 'O'-ring seal is not left in the crankshaft. Remove pulley, bearing thrust spring, clutch release fork return spring, clutch housing cover, and thrust ball bearing. Remove clutch using special puller 8.0203A (See Fig.B8).

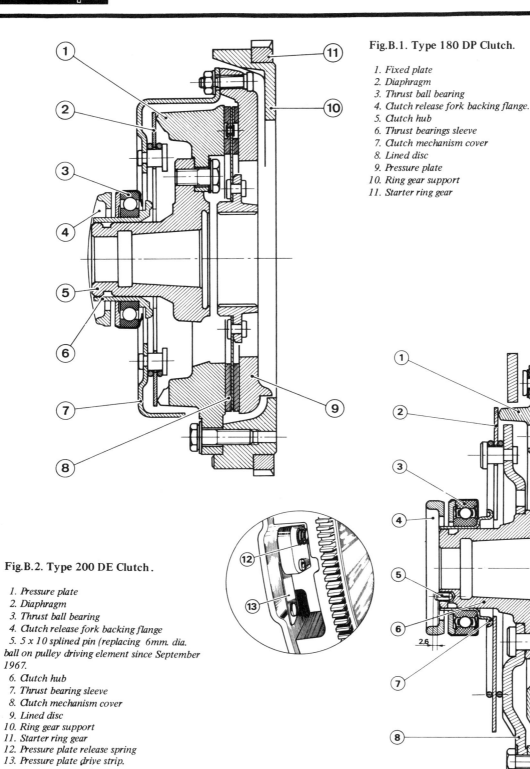

Fig.B.1. Type 180 DP Clutch.

1. *Fixed plate*
2. *Diaphragm*
3. *Thrust ball bearing*
4. *Clutch release fork backing flange.*
5. *Clutch hub*
6. *Thrust bearings sleeve*
7. *Clutch mechanism cover*
8. *Lined disc*
9. *Pressure plate*
10. *Ring gear support*
11. *Starter ring gear*

Fig.B.2. Type 200 DE Clutch.

1. *Pressure plate*
2. *Diaphragm*
3. *Thrust ball bearing*
4. *Clutch release fork backing flange*
5. *5 x 10 splined pin (replacing 6mm. dia.
ball on pulley driving element since September
1967.*
6. *Clutch hub*
7. *Thrust bearing sleeve*
8. *Clutch mechanism cover*
9. *Lined disc*
10. *Ring gear support*
11. *Starter ring gear*
12. *Pressure plate release spring*
13. *Pressure plate drive strip.*

*Note: Spare parts department supply 200DE clutches
with driving pin 5 Check that pin protrusion is 2.6mm before
installing clutch.*

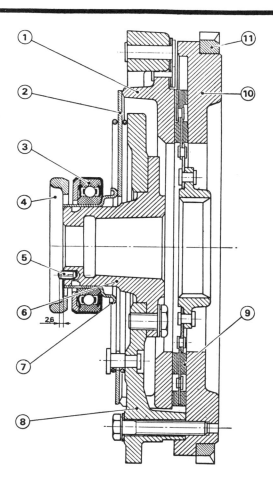
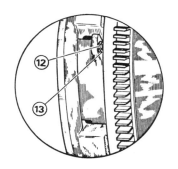
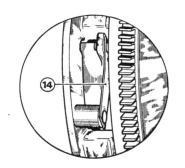

Fig.B3. Type TS190 Clutch.

1. Pressure plate
2. Diaphragm
3. Thrust ball bearing
4. Clutch release fork backing flange
5. 5 x 10 splined pin (replacing 6mm. diam. ball as pulley driving element since September 1967)
6. Clutch hub
7. Thrust bearing sleeve
8. Clutch mechanism cover
9. Driven disc
10. Ring gear support
11. Starter ring gear
12. Release spring guide
13. Pressure plate release spring
14. Pressure plate drive strip

Fig.B.4. Unlocking pulley attachment screw.

Fig.B.5. Bending tablock with special tool.

Fig.B.6. Clutch adjusting mechanism.

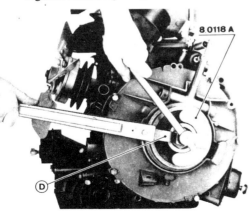

Fig.B.7. Removing crankshaft pulley attachment screw.

Fig.B.8. Removing 180 DP clutch.

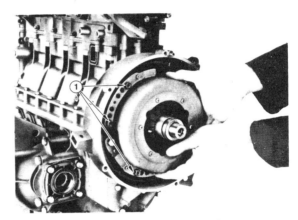

Fig.B.9. Refitting 180 DP clutch.

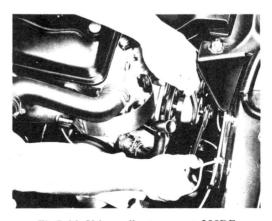

Fig.B.10. Using puller to remove 200DE or TS190 clutch.

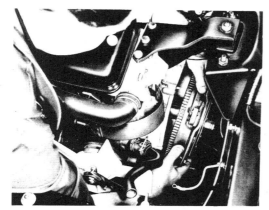

Fig.B.11. Removing 200 DE or TS 190 clutch.

Fig.B.12. Crankshaft reference hole.

Fig.B.13. Lining up clutch on crankshaft.

Fig.B.14. Tightening crankshaft attachment screw.

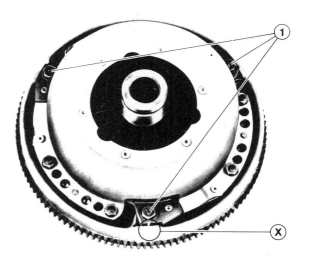

Fig.B.15. Reference marks on ring gear support and fixed plate.

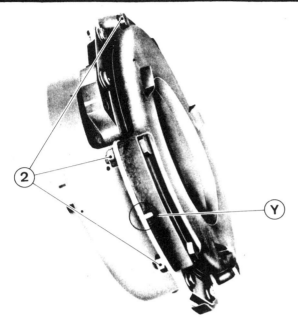

Fig.B.16. Reference marks on moving plate and clutch mechanism cover.

Fig.B.17. 180 DP clutch - exploded view.

Fig.B.18. 200 DE clutch reference marks.

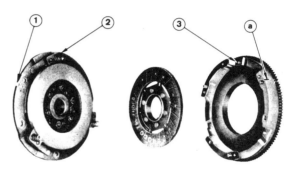

Fig.B.19. 200 DE clutch exploded view.

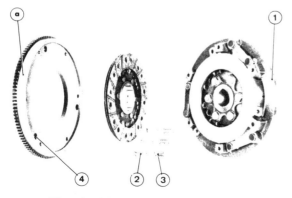

Fig.B.20. 190 TS clutch - exploded view.

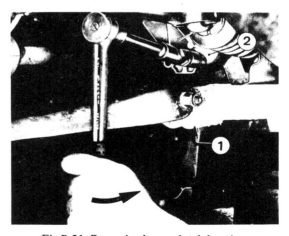

Fig.B.21. Removing lower clutch housing securing bolts.

180DP CLUTCH -Refitting

Clean Polygon cone carefully. Using a Molykote 321 aerosol spray, apply a thin lubricating film over the whole surface of the Polygon cone and power take-off pinion splined hub. Position clutch against crankshaft, and rotate clutch back and forth slightly to engage the driven disc on the power take-off pinion. Bottom hub on Polygon cone. Tighten assembly nuts (ref.1 Fig.B9) to 1mkg. (7.25 lb.ft.) torque. Pack clutch hub extractor groove with Multi-purpose Grease. Install thrust ball bearing. Install clutch housing cover, ensuring that flat side of clutch release fork backing flange is facing thrust bearing. Tighten clutch housing cover attachment screws to 1mkg. (7.25 lb.ft.). torque. Install bearing thrust spring, crankshaft pulley and attachment screw fitted with a new tablock and a new 'O–ring seal. Tighten screw to 6.5mkg. (47 lbft). torque using a torque wrench fitted with special socket 8.0118D, and holding the pulley with special jaw 8.0118A. Bend tablock over.

200DE AND TS190 CLUTCH - Removal

The 200DE and TS190 clutches may be removed without removing the power unit from the vehicle. Remove accessories as described for removal of Clutch Thrust Bearing. Remove crankshaft pulley, bearing thrust spring (if fitted), clutch housing cover, and thrust ball bearing. Align clutch mechanism cover notch with the 8mm. pin hole in the clutch housing. Remove clutch using special puller 8.0206A (see Figs.B10 and B11).

200DE AND TS190 CLUTCH - Refitting

The 200DE and TS190 clutches may be removed without removing the power unit from the vehicle. Remove accessories as described for removal of clutch Thrust Bearing. Remove crankshaft pulley, bearing thrust spring (if fitted), clutch housing cover, and thrust ball bearing. Align clutch mechanism cover notch with the 8mm.-pin hole in the clutch housing. Remove clutch using special puller 8.0206A (see Figs. B10 and B11.).

200DE AND TS190 CLUTCH - Refitting

Carefully clean Polygon cone. Using Molykote 321 aerosol spray, apply a thin film of lubricant over the whole surface of the Polygon cone and drive pinion splined hub, taking care not to spray the drive pinion oil seal surface. Ensure crankshaft reference hole (ref.1, Fig.B12) is aligned with the top of the cylinder. *Note:* Reference hole '1' indicates T.D.C. of cylinder 1 and 4 when in top position. Position clutch on crankshaft, ensuring that notch (ref.2, Fig.B13) on clutch mechanism cover faces pin hole (Ref.3) in clutch housing. Rotate clutch back and forth slightly to engage the clutch disc over the pinion. *Note:* The six clutch mechanism assembling screws must not be tightened or proper centring of the driven disc cannot be effected. Install crankshaft pulley temporarily. Tighten attachment screw slightly, to fully engage clutch. Tighten the six clutch mechanism assembling screws to 2.5 mkg. (18 lb.ft.) torque. Remove crankshaft pulley. Pack clutch hub extractor groove with Multipurpose Grease. Install thrust bearing, and if fitted, bearing thrust spring. *Note:* To fit a bearing thrust spring where not previously fitted, the thrust bearing and crankshaft pulley must be replaced. Install clutch housing cover, ensuring that flat side of clutch release fork backing flange is

facing thrust bearing. Tighten clutch housing cover screws to 1 mkg. (7.25 lb.ft.) torque. Re-install crankshaft pulley, ensuring that it engages the locking ball on the clutch hub. Install attachment screw fitted with new tablock, and tighten to 6.5 mkg. (47 lb.ft.). torque using a torque wrench fitted with extension socket 8.0118M, and holding pulley with special jaw 8.0118A (See Fig.B14). Bend tablock using special tool 0.0134. Refit accessories. Re-install ancilliary equipment, and adjust fan belt tension and clutch free travel, as described under refitting clutch thrust bearing.

180DP CLUTCH - Dismantling

The three main clutch parts, i.e. fixed plate and clutch mechanism, moving plate and ring gear support cannot be replaced separately. Since the assembly is accurately balanced, it is imperative that all parts must be re-assembled according to the initial fitting. Only the starter ring gear and driven gear may be replaced separately.

Check reference marks (ref.X. Fig.B.15) on ring gear support and fixed plate. The reference mark on the ring gear support may be a figure, letter, or line. Disconnect ring gear support by removing the three screws (Ref.1.). *Note:* If screws removed are identified by a figure '80', then they must be replaced by screws identified by a figure '100'. Check for reference marks (Ref.Y), Fig.B16) between moving plate and clutch mechanism cover. If there are no reference marks, then make marks before dismantling. Disassemble moving plate and clutch mechanism by removing the six bolts (Ref.2). *Important:* Never separate the fixed plate from the hub.

180DP CLUTCH - Re-assembly

Place clutch mechanism horizontally on bench with fixed plate (Ref.3, Fig.B17) facing upwards. Place lined disc (Ref.4) on fixed plate with offset section turned upwards. Place pressure plate (Ref.5) on driven disc, taking care to align the reference marks (**Ref.7**)on the moving plate and clutch cover. Assemble the two sub-assemblies, using the six special bolts fitted with new Onduflex washers. Do not tighten nuts, so that driven disc can be centred correctly when re-installing clutch on engine. Align the marks (Ref.X) on ring gear support (Ref.6) and fixed plate (Ref.3). Secure the moving plate driven disc clutch mechanism assembly to ring gear support (Ref.6) using attachment screws (marked '100' on the hexagon head)(Ref.3) Tighten attachment screws to 2.75 mkg. (19.9 lb.ft.) torque.

200DE CLUTCH - Dismantling

The two main clutch parts, i.e. clutch mechanism and ring gear support, cannot be replaced separately. Since the assembly is accurately balanced, it is imperative that all parts must be re-assembled according to the initial fitting. Only the starter ring gear and clutch driven disc may be replaced separately.

Draw a reference line (Ref'a'. Fig.B18) on ring gear support in alignment with notch (Ref.1) in clutch cover. Slacken and remove the six assembling screws. *Important:* Never separate the clutch cover mechanism from the hub.

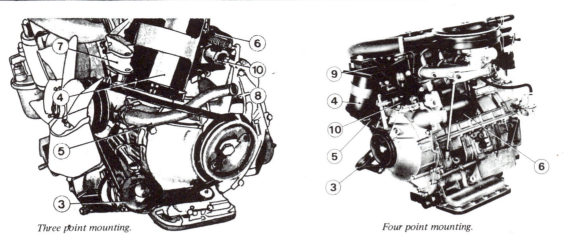

Three point mounting.   *Four point mounting.*

Fig.B.22. Power unit.

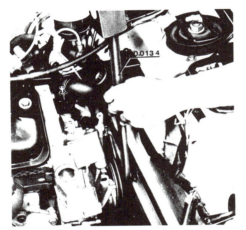

Fig.B.23. Releasing crankshaft pulley bolt.

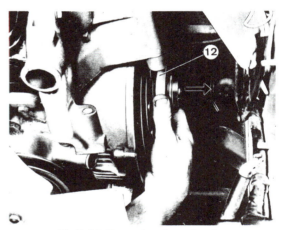

Fig.B.25. Removing thrust bearing.

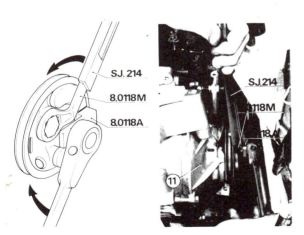

Fig.B.24. Removing crankshaft pulley bolt.

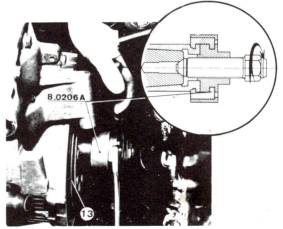

Fig.B.26. Removing clutch mechanism.

Fig.B.27. View on drive pinion with clutch removed.

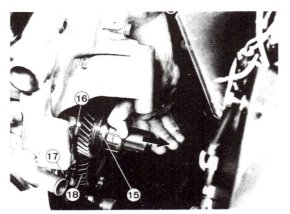

Fig.B.28. View on drive pinion with clutch cover removed.

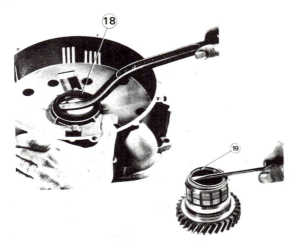

Fig.B.29. Removing seals.

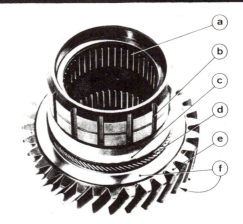

Fig.B.30. Drive pinion.

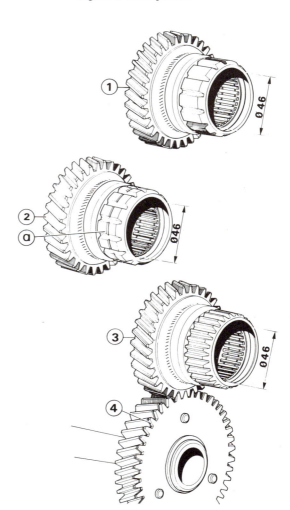

Fig.B.31. Drive pinions.

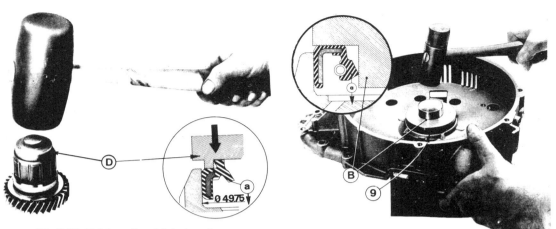

Fig.B.32. Driving oil seal into housing.

Fig.B.34. Fitting seal into clutch housing.

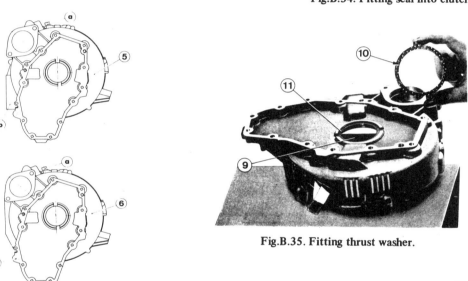

Fig.B.35. Fitting thrust washer.

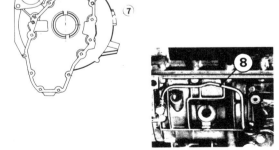

Fig.B.33. Clutch housings.

Fig.B.36. Locking thrust washer in housing.

200DE CLUTCH - Re-assembly

Place ring gear support horizontally on bench. Place driven disc on ring gear support, with offset section of driven disc hub turned downwards. Install the three pressure plate release springs (Ref.2 Fig.B19) on positioning studs (Ref.3). Install clutch cover, taking care to align notch(Ref.1) with mark (Ref.a) drawn on the ring gear support before dismantling. Check that the three pressure plate release springs (Ref.2), are correctly positioned in the corresponding recesses of the pressure plate. Install the six assembling screws, fitted with new Onduflex washers, but do not tighten screws so that driven disc can be centred correctly when re-installing clutch on engine.

190 TS CLUTCH - Dismantling

The two main clutch parts, i.e. clutch mechanism and ring gear support, cannot be replaced separately. Since the assembly is accurately balanced, it is imperative that all parts must be re-assembled according to the initial fitting. Only the starter ring gear and driven disc may be replaced separately. Draw a reference line(Ref.'a').Fig.B20) on ring gear support in alignment with notch in clutch cover (Ref.1). *Important:* Never dismantle the clutch hub.

190TS CLUTCH - Re-assembly

Place ring gear support horizontally on bench. Place driven disc on ring gear support, with offset section of driven disc hub facing downwards. Install guides (Ref.2 Fig.B20) and pressure plate release springs(Ref.3) in pressure plate recesses (Ref.4). Install clutch cover on ring gear, by aligning notch (Ref.1) with mark (Ref.a) drawn on ring gear support during dismantling. Check that guides (Ref.2) are correctly positioned in the corresponding recesses of the clutch mechanism cover. Install the six assembling screws fitted with new Onduflex washers, but do not tighten screws in order that driven disc can be centered correctly when re-installing clutch on engine.

200DE and TS190 CLUTCH

DRIVE PINION SEAL - Replacement

Drain oil and water from power unit. Support power unit under the left hand side of the oil sump (Ref.1 Fig.B21). Remove the fine bolts securing the lower part of the clutch housing (Ref.2). Disconnect battery, and remove regulator, air filter, radiator, tensioner roller (Ref.3 Fig.B22), generator (Ref.4), heater hose (Ref.5), and starter (Ref.6) without disconnecting it. Remove tie-link lug (Ref. 7), and right-hand mounting block (Ref. 8) (3 point mounting) or upper support (Ref.9) (4 point mounting). Remove clutch slave cylinder (Ref. 10) without disconnecting hydraulic lines.

Removal of Drive Pinion

Release crankshaft pulley bolt with special tool 0.0134 (See Fig.B23,) and remove using special socket 8.0118M with a Facom SJ214 extension, or similar (see Fig.B24), holding pulley with special jaw 8.0118A. Remove pulley and thrust spring, where fitted. Remove clutch housing cover (Ref.11. Fig.B24), Remove thrust bearing (Ref.12 Fig.B25). Withdraw clutch mechansim (Ref.13 Fig.B26) using special puller 8.0206A.

Remove the eight bolts (Ref.14, Fig.B27). Withdraw clutch housing carefully while holding drive pinion (Ref.15) in place. Remove drive pinion (Ref. 15, Fig.B27 and B28), thrust washer (Ref.16, Fig.B28) and housing seal (Ref. 17). Check condition of thrust washer (Ref.16), crankshaft, input pinion (Ref.18) and mating face.

Removal of Seals

Warning: Place components on a soft faced flat surface, i.e. cardboard, wood, etc. Carefully remove seals (Ref.18 and 19, Fig.B29). Do not remove grease from drive pinion needle roller bearing. Visually check pinion needle bearing (Ref, a Fig.B30) for wear, splines(Ref.'b') for burring or wear, oil seal bearing face(Ref.'c'),for impact marks or scratches, oil thrower (Ref.'d'), teeth (Ref.'e'), for sealing or wear, and thrust washer bearing faces (Ref.'f'),for impact marks or scratches.

Check the housing mating face for impact marks or scratches, and that it is not distorted by more than 0.1mm. between two points more than 100 mm. apart, or by more than 0.05mm. between two points less than 100mm. apart, by using a surface plate and feeler gauges. Check pinion thrust bearing for wear.

Refitting Seal on Drive Pinion

Warning: There are three different types of drive pinion, and they are not interchangeable.

204 Vehicles with petrol engines: Fit pinion (Ref.1, Fig.B31) with 14 splines without a groove in them.

304 Vehicles: Fit pinion (Ref.2) with a groove (Ref.'a'), on the splines.

204 Diesel Breaks: Fit pinion (Ref.3) with 28 splines, and an input pinion with a play take-up device (Ref.4). If no play take-up device is fitted, change the input pinion for one with the play take-up device. The play take-up device should not be fitted to a pinion not so fitted.

Grease oil seal housing. Drive seal well down into its housing, with the lip (Ref.'a'. Fig.B32) facing inwards.

Refitting Seal in Clutch Housing

Warning: Three housings with a timing setting hole(Ref.'a')Fig. B33) exist.

Three point mounted 204 engines: Use housing (Ref.5) with flange (Ref.'b') for securing rear left hand engine support block.

Four point mounted petrol and diesel engines with BB1 gearbox fitted. Use housing (Ref. 6) which has no flange, and which includes an oil duct sealing boss (Ref.'c').

204 and 304 vehicles fitted with BB6 gearbox (exterior lubrication line (Ref. 8) at rear): Use housing (Ref. 7) which has no oil duct sealing boss.

Place housing (Ref. 9, Fig.B34) bearing on its centre, on a piece of wood. Grease seal housing. Drive seal well down into its housing, with the lip (Ref.'a') facing downwards.

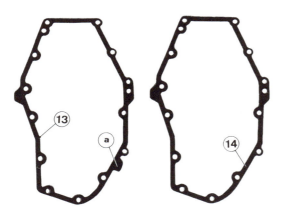

Fig.B.37. Clutch housing gaskets.

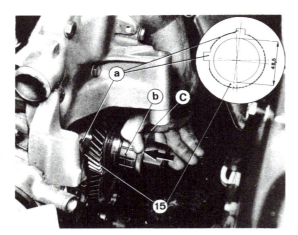

Fig.B.38. Fitting drive pinion.

Fig.B.40. Clutch housing securing bolts.

Fig.B.39. Fitting clutch housing.

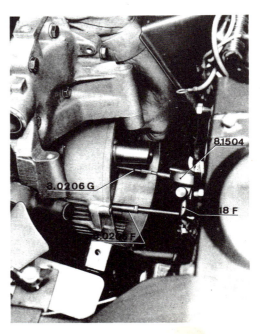

Fig.B.41. Measuring pinion end-float.

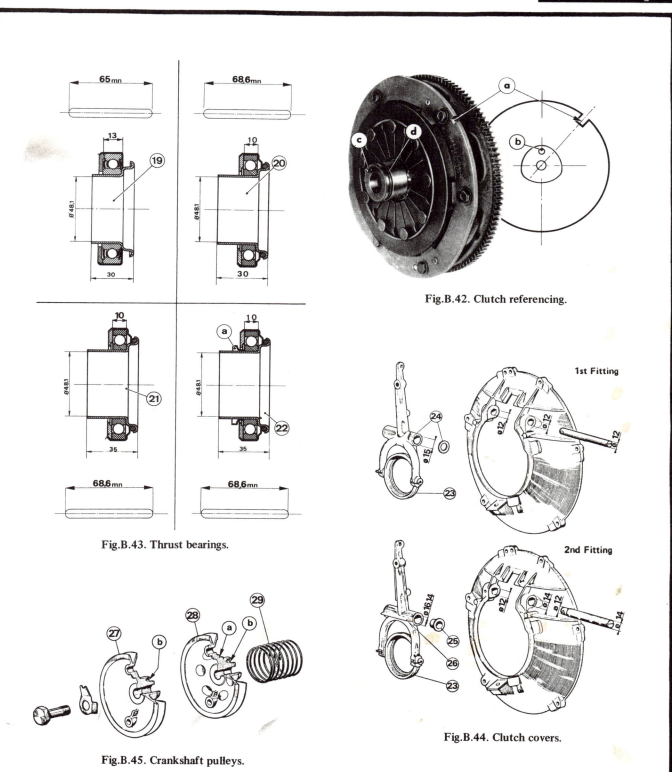

Fig.B.42. Clutch referencing.

Fig.B.43. Thrust bearings.

1st Fitting

2nd Fitting

Fig.B.44. Clutch covers.

Fig.B.45. Crankshaft pulleys.

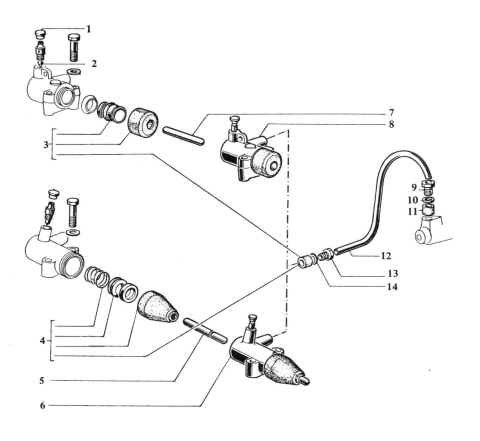

1. Dust cap
2. Bleed screw
3. Repair kit
4. Repair kit
5. Push-rod
6. Cylinder (30 mm.)
7. Push rod

8. Cylinder (27 mm.)
9. Union
10. Seal
11. Rubber bush
12. Nylon tube
13. Union
14. Seal

Fig. B.46 Exploded details of clutch release cylinder

Adjusting Pinion Side Play

Place housing on a piece of wood (Ref.9 Fig.B35). If necessary, fit new thrust washer (Ref.10) on top of shims previously fitted (Ref.11) or without shims if it is a new housing. Insert the washer well down in its housing and lock it with three light punch marks at 120º on the housing (Ref.12, Fig. B36). Place a new gasket, dry, on the cylinder block. *Warning:* Two types of gasket exist. Fit gasket (Ref.13, Fig.B37) with sealing tab (Ref.'a') for oil passage only on 204 vehicles fitted with BB1 gearbox. Fit gasket (Ref.14) only on 204 and 304 vehicles fitted with BB6 gearbox.

Refit thrust washer (Ref. 15, Fig.B38), after oiling it, with tabs (Ref.'a') in their housings. Oil drive pinion splines (Ref.'b'). Place drive pinion to bear against washer (Ref.15), using bush (Ref. C). Remove bush (Ref.C.), holding pinion carefully in place. *Warning:* Any sideways movement of the fitting bush (Ref.C) will damage the oil seal. Lightly oil the cone (Ref.E, Fig.B39), and place it over the pinion. Carefully position the housing (to facilitate passing it in front of the master cylinder (Ref.16) pull engine towards the front). Tighten the eight bolts (Ref.17, Fig. B40) to 1.25 mkg. (9 lb.ft.). torque. Remove bolt (Ref.'a'). Position dial indicator with extension so that it is bearing on pinion (see Fig.B41): Push pinion in as far as possible, and set dial indicator to zero at this position . Pull on pinion, and note difference in reading. The pinion end float should be between 0.25 mm. 0.40mm. (0.0098 and 0.0157 in).

If the pinion end float is not within the tolerance, refit the cone and remove the housing while holding the pinion in place. Add or remove shims between the thrust washer and housing to obtain the correct end float. Refit and lock the washer. Shims are available in thicknesses of 0.07, 0.15, 0.20, 0.25 and 0.50 mm. Refit clutch housing and tighten the eight bolts to 1.25 mkg. (9 lb.ft.). torque. Check pinion end float. Spray a fine coat of Molykote 321 on the Polygon and splined sleeve, taking care not spray the oil seals and their bearing faces.

Refitting the Clutch

Take care with positioning of the notch(Ref.'a') Fig.B42) in relation to the reference hole(Ref.'b')in the crankshaft. *Note:* The clutch mechanism for the 204Diesel Break has no notch, it is fitted with a ring gear with 100 teeth (as opposed to 121),and must incorporate a lined disc with 28 splines on the hub. Ensure that the pulley positioning ball on pin (Ref.'c') is in place. Lightly grease the clutch hub withdrawal groove (Ref.'d') with Multipurpose Grease.

Refitting Ball Thrust Bearing

Warning: Four different thrust bearings exist (See Fig.B43). Only use thrust bearing (Ref.22) for replacement. When replacing thrust bearing of type Ref 19, also replace slave cylinder thrust rod with one 68.6 mm. (2.7 in.) long. If fitting a thrust spring where not previously fitted, replace thrust bearing with type Ref. 22.

Refitting Clutch Cover

Warning: There are two fittings (see Fig. B44). The thrust bearing (Ref.23, Fig. B44) are common to both fittings, the other parts not being separately interchangeable. The other parts are identifiable by the bushes (Ref.24) being in calcinated bronze, and nylon washers, bushes (Ref.25) being in Rilsan, and the second fitting have visible ribbing for identification. 304 vehicles are equipped with the second fitting. 204 Diesel Breaks are fitted with a fork in cast iron as opposed to light alloy. Tighten cover bolts to 1 mkg. (7.25 lb.ft.).

Crankshaft Pulley

Warning: There are two models of crankshaft pulley.
(1)   Pulley without a shoulder for the thrust spring (Ref. 27 Fig. B45).

(2)   Pulley with a shoulder(Ref.'a') for the thrust spring (Ref. 28). If a thrust spring (Ref.29) is fitted where not fitted previously, pulley (Ref. 28) must be used.

Refit crankshaft pulley, adjust clutch play, secure power unit, fit and adjust fan belt as previously described. Fill oil sump with 7 pints (4 litres) of approved engine Oil 20W/30/40. Refit accessories, and fill cooling system.

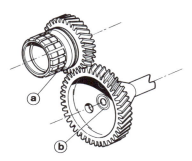

Fig.C.1. Identification of 32 x 43 input gearset.

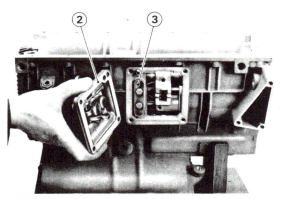

Fig.C.2. Removing gearchange mechanism cover.

Fig.C.3. Removing reverse gear forkshaft.

Fig.C.4. Removing input and layshaft coupling pin retaining spring.

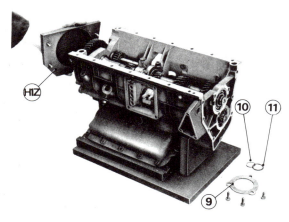

Fig.C.5. Installing retaining plate.

Fig.C.6. Removing layshaft ball bearing.

Gearbox

Two types of gearbox have been fitted to 204 vehicles, namely the BB1 and BB6 gearboxes. 304 vehicles have only BB6 type gearboxes fitted. The BB1 gearbox was fitted to 204 vehicles up to serial Nos:

204 Luxe 6071 924	204 C 6416 515
204 GL 8703 200	204 Co 6482 896
204 B 6770 600	204 U4 6502 726
204 BD 6638 250	

The BB6 gearbox fitted to 204 vehicles has an input gearset of 32 x 44, whereas the BB6 gearbox fitted to 304 vehicles has an input gearset of 32 x 43. The two gearsets are not interchangeable.

The 32 x 43 gearset is identified by a groove (Ref.'a', Fig.C1) on the drive pinion, and a groove(Ref.'b') on the input pinion.

BB1 GEARBOX/DIFFERENTIAL - Dismantling

Remove oil sump and oil pump strainer. Place gearbox on support base 8.0306Z, or similar. Slacken, and remove right and left-hand differential cover attachment screws, and differential housing attachment screws. Remove differential assembly. Remove oil deflector where fitted. Remove gear change mechanism cover (Ref,2 Fig.C2). Remove locking mechanism plate (Ref.3) and recover the three locking springs and the three locking balls. Drive out the Rollpins from the selector (Ref,4 Fig.C3) and from reverse gear fork (Ref.5). Remove reverse gear fork shaft (Ref.6), working towards the right.

Gearboxes Equipped with Input and Layshaft of the 1st Fitting

(No marking on 4th gear pinion).

Remove input shaft and layshaft coupling pin retaining spring (Ref.7, Fig.C4) towards the left, using a screwdriver by rotating the input shaft (Ref. 8). Drive the pin out in a slanted position so as to avoid any contact with the drive pinion. Remove layshaft ball bearing cover (Ref. 9 Fig.C5). Remove circlip (Ref. 10) and spring washer (Ref. 11). Strike end of input shaft with a mallet to loosen layshaft ball bearing and thereby facilitate extraction. Install special plate (Ref. H1Z) using gearbox cover mechanism attachment screws, tightening the four screws to 1 mkg. (7.25 lb.ft.) torque. *Important:* Ensure that end of the shaft is not burred, especially around the circlip neck. Smooth out using a fine stone if necessary. Drive out layshaft ball bearing, using special extractor (Ref.G Fig.C6). Remove special plate H1Z, input shaft (Ref. 8 Fig.C4) by pulling pinion out, bearing cap, and layshaft.

Gearboxes Equipped with Input and Layshaft of the 2nd Fitting

(4AL marking on 4th gear pinion).

Remove layshaft ball bearing cover (Ref. 9, Fig.C7). Remove circlip (Ref. 10), and spring washer (Ref. 11). Strike end of input shaft with a mallet to loosen layshaft ball bearing, and thereby facilitate extraction. Install special plate (Ref. H1Z), using the gear change cover mechanism attachment screws,

tightening the four screws to 1 mkg. (7.25 lb.ft.) torque. On diesel vehicles with a gearbox having an input shaft with a play take-up device, special spacers 8.0305 H2 and H3 should be inserted between the gearbox housing and special plate H1Z. Drive out layshaft ball bearing, using special extractor (Ref.G, Fig.C8). Remove special plate (Ref. H1Z). While removing the layshaft ensure that the circlip is in position, in both the input shaft and layshaft. If this precaution is not taken, the layshaft displacement is such that the 2nd and 4th gear pinions butt against the corresponding synchro cone, and may damage the cones. Compress the circlip using a pair of pliers, and remove the layshaft (Ref.8, Fig.C9), by pulling the pinion outwards. Remove the bearing cap and layshaft.

All Gearboxes: Unlock and remove reverse gear pinion shaft holding screw. Remove reverse gear pinion and shaft. Engage 2nd gear. Remove Rollpin from 1st/2nd gear fork using pin drift, working through gear change control orifice. With 3rd/4th gear fork in neutral, work out 1st/2nd gear fork shaft towards the right. Remove Rollpins from 3rd/4th gear fork and selector. Push 3rd/4th gear fork shaft (Ref.12, Fig.C11) towards the left, against the gearbox housing, so as to clear the 3rd/4th gear fork. Rotate shaft (Ref.12) by a quarter of a turn, so as to prevent the locking needle from falling downwards. Remove 3rd/4th gear fork. Work out 3rd/4th gear fork shaft to the right. Remove 3rd/4th gear selector and 1st/2nd gear fork.

Remove the two locking fingers from their housing (Fig. C12). Remove speedometer drive bush attachment screw. Remove speedometer drive bush using special pliers 8.0305J (See Fig.C13) by rotating the socket one half turn clockwise. Remove circlip and spring washers from each end of the mainshaft.

Remove speedometer drive worm and reverse gear pinion. Open mainshaft ball bearing circlip, using special pliers 8.0305J (see Fig.C14). Drive out shaft towards the left using a 20mm. (0.757 in.) dia. bronze drift. The sheet iron cap will be pushed out by the shaft. Remove 1st, 2nd, 3rd, and 4th gear pinions, bushes, hubs, and synchronizers. Keep washers and shims aside. *Note:* Do not separate synchro hubs from their dog sleeve. These are to be marked as regards their angular setting and initial position in the gearbox. Remove mainshaft outer bearing, using drift 8.0305R or similar (see Fig.C15).

Important: On the mainshaft of the 1st fitting ensure that ends of the shaft are not burred, especially around the circlip neck. If necessary, grind down carefully using a fine stone. Drive out the mainshaft ball bearing, using ball bearing extractor 8.0305G or similar (See Fig.C16). Drive out mainshaft taper bearing, using bearing extractor 8.0305K or similar (see Fig.C17).

DIFFERENTIAL ASSEMBLY - Dismantling

Remove the six assembling screws of the differential. Remove differential left hand casing, sun gear and its Celeron washers. Separate the crown wheel from the differential casing, using a mallet. Remove planet pinion spindle, planet pinions and their thrust washer, the second sun gear, and its Celeron washer. Remove differential bearings, using a taper roller bearing extractor with special tool 8.0312F (see Fig.C18).

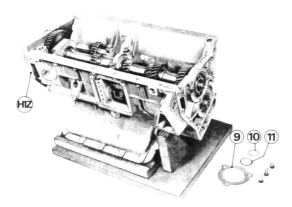

Fig.C.7. Installing retaining plate.

Fig.C.10. 1st/2nd and 3rd/4th gear forks.

Fig.C.8. Removing layshaft ball bearing.

Fig.C.11. Removing 3rd/4th gear fork.

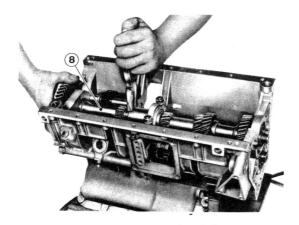

Fig.C.9. Removing layshaft.

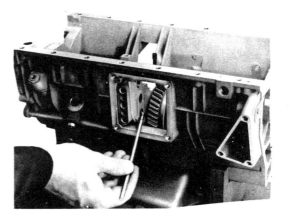

Fig.C.12. Removing locking fingers.

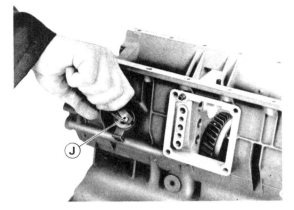

Fig.C.13. Removing speedometer drive bush.

Fig.C.14. Opening mainshaft ball bearing circlip.

Fig.C.15. Removing mainshaft outer bearing.

Fig.C.16. Driving out mainshaft ball bearing.

Fig.C.17. Driving out mainshaft taper bearing.

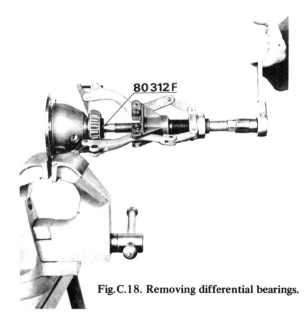

Fig.C.18. Removing differential bearings.

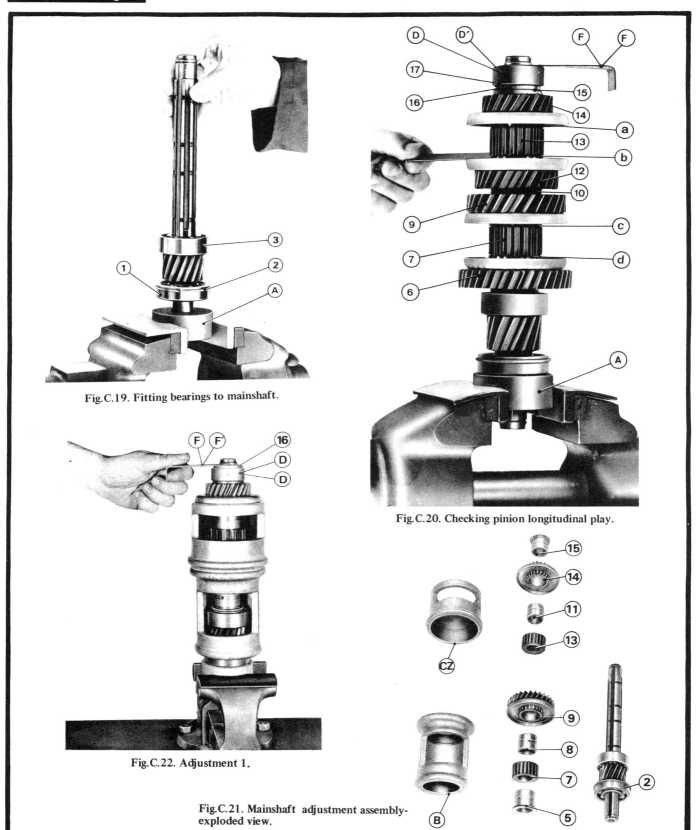

Fig.C.19. Fitting bearings to mainshaft.

Fig.C.20. Checking pinion longitudinal play.

Fig.C.22. Adjustment 1.

Fig.C.21. Mainshaft adjustment assembly-exploded view.

GEARBOX INPUT PINION BUSH

Due to extreme precision with which the reaming has to be performed when replacing an input pinion bush, it is essential that the work be given to a specialist who has the necessary machines for 'in-line' reaming, regrinding crankshafts, or machining of main bearings.

BB1 GEARBOX/DIFFERENTIAL - Re-assembly

The gearbox housing, differential housing, and layshaft control bearing cap, are machined after assembly. Consequently these parts must not be replaced separately. In order to make the pairing easier, all parts have been marked with a common reference since June 1965. On the first 204 gearboxes, the manufacturing number is inscribed on a boss located on the gearbox housing front end near the lower sump and the differential housing.

Use only a lint free cloth moistened with industrial grade methylated spirits for cleaning mating surfaces smeared with 'Perfect Seal'. Never use emery cloth or cutting tools. Before assembly all parts must be perfectly clean, and particular attention should be paid to the cleanliness of the oil passages for the input and layshaft bearings. Check the condition of the input shaft bush and half shells, replacing if necessary. All Onduflex washers must be replaced. Lubricate the components on installation.

Install ball bearing (Ref. 1 Fig.C19) with the groove facing the pinion, using a hollow drift. Fit a new circlip (Ref. 2). into the bearing groove for adjustment. Fit taper bearing (Ref.3) using a hollow drift. Hold special collar 8.0305A in a vice, and engage the mainshaft into the collar bore.

PINION LONGITUDINAL PLAY - Checking

Assemble 1st gear bush and pinion (Ref. 6 Fig.C20), synchro hub (Ref. 7,) 2nd gear bush and pinion (Ref. 9), spacer (Ref. 10), 3rd gear bush and pinion (Ref.12), synchro hub (Ref.13), pinion (Ref.14), 4th gear bush (Ref.15), and spacer (Ref.16), onto the mainshaft. Establish the number of shims (Ref.17) to be placed under the gauge 8.0305D (2nd fitting gauges are yellow bichromated) to obtain a tight assembly after insertion of fork 8.0305F in the groove provided for the snap ring. Check that the play at references 'a' 'b', 'c', and 'd' is between 0.35mm. 0.5mm. (0.0138 and 0.0197 in.) for gearboxes up to serial No. F74 634, or between 0.20 and 0.5mm. (0.0079 and 0.0197 in). for gearboxes from serial No. F74 635 or between 0.20 and 0.35 mm. (0.0079 and 0.0138 in.) or between 0.20 and 0.35mm (0.0079 and 0.0138 in.) for gearboxes fitted to Diesel vehicles from serial No. 6 636204. Replace the bushings if the play exceeds the appropriate values in either direction. Dismantle the assembly in order to perform the next adjustment.

Mainshaft Adjustment Procedure

Assemble the 1st gear pinion bush (Ref.5, Fig.C21), synchro hub (Ref.7), gauge 8.0305B (Ref.B), using snap ring (Ref.2) of the ball bearing as a support, 2nd gear pinion (Ref.9) and its bush (Ref.8), synchro hub (Ref.13), 3rd gear pinion bush (Ref.11), gauge 8.0305CZ (Ref. CZ), and 4th gear pin (Ref.14) and its bush (Ref.15), onto mainshaft.

Adjustment

Install gauge (Ref.D Fig.C22). Select a spacer (Ref.16) placed on the gauge, and if necessary a number of shims (Ref.17) to obtain a free fit after inserting fork (Ref.F) in the groove provided for the snap ring. The spacers (Ref.16) are available in thicknesses 2.50 mm. (Part No. 2357.23), 3.00mm. (P.N. 2357.24), 3.50mm. (P.N.2357.25), 3.93mm. (P.N.2357.26), and 3.25mm. (P.N.2357.27). Spacing shims (Ref.17) are available in thicknesses 0.15mm. (Part No.2357.05). and 0.50mm. (P.N.2357.06).

Adjustment 2

Determine the thickness of adjusting shim (Ref.10, Fig. C23) required between 3rd gear pinion bush (Ref.11) and 3rd/ 4th gear synchro hub (Ref.13), to eliminate all play. Leave shim in position to perform adjustment 3. *Note:* Shim (Ref.10) determined by adjustment 2 will be placed between 2nd gear bush pinion (Ref.9, Fig.C20) and 3rd bush and pinion (Ref.12) assemblies at final assembly. If the original assembly contained two spacers and an adjusting shim, they should be replaced with one of the new spacers. The spacers are available in 19 thicknesses.

Thickness	Part No.	Thickness	Part No.
2.50mm.	2318.22	3.00mm.	2318.32
2.55	2318.23	3.05	2318.33
2.60	2318.24	3.10	2318.34
2.65	2318.25	3.15	2318.35
2.70	2318.26	3.20	2318.36
2.75	2318.27	3.25	2318.37
2.80	2318.28	3.30	2318.38
2.85	2318.29	3.35	2318.39
2.90	2318.30	3.40	2318.40
2.95	2318.31		

Adjustment 3

Determine the thickness of adjustment shims (Ref.4, Fig. C24) required between the taper bearing (Ref.3) and the 1st gear pinion bush (Ref.5), to eliminate all play. Adjusting shims (Ref.4) are available in thicknesses 0.15mm. (Part No. 2318.15), 0.20mm. (P.N.2318.16), 0.25mm. (P.N.2318.17), and 0.50mm (P.N.2318.18).

Dismantle the assembly. Place shims (Ref.4, Fig.C24) obtained at adjustment 3, between 1st gear pinion bush (Ref.5) and taper bearing (Ref.3). Remove circlip mounted on the ball bearing for adjustment purposes, and install it in the housing. Assemble the 1st gear pinion (Ref.6, Fig.C20), hub (Ref. 7) and 1st/2nd gear synchro. (with reference grooves (Ref.'a' Fig. C25) facing the 1st gear pinion, the hub and its sleeve with their reference marks facing each other), the 2nd gear pinion (Ref.9, Fig.C20) and its bush (Ref. 8) in the housing. Bring the mainshaft into position, working from the left, and engage it in the assembly. Fit adjusting shim (Ref,10 Fig.C26) determined by adjustment 2. Fit bush (Ref.11), 3rd gear pinion (Ref.12), hub (Ref.13), and 3rd/4th gear synchro (with reference marks (Ref. 'a') facing 3rd gear pinion, and with reference marks on hub and its sleeve facing each other). Raise the assembly, slide 4th gear pinion (Ref14), and engage its bushing (Ref.14) through the bearing bore.

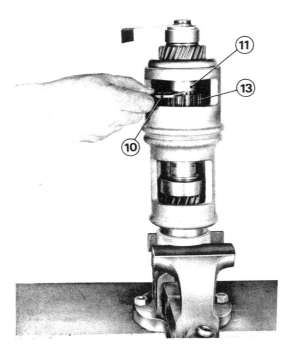

Fig.C.23. Adjustment 2.

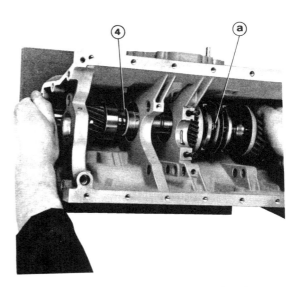

Fig.C.25. Fitting 2nd gear bush and pinion onto mainshaft.

Fig.C.24. Adjustment 3.

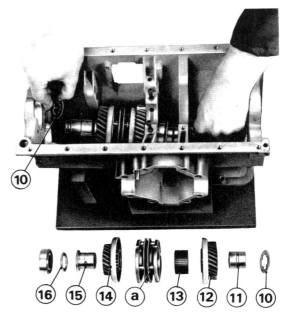

Fig.C.26. Fitting adjusting shim.

58

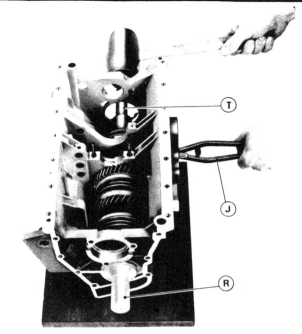

Fig.C.27. Engaging mainshaft.

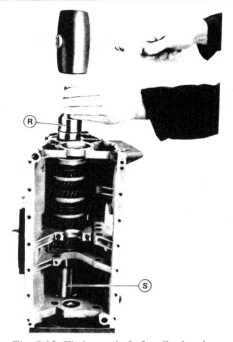

Fig. C.28. Fitting mainshaft roller bearing.

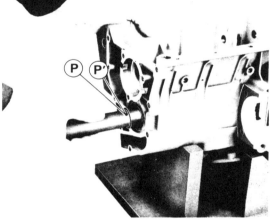

Fig.C.29. Centering mainshaft assembly.

Fig.C.30. Checking speedometer drive worm play.

Fig.C.32. Installing locking finger.

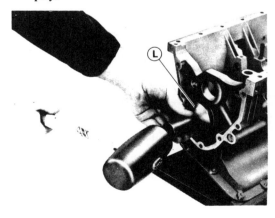

Fig.C.31. Installing sheet iron cap.

Fig.C.33. Installing ball bearing.

Fig.C.34. Pinning fork and reverse gear selector with Rollpin.

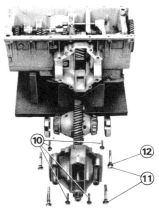

Fig.C.38. Installing differential.

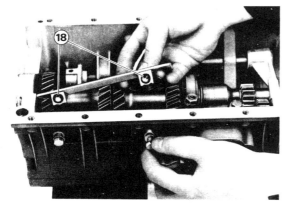

Fig.C.35. Fitting O-rings on oil deflector.

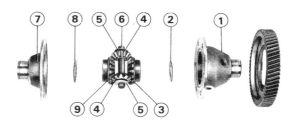

Fig.C.36. Differential - exploded view.

Fig.C.37. Installing differential bearing cones.

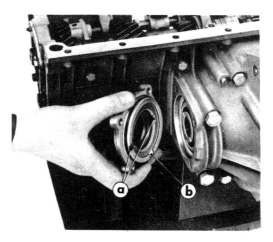

Fig.C.39. Installing right hand differential cover.

Engage drift (Ref.R, Fig.C27) in place of the bearing with the end of the shaft being guided into the drifts.

Make up a mainshaft installing tool by clamping a spacer (Ref.T, Fig.C27) between body and screw head of extractor 8.0305G. Open ball bearing circlip and hold it. To engage mainshaft use a mallet to strike on the end of the extractor. Continue striking until bearing groove protrudes from the circlips. Withdraw drift (Ref.R, Fig.C27). Install support rod (Ref.S, Fig.C28) at end of mainshaft, and hold it using installing plate H1Z screwed in and locked against the housing face. Place the gearbox vertically on plate H1Z. Install spacer and shims determined by adjustment 1. Fit mainshaft roller bearing using a mallet and drift (Ref.R. Fig.C28). Remove plate H1Z and support rod Ref.S. Move mainshaft towards left using drift until engagement of circlip into ball bearing groove. Install a new spring washer and a new circlip at the shaft end. Using drift (Ref.P, Fig.C29), position and centre the assembly by hand. Terminate the operation by striking a blow with the mallet. As a safety measure, the circlips should be tightened with a pair of pliers after they are fitted in position. Install reverse gear pinion and speedometer drive worm. Bring adjusting gauge (Ref.E Fig.C30) against the worm, and check for correct fitting with fork (Ref.F). Take up play, if any, using an adjusting shim (Ref.17, Fig.C22) of appropriate thickness. Remove yoke and gauge. If necessary, place shim between reverse gear pinion and speedometer drive worm. Install a spring washer and a new circlip, using a drift.

Install a new sheet iron cap smeared with Festinol compound using special drift 8.0305L (see Fig.C31). Rotate mainshaft by about half a turn. Re-install speedometer drive socket with a new 'O'-ring. Install 1st/2nd gear fork. Work fork shaft into position from the right with the locking notches facing upwards and the 1st gear locking notch alignment with the vertical locking finger hole. Install a locking finger in position (See Fig.C32). Ensure that this locking finger does not exceed the 3rd/4th gear shaft bore. Working from the right, bring 3rd/4th gear shaft into its bore, and at the same time install its selector with its flange facing towards the right. Bring it to bear against the housing centre wall, and fit locking needle held in position with grease. Engage 4th gear and fit 3rd/4th gear fork. Bring the shaft back into 3rd/4th gear fork, and position it with the flat facing upwards for a 1st fitting shaft, or with reference mark facing gear change mechanism cover for a 2nd fitting shaft (the 2nd fitting shaft has been fitted since February 1967). Release 4th gear to engage neutral, and pin the fork selector on the shaft. Rotate 1st/2nd gear shaft by a quarter of a turn outwards, and then bring the shaft pin hole in alignment with the fork pin hole, and fit the pin. Use new Rollpins. Fit reverse gear pinion and its shaft. Tighten pinion screw to 0.75 mkg. (5.4 lb.ft.) and then lock screw.

Gearboxes Equipped with an Input and Layshaft of 1st Fitting

The 1st fitting is on vehicles with serial numbers up to: 204 Luxe 6066 034, 204 Grand Luxe 6316 979, 204B (Break) 6 694 650, 204C (Convertible) 6 408 230, 204C (Coupe) 6 457 526, 204 U4 (Light Van) 6 500 911, and can be identified by the lack of marking on the 4th gear pinion.

Fit the layshaft and bearing cap (the half bearing shells should be free from defect). Tighten the nuts to 2.25mkg. (16 lb.ft.) torque. Install input shaft and special plate H1Z. Place gearbox vertically on plate H1Z. Install ball bearing with extraction groove facing outwards, using extractor body (Ref.G, Fig.C33). Fit a new spring washer and a new circlip,

using a drift. Remove plate H1Z. Install ball bearing cover and tighten the three screws to 1 mkg. (7.25 lb.ft.) torque. Move the retaining spring along the input shaft, as during dismantling. Fit a new input shaft layshaft coupling pin (length 33mm. (1.3 in.) Re-install the retaining spring. Ensure that layshaft rotates freely. If it does not, slacken bearing cap nuts, and tap gently with a mallet to properly position the layshaft until it rotates freely. Re-tighten the nuts to 2.25 mkg. (16 lb.ft.) torque.

Gearboxes Equipped with an Input and Layshaft of 2nd Fitting

The 2nd fitting is fitted as from gearbox number C80 383, and vehicles from serial numbers 204 Luxe 6 066 035, 204 Grand Luxe 6 316 980, 204B (Break) 6 694 651, 204C (Convertible) 6 408 231, 204C (Coupe) 6 457 527, 204 U4 (Light Van) 6 500 912, 204 BD from beginning of series, and can be identified by the marking 4AL on the 4th gear pinion.

Install the layshaft and bearing cap (the half bearing shells must be free from all defect). Tighten the nuts to 2.25 mkg. (16.6 lb.ft.) torque. Install a new circlip in the groove provided at the input shaft end. Engage input shaft end onto layshaft. Compress the circlip using a pair of pliers, and insert the input shaft until the circlip falls into its groove on the layshaft. Fit special plate H1Z. On petrol engine vehicles with a gearbox with a one piece input shaft (fitted in production since July 1968, insert box plug 8.0312F between plate H1Z and input shaft pinion, by centring the base plug in the 8.2 mm. dia. hole provided in the centre of plate H1Z. On diesel engine vehicles with a gearbox incorporating an input shaft with an automatic play take-up device, insert spacers 8.0305 H2 and H3 between the gearbox housing and plate H1Z. Place gearbox vertically on plate H1Z. Install the ball bearing with extraction groove facing outwards, using extractor body (see Fig.C33). Place a new spring washer and a new circlip, using a drift. Remove plate H1Z. Install ball bearing cover, and tighten the three screws 1 mkg. (7.25 lb.ft.). torque. Ensure layshaft rotates freely. If it does not, slacken bearing cap nuts, and tap gently with a mallet to properly centre the layshaft until it rotates freely. Re-tighten the nuts to 2.25 mkg. (16 lb.ft.). torque.

All Gearboxes: Install the 2nd locking finger. Install reverse gear fork. Engage shaft into position on the fork, working from the right (with locking notches facing rearwards). Fit the selector. Pin the fork and reverse gear selector, using new Rollpins (see Fig.C34). Install the three locking balls and the three locking springs. Fit the gearbox locking plate, and tighten the screw to 0.75 mkg. (5 lb.ft.). torque. Install gear change mechanism cover and gasket. Tighten screw 1 mkg. (7.25 lb.ft.) torque. On gearboxes equipped with an oil deflector fit new 'O'-rings (Ref.18, Fig.C35) held in position with grease. Tighten the screws to 1 mkg. (7.25 lb.ft.). torque.

DIFFERENTIAL - Re-assembly

Place the Celeron washer (Ref.2, Fig.C36), sun gear (Ref.3) planet gears (Ref.4,) and their thrust washer (Ref.5), in the differential case (Ref.1). Install planet gear shaft (Ref.6). Place the Celeron washer (Ref,8), and sun gear (Ref,9), on the differential cover (Ref,7). Assemble differential.

Install the crownwheel on the differential case. Use new assembling bolts equipped with new Blocfor washers, and tighten to 5.75 mkg. (42 lb.ft.) torque. Using a press, install the differential bearing cones, using fitting tool 8.0312G on

Fig.C.40. Determining shims for differential.

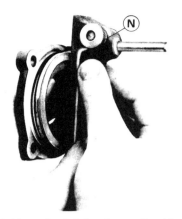

Fig.C.41. Measuring left hand cover for shim determination.

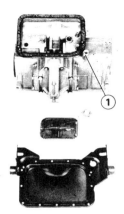

Fig.C.42. Oil pump strainer and sump.

Fig.C.43. Removing gear change mechanism cover plate.

Fig.C.44. Removing Rollpin from reverse gear fork.

Fig.C.45. Fitting special retaining plate.

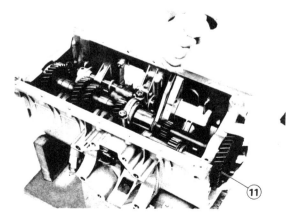

Fig.C.46. Removing input shaft.

the top of the bearing as shown in Fig.C37. Smear the differential bearing surfaces with Perfect Seal. Install the differential assembly and differential cover. Install, without tightening, the four 8mm. dia. screws (Ref.10, Fig.C38) with new Onduflex washers, and the four 10mm. dia. screws (Ref.11) with new Onduflex washers and new 'O'-rings (Ref.12), part no. 0165.07.

Differential Adjustment

Install a new 'O'—ring smeared with tallow, and a seal ring into the right hand differential cover. Fit the right hand differential cover after smearing its bearing surface with Perfect Seal, positioning notches (Ref.'a' Fig.C39) horizontally, and the oil drain groove (Ref.'b')facing downwards. Tighten the cover screws to 2 mkg. (14.5 lb.ft.) torque. Install locking clamp (Ref.M, Fig. C40), and bring the left hand bearing outer race to bear on the roller cage, without applying force. Place adjusting gauge (Ref. N) against the mating surface, bring the feeler to rest on the bearing outer race, and lock feeler in position. Determine the number of shims required by comparison with the left hand cover (Fig.C41). and add one 0.1 mm. shim. Remove clamp (Ref. M). Slacken right hand cover securing bolts. Tighten the 8mm. dia. bolts to 2mkg. (14.5 lb.ft.) torque, and the 19mm. dia. bolts to 4mkg. (29 lb.ft.) torque. Place a new 'O'-ring, smeared with tallow, and a new seal ring on the left hand cover. Smear the cover left hand bearing face with Perfect Seal, and fit the left hand cover (same positioning as the right hand cover) while inserting the adjusting shims. Tighten the cover securing bolts 2 mkg. (14 lb.ft.) torque. Refit oil pump strainer. Refit sump plate with a new gasket. Check all gears for free engagement before re-installing gearbox on the engine.

BB6 GEARBOX/DIFFERENTIAL - Dismantling

Remove oil sump and oil pump strainer. *Note:* The spacer (Ref. 1, Fig.C42) for the right hand drain plug is secured with 'Hard Holding Loctite' at the factory, and must not be removed. Place gearbox on support 8.0306Z, or similar. Slacken and remove bolts of left and right hand covers and differential housing. Remove differential assembly. Remove the two union bolts (Ref.2, Fig.C43), oil pipe (Ref.3), gear change mechanism cover plate(Ref.4), gasket (Ref.5), locking springs (Ref.6), and balls. Engage reverse gear. Remove Rollpin (Ref.7),Fig.C44) from reverse gear fork. Recover ball and spring from reverse gear selector by pivoting selector upwards. Remove Rollpin from reverse gear selector. Recover reverse gear fork, shaft, and reverse gear selector.

Remove layshaft bearing retaining plate (Ref.8, Fig.C45). Remove snap ring (Ref.9), and spring washer (Ref.10). Tap end of input shaft to free bearing and facilitate removal. Fit special plate H1Z using gear selector cover plate bolts. For diesel engine gearbox, fit spacers 8.0305H2 and H3 between housing and plate H1Z. Tighten the four bolts to 1mkg. (7.25 lb.ft.) torque. Remove layshaft bearing using extractor 8.0305G or similar. When removing layshaft bearing, the snap ring must be in position in the input and layshaft. If not, the movement of the layshaft will cause the 2nd and 4th gear pinions to damage the corresponding synchroniser cones, by butting into them. Remove plate H1Z. Close up snap ring with a pair of pliers, and withdraw input shaft (Ref.11, Fig.C46). Remove central bearing cap and layshaft.

Engage 4th gear. Remove Rollpins from 3rd/4th gear selector (Ref.12,Fig.C47), 3rd/4th gear selector fork (Ref.13), and reverse gear sliding pinion shaft (Ref.14). Remove reverse gear shaft (Ref.14), and sliding pinion (Ref.15). Remove 3rd/ 4th gear selector fork shaft (Ref.16) after rotating it quarter of a turn to prevent locking finger falling out. Remove 3rd/4th gear selector (Ref.12). Engage 2nd gear. Remove Rollpin from 1st/ 2nd gear.selector fork (Ref.17, Fig.C48). Remove 1st/2nd gear selector fork shaft, 3rd/4th gear selector fork (Ref.13) and 1st/ 2nd gear selector fork (Ref.17). Recover the two locking fingers (see Fig.C49). Withdraw screw securing speedometer drive bush. Remove speedometer drive bush, using special pliers 8.0305J, by turning it half a turn clockwise. Remove snap rings and spring washers from both ends of mainshaft. Remove speedometer drive worm and reverse pinion. Refit special plate 8.0305 H1Z, using gear selector cover plate bolts. Fit a thrust rod in a press 20mm (0.787 in.) dia. max. and install housing in press, resting it on plate H1Z. Spread mainshaft bearing circlip using special pliers 8.0305J. Drive out shaft until plug in housing is pushed out by shaft. Release press. Remove needle roller bearing inner race (Ref.18 Fig.C50), 4th gear spacer (Ref.19), and 4th gear pinion and bush (Ref.20). Fit a flat thrust pad in press. Place pad 8.0312B or similar on needle roller bearing outer race with grooved face downwards. Remove needle roller race. Recover race and pad 8.0312B.

Place housing on its support on workbench. Remove plate H1Z. Recover mainshaft with its two bearings, 3rd/4th gear synchroniser and hub, 3rd gear pinion and bush, spacer (Ref.21 Fig.C51), 2nd gear pinion and bush, 1st/2nd gear synchroniser and hub, and 1st gear pinion bush and shims. *Note:* Do not separate synchronisers and hubs which must be marked according to their relative positions in the gearbox. Remove ball bearing from mainshaft using extractor 8.0305G or similar. Remove roller bearing from mainshaft using extractor 8.0305K or similar.

DIFFERENTIAL - Dismantling

Remove the six bolts retaining the crown wheel. Remove left hand half casing, sun gear, and 'Celeron' washer. Drive crown wheel off the casing, using a mallet. Remove planet gear shaft and the two thrust washers, second sun gear and 'Celeron' washer. To remove differential bearings, use a roller bearing extractor and special thrust pad 8.0312F or similar (see Fig.C.18).

GEARBOX INPUT PINION BUSH

Due to extreme precision with which the reaming has to be performed when replacing an input pinion bush, it is essential that the work be entrusted to a specialist who has the necessary machines for 'in-line' reaming, regrinding crankshafts, or machining of main bearings.

BB6 GEARBOX/DIFFERENTIAL - Re-assembly

The gearbox housing, differential housing, and layshaft central bearing caps, are machined after assembly. Consequently these parts must not be replaced separately. In order to make the pairing easier all parts are marked with a common reference.

Use only lint free cloth moistened with industrial grade methylated spirits for cleaning mating surfaces which are to be sealed with Perfect Seal.

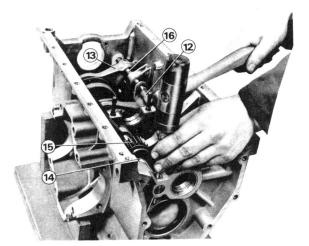

Fig.C.47. Removing Rollpin from reverse gear sliding pinion shaft.

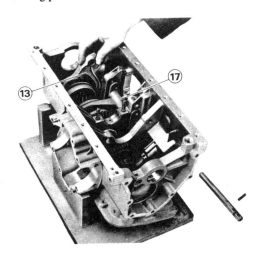

Fig.C.48. Removing 3rd/4th gear selector fork.

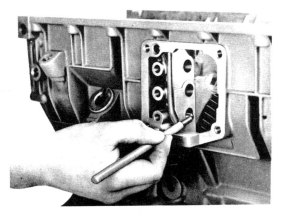

Fig.C.49. Recovering locking fingers.

Fig.C.50. Removing mainshaft.

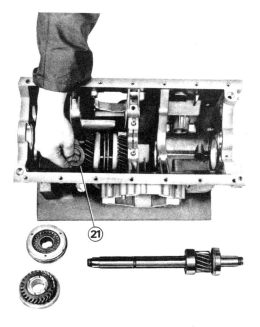

Fig.C.51. Removing spacer.

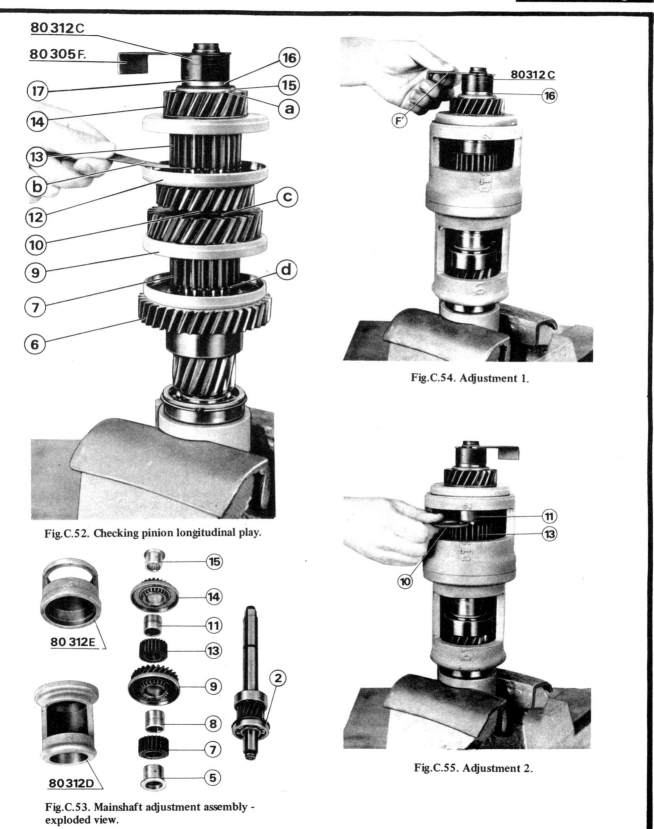

80 312 C

80 305 F.

Fig.C.52. Checking pinion longitudinal play.

80 312 E

80 312 D

Fig.C.53. Mainshaft adjustment assembly -
exploded view.

Fig.C.54. Adjustment 1.

80 312 C

Fig.C.55. Adjustment 2.

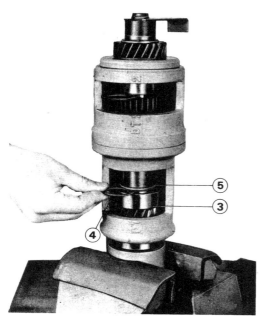

Fig.C.56. Adjustment 3.

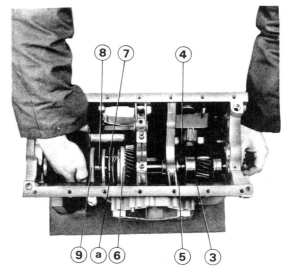

Fig.C.57. Fitting 2nd gear pinion to mainshaft assembly.

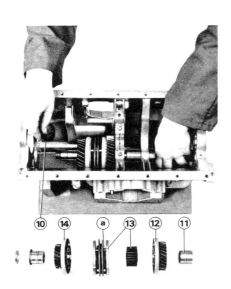

Fig.C.58. Fitting spacer to mainshaft assembly.

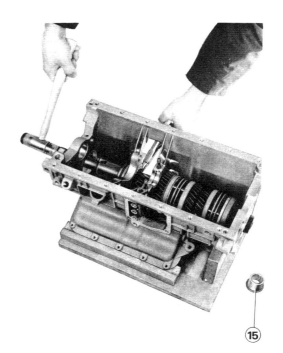

Fig.C.59. Driving mainshaft into housing.

Never use emery cloth or cutting tools. Before assembly, all parts must be perfectly clean and particular attention should be paid to the cleanliness of the oil ducts and plain bearings of layshaft and input shaft. Ensure that the input shaft bush and half shells are in perfect condition. Replace all Onduflex washers. Lubricate the components on installation.

Fit ball bearing on mainshaft with the groove towards the pinion, using body of extractor 8.0305G. Fit a new circlip in the groove. Fit roller bearing, using body of extractor 8.0305K. Clamp special sleeve 8.0305A in a vice, and place mainshaft in sleeve bore.

PINION LONGITUDINAL PLAY - Checking

Assemble, in the order given, 1st gear bush and pinion (Ref.6, Fig.C52), synchroniser hub (Ref.7), 2nd gear bush and pinion (Ref, 9). spacer (Ref,10), 3rd gear bush and pinion (Ref,12), synchroniser hub (Ref. 13), 4th gear pinion (Ref.14), and bush (Ref.15), and spacer (Ref,16), onto the mainshaft. Determine the number of shims (Ref,17), to be placed under the gauge 8.0312C, to obtain a tight assembly with the fork 8.0305F, inserted in the snap ring groove. Check the play at references 'a' 'b' 'c' and 'd' which should be between 0.20mm. 0.35mm. (0.0079 and 0.0138 in). Replace pinion bushes if the play exceeds these values in either direction. Dismantle this assembly to perform adjustment 1.

To perform adjustments 1 to 3, assemble in the order given, 1st gear bush (Ref,5, Fig.C53), synchroniser hub (Ref.7), gauge 8.0312D, resting on circlip (Ref.2), 2nd gear pinion (Ref.9) and bush (Ref. 8), synchroniser hub (Ref,13), 3rd gear bush (Ref,11), gauge 8.0312E, 4th gear pinion (Ref.14), and bush (Ref.15).

Adjustment 1

Install gauge 8.0312C (See Fig.C54). Select a spacer (Ref. 16), and place it under gauge, if necessary using one or two shims(Ref.17), to obtain a tight fit without play when the fork (Ref.F) is inserted in the groove for the snap ring. The spacer (Ref.16) is available in the thicknesses. 3.2mm. (Part No.2357. 39), 3.6mm. (P.N. 2357.40), 4.0 mm. (P.N. 2357.41), 4.4mm. (P.N. 2357.42), and 4.8mm. (P.N.2357.43). The shim (Ref.17) is 0.15mm. thick (Part No. 2357.05).

Adjustment 2

Determine the thickness of the spacer (Ref.10) Fig.C.55) between the 3rd gear bush (Ref.11) and the 3rd/4th synchroniser hub (Ref.13) to eliminate play. Leave this spacer in position for adjustment 3. *Note:* The spacer (Ref.10) will be assembled between the 2nd gear bush (Ref.9, Fig.C52), and 3rd gear bush (Ref.12, Fig.C52), during final assembly. Spacer (Ref.10) is available in 19 different thicknesses from 2.00mm. to 2.90mm. varying by .05mm. increments.

Adjustment 3

Determine the thickness of the shims (Ref.4, Fig.C56) between the roller bearing (Ref, 3) and 1st gear bush (Ref, 5), to eliminate play. Shim (Ref, 4) is available in thicknesses 0.15mm. (Part No. 2318.15), 0.20mm. (P.N.2318.16), 0.25mm. (P.N.2318.17), and 0.50mm. (P.N. 2318.18).

Dismantle the assembly. Place shims (Ref. 4 Fig.C57) determined by adjustment 3 between roller bearing (Ref.3) and 1st gear bush (Ref. 5). Remove circlip from ball bearing and place it in its groove in the housing. Engage mainshaft partly in housing, and fit, in order given, 1st gear pinion (Ref. 6), 1st/2nd gear synchroniser (Ref. 7), and hub with reference groove (Ref.a), on 1st gear side, and hub synchro reference marks in line, 2nd gear bush (Ref, 8), and 2nd gear pinion (Ref, 9). Fit spacer (Ref. 10, Fig.C58) determined by adjustment 2. Fit 3rd gear bush (Ref. 11) and pinion (Ref.12), hub (Ref. 13), and 3rd/4th synchroniser with groove (Ref'a') and reference marks in line.

Raise the shaft slightly, and fit 4th gear pinion (Ref.14). Engage special ring 8.0312B in the housing in the needle roller bearing housing, ground side facing outwards, to guide the mainshaft into the bearing. Assemble fitting tool for the mainshaft securing spacer 8.0305T or similar between the head and base of the extractor bolt 8.0305G. Open up ball bearing circlip, and hold open. Engage mainshaft using a mallet and fitting tool (See Fig. C59). Continue driving mainshaft in until the circlip engages in the groove in the bearing. Withdraw ring 8.0312B. Engage 4th gear bush (Ref.15, C59) through needle roller bearing bore. Fit reverse gear pinion with small shoulder against bearing. Fit speedo-meter drive worm. Place special gauge 8.0305E against worm, and check side play with special fork 8.0305F, (See Fig. C60). Take up any excessive play using appropriate shim. Shims are available in thicknesses 0.15 mm. (Part No. 2357.05), and 0.50 mm. (Part No. 2357.06). Remove fork and gauge. If required, place shim between reverse gear and worm. Fit a new spring washer and snap ring, using a drift.

Place special adjustable pad 8.0312A on mainshaft end. Fit special plate 8.0305H1Z, taking care to position flats of pad 8.0312A in the groove in the lower part. Secure plate with gear change mechanism cover plate bolts.

Tighten bolts to 1 mkg. (7.25 lb.ft.) torque. Unscrew pad 8.0312A until the nut butts against plate 8.0305 H1Z. Hand-tighten. Do not use a tool for this. Place gearbox on a press plate resting on plate 8.0305H1Z. Position the spacer; and if required, shims determined by adjustment 1 on the shaft. Place needle roller bearing on end of shaft with the inscription facing upwards. Press the bearing into the housing until it butts against the shaft. Do not exceed 1 ton pressure. Place a new washer and circlip on end of shaft. Engage the snap ring in the groove, using a press and tubular drift. Again do not exceed 1 ton pressure. Close up snap ring with a pair of pliers, and check that the outer diameter of the snap ring does not exceed 22.6mm. (0.8898 in.). Remove plate 8.0305 H1Z and thrust pad 8.0312A.

Fit a new sheet metal plug smeared with Festinol, using special drift 8.0305L or similar. Refit speedometer drive bush, fitted with a new oil seal, turning it through one half turn. Position 1st/2nd and 3rd/4th gear selector forks in their corresponding synchronisers. Engage 1st/2nd selector fork shaft from the right, ensuring that the locking notch is on the axis of the vertical hole. Insert a locking finger. Ensure that the locking finger is in place, and that it does not protrude into the 3rd/4th selector shaft hole. Place 3rd/4th selector shaft in position, positioning it with the two flats facing upwards, and insert the locking finger, after greasing it. Insert the shaft in this position from the right, fitting the selector control, with its ramp facing upwards, until it is in line with the 1st/2nd shaft. Rotate the 3rd/4th shaft quarter of a turn towards the selector mechanism cover opening. The correct positioning is when the reference notch (Ref.a, Fig.C61) is parallel to the opening. Pin the shafts, forks and selector controls, using new Rollpins. Insert reverse gear sliding pinion shaft in housing.

Fig.C.60. Checking side play of speedometer drive worm.

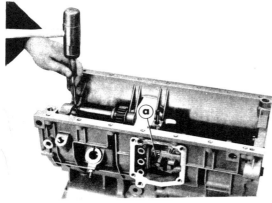

Fig.C.61. Pinning the shafts forks and selector controls.

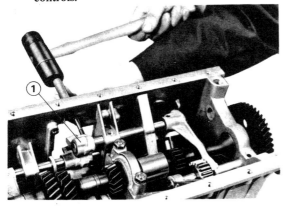

Fig.C.62. Pinning reverse gear selector control.

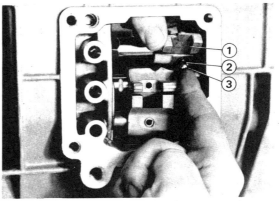

Fig.C.63. Positioning spring and ball in selector.

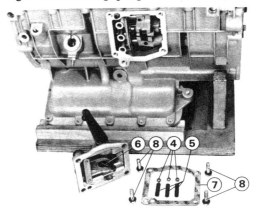

Fig.C.64. Gear selector mechanism.

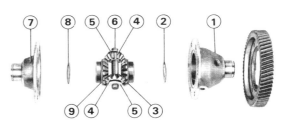

Fig.C.65. Differential - exploded view.

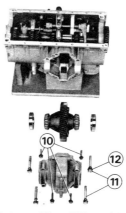

Fig.C.66. Assembling differential to gearbox.

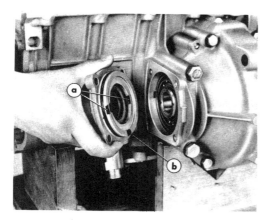
Fig.C.67. Determining shims for differential.

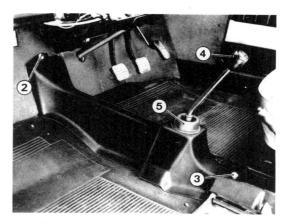
Fig.C.70. Interior view of gear change lever mechanism cover.

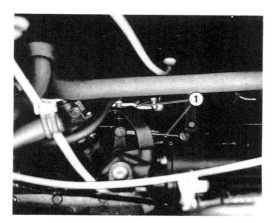
Fig. C.69. Floor mounted gear change lever links.

Fig.C.68. Measuring left hand cover for shim determination.

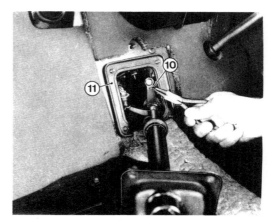
Fig.C.71. Disconnecting the return spring.

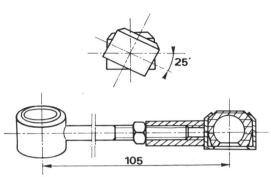

Fig.C.72. Link adjustment.

Fig.C.73. Gear change mechanism links.

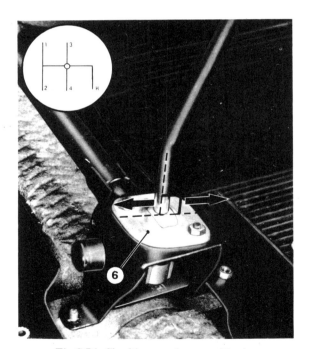

Fig.C.74. Checking gear lever positioning.

Fit reverse gear sliding pinion with the groove facing outwards. Secure shaft using a new Rollpin. Fit layshaft and central bearing, ensuring beforehand that the bearing shells are clean and free from faults. Tighten the nuts to 2.25 mkg. (16 lb.ft.). torque.

Place a new snap ring in the groove on the end of the input shaft. Engage input shaft in layshaft. Compress the snap ring with a pair of pliers, and push the input shaft in until the snap ring engages in the groove in the layshaft. On petrol engine gearboxes, fit special plate 8.0305H1Z with special pad 8.0312F inserted between the input pinion and plate H1Z, with its centring pin in the 8.2mm. dia. hole in the plate. On diesel engine gearboxes, fit special plate 8.0305H1Z with spacers 8.0305H2 and H3 inserted between the housing and plate H1Z. Place gearbox upright, resting on plate H1Z. Fit ball bearing with groove facing outwards, using a drift and mallet. Fit a new cup washer and snap ring, using a drift. Compress the snap ring, using a pair of combination pliers. Its outer diameter must not exceed 22.6mm. (0.8898 in.). Remove plate H1Z. Fit bearing retaining plate and tighten the bolts to 1 mkg. (7.25 lb.ft.) torque. Ensure that the layshaft turns freely. If it does not, slacken the bearing cap nuts, and tap lightly until the shaft turns freely. Re-tighten the nuts to 2.25 mkg. (16 lb.ft.). torque.

Position 2nd locking finger. Fit reverse gear selector fork. Engage shaft from right, with locking notches facing rear of gearbox. Fit and pin selector control (Ref.1, Fig.C62), using a new Rollpin. Push selector to right, pivoting it upwards. Position spring (Ref 2, Fig.C63) of free height 26.15mm. (1.03 in.) and ball (Ref.3) in selector (Ref.1). Compress spring while lowering selector. Return selector (Ref. 1) to neutral. Pin reverse gear fork to its shaft with a new Rollpin. Place locking balls (Ref.4 Fig.C64), and springs (Ref. 5), in position, (spring free height is 29.5mm. (1.161 in.). Fit selector mechanism cover (Ref. 6), after fitting a new gasket (Ref. 7), and using new Onduflex washers. Tighten bolts (Ref. 8) to 1 mkg. (7.25 lb.ft.) torque.

DIFFERENTIAL - Re-assembly

Position 'Celeron' washer (Ref. 2 Fig.C65), sun gear (Ref.3), planet gears (Ref. 4), and their thrust washers (Ref. 5), in the differential casing (Ref. 1). Fit planet gear spindle (Ref, 6). Position 'Celeron' washer (Ref. 8), and sun gear (Ref. 9), in differential casing (Ref, 7), Assemble differential. Fit crown wheel on differential casing, using new bolts and Blocfor washers. Tighten bolts to 5.7 mkg. (42 lb.ft.). Fit differential bearing races using a press and suitable press pad. Smear Perfect Seal on differential housing mating faces. Install differential and cover. Fit, without tightening the four 8mm. diameter bolts (Ref. 10, Fig.C66) with new Onduflex washers, and the four 10mm. diameter bolts (Ref.11) with new Onduflex washers and 'O'-rings (Ref.12) (Part No. 0165.57).

Differential Adjustment

Place a new, tallowed, 'O'-ring, and a new oil seal on right hand differential cover plate. Fit right hand cover plate, having coated the bearing face with Perfect Seal, taking care to position the notches (Ref, a, Fig.C67) horizontally, and the outlet groove (Ref, b) facing downwards. Tighten cover plate bolts to 2 mkg. (14.5 lb.ft.) torque. Fit special clamp 8.0305M, and bring the left hand bearing outer race to bear onto the roller cage without applying force (See Fig.C68). Place special gauge 8.0305N on the mating face, bringing the feeler into contact with the outer race, and tighten the knurled wheel. Determine

the number of shims required by comparison with the left hand cover (See Fig.C69), and add one 0.1mm. shim. Remove clamp 8.0305M. Slacken right hand cover plate bolts. Tighten the 8mm. dia. housing bolts to 2 mkg. (14.5 lb.ft.) torque, and the 10mm. dia. housing bolts to 4mkg. (29 lb.ft.) torque. Place a new, tallowed, 'O-ring, and a seal ring on the left hand plate. Smear Perfect Seal on left hand plate mating face. Fit left hand cover plate (same positioning as right-hand cover plate), inserting the shims at the same time. Tighten the bolts to 2 mkg. (14.5 lb.ft.). torque.

Fit the oil pump strainer, and tighten the three bolts to 0.6 mkg. (3.5 lb.ft.) torque. Ensure that the mating surfaces of the gearbox housing and oil sump are in good condition. Ensure that the two polarising pins are in place. Fit a new gasket and sump plate. Place the eight 7mm. dia. bolts and their thrust plates, the two 8mm. dia. bolts with the polarising pin cover plates, and the three 8mm. dia. bolts with the polarising pin cover plates, and the three 8mm. dia. bolts in position. Tighten the 7mm. dia. bolts to 1 mkg. (7.25 lb.ft.) torque, and the 8mm. dia. bolts to 1.75 mkg. (13 lb.ft.) torque. Fit the limiting stops on the side supports of the sump plate, and tighten them 3.25 mkg. (23.5 lb.ft.) torque. Fit to the right hand drain plug spacer, a new locking washer and a thin 36 mm. across flats nut. Tighten nut 3.5 mkg (25 lb.ft.) torque, and bend lock washer up around the nut. Ensure that the exterior oil line is in perfect condition. Replace the four copper washers, and tighten the two union bolts to 1.75 mkg. (13 lb.ft.) torque. Check all gears for free engagement before re-installing gearbox on the engine.

FLOOR MOUNTED GEAR CHANGE LEVER 204-304 -
Removal

Disconnect battery, and remove links (Ref. 1, Fig.C69). Move front seats completely back. Remove the rubber mat from the bulkhead. Remove the nut (Ref.2, Fig.C70), and the bolt (Ref.3), securing the plastic cover. Remove the gear lever knob (Ref.4). Remove the gaiter (Ref.5). Rotate the plastic cover away from the pedal side, and remove it. Remove the two nuts securing gear change mechanism (located at base of gear lever support). Remove the four nuts securing the gear change mechanism to the bulkhead. Disengage the cover plate from the bulkhead, towards the rear. Remove gear change mechanism after disconnecting the return spring (Ref.10 Fig.C71). Remove the gasket (Ref.11).

FLOOR MOUNTED GEAR CHANGE LEVER 204-304 -
Refitting

Refit gasket and lever assembly. Engage cover plate, and tighten the four nuts to 1 mkg. (7.25 lb.ft.) torque. Tighten the two securing nuts to 2 mkg. (14.5 lb.ft.) torque.

Check condition of links and in particular the ball sockets for cracks, etc. Adjust the length and angle of the selector link, as shown in Fig.C72 (measurements in mm.). Select neutral (the two levers on the cover in the central position). Fit selector link (Ref.3. Fig.C73). Fit jack lever link without tightening the nut (Ref.4). Push the jack lever (Ref.5) to the right until the gear change lever butts against the reverse selector stop. Tighten the nut (Ref.4). Hook the spring (Ref.6) in the hole in the jack lever (Ref.5).

With the engine running, the lever should be between 3rd and 4th when in neutral. When the lever is pushed fully to the left, it should be between 1st and 2nd. If it is not, adjust on the jack lever positioning. Check that all five gears engage, (particularly reverse and 1st). the locking should take place without the lever touching the clamp (Ref.6 Fig.C74). Lengthen the selector link to move the lever backwards, or shorten it to move it forwards. In neutral the lever should be at right angles to the clamp as shown in Fig.C74. Correct the lever position by moving the clamp to the left or right. Refit the plastic cover and rubber mat.

Technical Data

TRANSMISSION

Type	Front wheel drive	
Clutch	Verto 200 DE or Luk TS 190 diaphragm spring type	Verto 200 DE
Gearbox	4 forward speeds, all synchromesh	
Gearbox ratios	Top: 1.009:1, 3rd: 1.486:1, 2nd: 2.268:1, 1st: 3.731:1, Rev. 4.032:1	Top 0.986:1, 3rd: 1.451:1, 2nd: 2.217: 1 1st 3.650:1, Rev. 3.953:1
Driving axles	Homokinetic shafts with inner slides	Two CV joints (Glaenzer Spicer) one sliding
Final drive gear	Bevel	
Final drive ratio	4.07:1 (61 x 15)	

Final Drive

IDENTIFICATION AND CHARACTERISTICS

1st Fitting (Fig.D1): Drive shaft incorporating a double cardan spider joint (Ref.1) - wheel side - and a tulip joint with roller sliding motion (Ref.2) - front axle side.

2nd fitting (Fig.D2). Drive shaft incorporating a roller joint, outer (Ref.1) - wheel side - and a tulip joint with roller sliding motion (Ref.2) - front axle side.

Interchangeability: 2nd fitting drive shafts are interchangeable with 1st fitting drive shafts. Consequently the spare parts department supplies only 2nd fitting drive shafts. When replacing a 1st fitting drive shaft with a 2nd fitting drive shaft, check that the outer joint freely rotates on the steering knuckle with a 0.5mm. shim. If the play is less than 0.5mm. the appropriate points must be carefully ground until the gap is 0.5mm. (see Fig.D3).

HALF SHAFT - Removal

Drain engine sump. Raise and block up the vehicle under the rear part of the engine cradle (Ref.1, Fig.D4). Remove the wheel. Carefully clean the axle cover and knuckle to prevent impurities getting in during removal. Unscrew and remove hub nut, holding it with special tool 8.0606A. Uncouple anti-roll bar tie-link (Ref.2) from the triangle, where necessary. Remove triangle pins. Pull suspension element towards you, and separate drive shaft from hub. Remove axle drive shaft, taking care not to damage the seal ring lips. *Important:* Avoid knocking the seal ring mating surfaces (Ref.3 Fig.D5).

HALF SHAFT - Refitting

Each time the drive shaft is replaced, the differential bearing cover seal ring must be replaced. Tallow or grease the clearance between the axle ring lips and the knuckle. Carefully engage shaft on the axle. Smear shaft grooves with Molykote, hub side. Pull the suspension element towards you, and engage shaft in the hub, taking care not to damage the seal ring. Engage the anti-roll bar tie-link (Ref.2) in the corresponding triangle hole, where necessry. Place the triangle in position on the cradle, inserting four new 'Vulkollan' washers between the elastic bushings and the triangle yokes. Tallow and insert spindles. Screw on new Nyloc nuts without tightening them. Fit hub washer and new nut. Tighten hub nut. Tighten hub nut to 25 mkg. (181 lb.ft.) torque, using extension Facom SJ214 or similar, and holding the hub with special tool 8.0606A. *Note:* Facom extension S5214 doubles the tightening torque wrench, therefore set torque wrench to 12.5 mkg. (90.5 lb.ft.). Remove tool 8.0606A. Lock hub nut in appropriate grooves with locking tool 8.0606D or similar. Refit wheel. Lower vehicle back onto its wheels, and tighten wheel nuts to 6 mkg. (43.5 lb.ft.) torque.

Ensure that the anti-roll bar tie-link is correctly fitted, and that the tubular spacer is in place. Fit a new Nyloc nut without tightening. Push the vehicle a few feet to give it its own balancing. Tighten triangle spindle nuts 2.75mkg. (20 lb.ft.) torque. Tighten anti-roll bar tie-link lower nut to 1.25 mkg. (9 lb.ft.) torque. Refill engine with 7 pints (4 litres) approved engine Oil 20W/30/40.

DRIVE SHAFT - Dismantling

Only the following operations can be performed:

Changing the protector assembly, axle side only. Changing the protector assembly, wheel side, necessitates changing the axle side also.

Renewing the 'inner' joint (axle side) - also necessitates replacing the protector assembly axle side.

Renewing the 'outer' joint wheel side is not possible.

Protect the ends of the seal ring mating faces with masking tape. Moderately tighten the 'inner' joint (axle side) in a vice, using support 8.0403U or similar (See Fig.D7). Carefully unfasten the steel cap. Tighten the drive shaft by the link shaft in lead jaws, and remove the steel cap. Remove the sleeve (Ref.2 Fig.D8), thrust cup (Ref.3) and its spring (Ref.4). Hold the rollers on the shaft (Ref.5) with an elastic band (the assembly must not be separated). Remove the circlips (Ref.6) Etch a reference mark on one of drive shaft grooves with an electric pencil, to relate the position of the tulip with respect to the shaft. The reference mark is necessary when refitting, because the 'inner tulip' rollers must be line with the 'outer' ones. Remove the tulip. Remove tulip thrust ring.

Remove the rubber protector elastic holding ring (Ref.8 Fig.D9). Remove the protector assembly (Ref.9) and the ring (Ref.8). Tighten the 'outer' joint (wheel side) in jaws of vice, and carefully unfasten the steel cap. Remove the rubber protector elastic holding bushing (Ref.10, Fig.D10). Remove the protector assembly (Ref.11) from the free end of the shaft. Do not separate the link shaft (Ref.12) from the 'outer' joint (Ref.13).

DRIVE SHAFT - Re-assembly

Carefully clean and dry all parts, and replace any parts showing signs of wear.

Outer Joint: Fit the new rubber protector and steel cap assembly (Ref.14 , Fig.D11) on the free end of the shaft. Fit the gaiter lips in the corresponding grooves on the link shaft (Ref.15). Fit the new '0'-ring (Ref.16 Fig.D12) in its groove. This is in the set of parts supplied as part No. 3293.06. Fill the cap with two 120g. tubes of Esso LADEX HPF 2 grease (also supplied in set of parts). Fit the 'outer' joint until it is 2mm. (0.08 in.) below the top of the cap, using a mallet if necessary. Immobilise it by bending the cap down at four equi-spaced points. Using a block of wood, drive the cap home with light glancing blows on the outside towards the centre. Avoid knocking the seal ring mating surface. Check that the outer diameter of the cap does not exceed 88.8mm. (3.496 in) at the '0'-ring level. Insert a round headed brass feeler under the gaiter lips to let out excess air. Ensure gaiter tightness by fitting rubber ring from the set of parts part No. 3293.06.

Inner Joint: Fit the rubber ring (Ref.19. Fig.D13) on the shaft. Fit the rubber protector/cap assembly (Ref.20). Fit the end of the gaiter in its groove. Fit a new snap ring (Ref.21). Fit the tulip, ensuring that the reference marks line up.

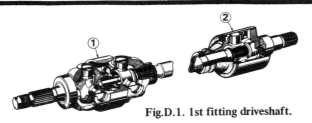

Fig.D.1. 1st fitting driveshaft.

Fig.D.2. 2nd fitting driveshaft.

Fig.D.5. Removing axle drive shaft.

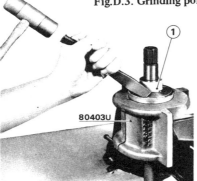

Fig.D.3. Grinding points to reduce play.

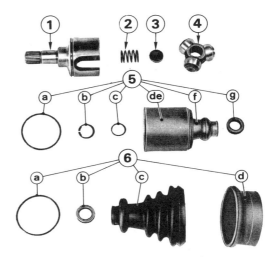

Fig.D.6. Drive shaft parts supplied by spare parts department.

1. Outer joint sleeve   P.N.3275.12
2. Play take up spring   P.N3276.03
3. Thrust cap   P.N.3277.03
4. Assembled tulip   P.N.3279.06
5. Protector assembly
   axleside   P.N.3287.07
   incorporating a. O-ring
              b. tulip holding circlip
              c. tulip stop ring
              d. steel cap
              e. assembly hoop   supplied
              f. rubber protector   assembled
              g. rubber ring

6. Protector assembly, wheelside   P.N.3293.06

comprising: a 0-ring
               b rubber ring
               c rubber protector
               d steel cap

Fig.D.7. Unfastening the steel cap.

80403U

80606A

Fig.D.4. Removing hub nut.

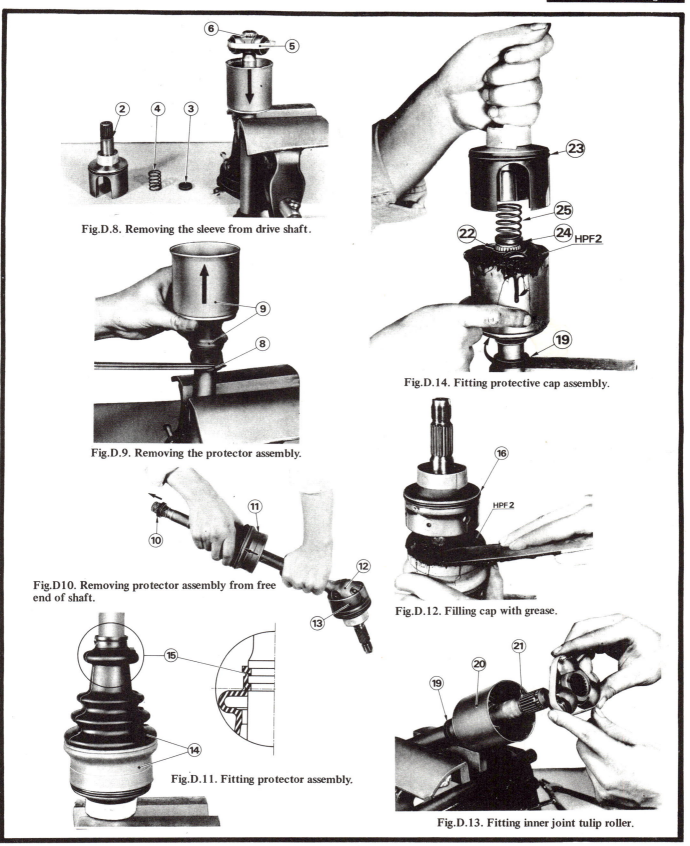

Fig.D.8. Removing the sleeve from drive shaft.

Fig.D.9. Removing the protector assembly.

Fig.D10. Removing protector assembly from free end of shaft.

Fig.D.11. Fitting protector assembly.

Fig.D.14. Fitting protective cap assembly.

Fig.D.12. Filling cap with grease.

Fig.D.13. Fitting inner joint tulip roller.

New Tulip: Push the stop ring past its groove. Fit the new tulip over the old one to line up the rollers. Note the position of the new tulip in relation to the shaft. Put the stop ring back in its groove. Finally, fit the new tulip respecting its angular position. Fit the new circlip (Ref.22, Fig.D14) in its groove. Fill the protective sleeve with a 120g. tube of Esso LADEX HPF 2 grease (supplied as part of spare parts kit). Fit a new 'O'-ring (Ref.23) on the sleeve. Fit the cup (Ref.24), spring (Ref.25), and the sleeve. Fit the sleeve in the steel cap until it meets the rubber protector holding hoop. Immobilise the cap by bending down the rim at four equi-spaced points. Finally fit cap in the same manner as for the 'outer' joint. Insert a round headed brass feeler under the gaiter lips to let out excess air. Ensure gaiter tightness by fitting elastic ring (Ref.19).

Rear Axle

CHARACTERISTICS

On vehicles manufactured up to September 1970, the toe-in was 1.5 ± 2mm. (0.059 ± 0.079 in.), and the camber angle was -0°30' ± 1°.

On vehicles manufactured from September 1970 to May 1971, the toe-in was 3 ± 1.5mm. (0.118 ± 0.059 in.) and the camber angle was -0°30' ± 1°.

On vehicles manufactured since May 1971, the toe-in is 3 ± 1.5mm. (0.118 ± 0.059 in) and the camber angle is -2° ± 1°.

REAR AXLE - Removal

Raise rear of vehicle, and chock under the side members near the crossmember. Remove rear seat cushion and back rest, rear wheels and exhaust pipes. Slacken, disconnect, and uncouple from the bodywork the cables and sleeve of the hand brake. *Note:* There are two fittings, the first with the counter lever on rear crossmember requires the brake cable (Ref.3 Fig.E1) to be removed from the counter lever; the second with the counter lever on the brake lever requires the hand brake lever (Ref.4) to be removed to uncouple the cables (Ref.5) from the counter lever. Disconnect the left and right brake hoses, and plug the piping (Ref.6 Fig.E2). Slacken the pivots (Ref.7) on 204 with aluminium alloy arms (Ref.a). With the aid of a bronze drift, drive out the pins until the splines are released. Remove the screws (Ref.8 Fig.E3) or nuts (Ref. 9) on the crossmember of the bodywork, from each side. Lower the crossmember and remove the shock absorber pivots.

REAR AXLE - Refitting

Position rear axle under vehicle and engage shock absorbers in their yokes (Ref. 1 Fig.E4). Fit shock absorber pivots, with head towards the inside, using new Nyloc nuts. *Note:* There are two types of pivot. Fit the pivots without splines (Ref. 2), on sheet metal arms (Ref.3). Fit pivots with splines (Ref.4), on aluminium alloy arms, leaving the splines (Ref. a) visible (See Fig.E2). Chock the arms at 90° to the shock absorbers (See Fig.E5), and tighten the Nyloc nuts on the pivots to 5.5 mkg. (40 lb.ft.) torque. Fit rear crossmember on the bodywork. To facilitate the centring of the crossmember, insert two rods in the holes (Ref.5 Fig.E6), and in the corresponding holes in the crossmember supports. Plug the central holes (Ref.5) with filler. Fit the counter plates (Ref.6) and new tab washers (Ref.7). *Note:* On Breaks, the rear back rest hinge frames are held in place on each side by two of the four bolts of the rear crossmember. The rear crossmember should always be fixed to the bodywork by its eight bolts.

There are two types of crossmember supports (See Fig. E7). Fitting 1. Crossmember supports (ref. 8) with four threaded holes. Tighten the eight bolts to 1.75 mkg. (13 lb.ft.) torque. Fitting 2: Crossmember supports (Ref. 9) with four studs. Tighten the eight nuts to 2.75 mkg. (20 lb.ft.) torque. The crossmember supports with studs can be used to replace the supports with threaded holes, but not vice-versa. If changing from a threaded hole support to a stud support, the crossmember must be fitted with the corresponding flexible bushings (Ref.10) and pivots (Ref.11). The holes in the bodywork will need to be enlarged to 10.5mm. (0.413 in.) diameter. Tighten the Nyloc nuts (Ref. 12) to 3.5 mkg. (25 lb.ft.) torque.

Re-install exhaust pipe. Connect brake piping. Refit hand brake lever, and tighten nuts to 2 mkg. (14.5 lb.ft.) torque. Refit wheels, and tighten wheel nuts to 6 mkg. (43 lb.ft.) torque. Bleed and adjust brakes. Refit rear seat cushion.

REAR HUBS FITTED WITH BALL BEARINGS - Removal

Ball bearings are fitted only to rear hubs fitted on aluminium alloy suspension arms, except that hubs with 64mm. diameter ball bearings must be fitted on sheet steel arms which have been used to replace aluminium ones.

Raise rear of vehicle and chock under the rear crossmember. Remove the wheel and hub-drawn assembly.

EXTERNAL BEARING - Removal

Using special extractor from tool chest 8.0518Y or similar, remove external bearing (see Fig.E8). Tighten bolt (Ref.A) until the bearing race (Ref.3) is completely extracted.

INNER BEARING - Removal

Remove inner bearing using special extractor from tool chest 8.0518Y or similar (See Fig.E9). The extractor (Ref.BZ) should engage on its shoulders (Ref.a). Fit the anvil (Ref.DZ) without the spacer (Ref.G) for hubs of external diameter 70mm. (2.756 in.) instead of 72mm. (2.835 in). Extract the bearing race (Ref.4), ball cage and seal (Ref.5), simultaneously.

To remove the race and spacer from the stub axle, extract the spacer (Ref. 6 Fig.E10) and internal race (Ref. 7) simultaneously, using special extractor 8.0518EY or similar.

REAR HUBS FITTED WITH BALL BEARINGS - Refitting

The components of a bearing are paired, and must never be interchanged. Fit new bearings without degreasing.

OUTER BEARING - Re-installation

Fit the anvil (Ref.DZ, Fig.E11) without the spacer (Ref.9) for hubs of external diameter 70mm. (2.756 in.) instead of 72mm. (2.835 in). Screw the control bolt (Ref.A) until the outer race (Ref.3) fits perfectly as far as it will go.

INNER BEARING - Re-installation

Do not use the spacer (Ref.F Fig.E12) for bearings with a diameter of 62mm. (2.441 in.) instead of 64mm. (2.52 in). Screw the control bolt (Ref.A) until the outer race (Ref.4) fits perfectly as far as it will go.

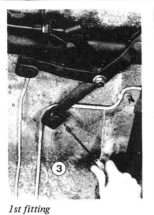

1st fitting *2nd fitting*

Fig.E.1. Two fittings of handbrake counter lever.

Fig.E.2. Shock absorber pivot and brake piping.

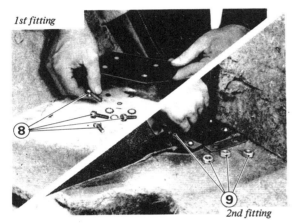

1st fitting *2nd fitting*

Fig.E.3. Crossmember bodywork fixings-two fittings.

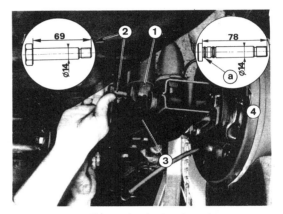

Fig.E.4. Fitting shock absorber pivots.

Fig.E.5. Chocking arms to give correct positioning.

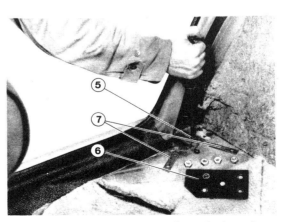

Fig.E.6. Fitting rear crossmember to bodywork.

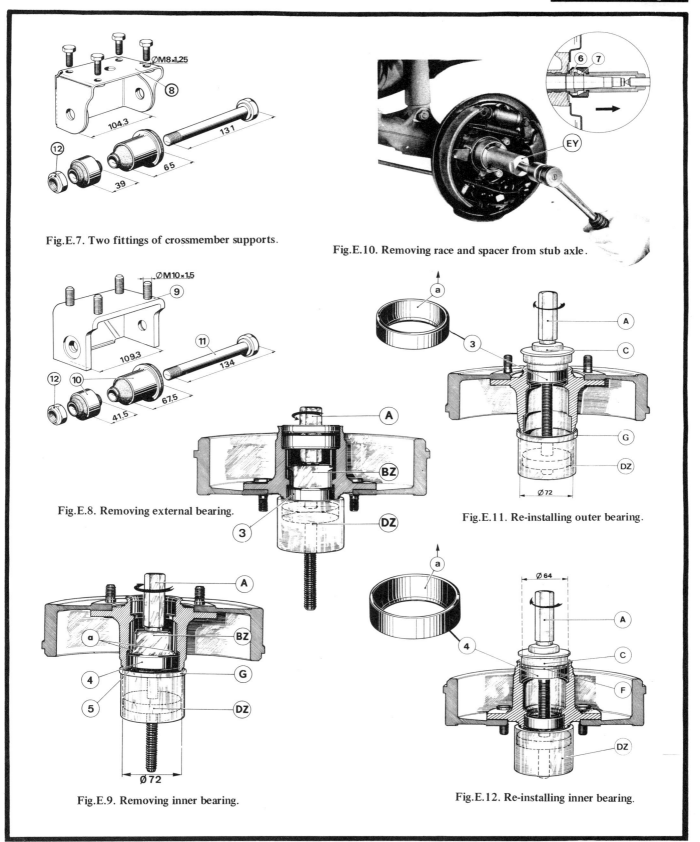

Fig.E.7. Two fittings of crossmember supports.

Fig.E.10. Removing race and spacer from stub axle.

Fig.E.8. Removing external bearing.

Fig.E.11. Re-installing outer bearing.

Fig.E.9. Removing inner bearing.

Fig.E.12. Re-installing inner bearing.

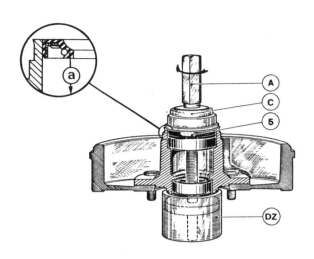

Fig.E.13. Fitting oil seal.

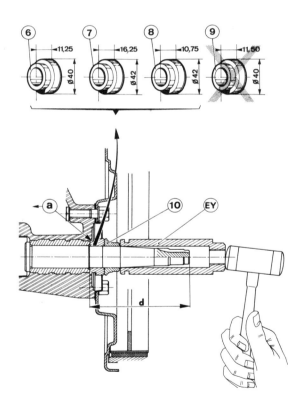

Fig.E.14. Refitting inner race and spacer on stub axle.

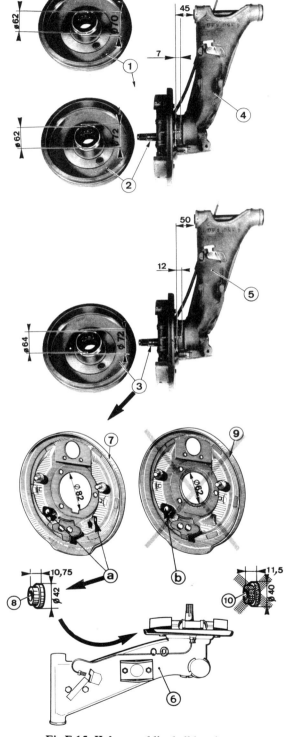

Fig.E.15. Hub assemblies-ball bearings.

Fit the ball cage. Fit an appropriate new oil seal (Ref.5 Fig.E13), according to the size of bearing, with lip (Ref.'a'). towards the inside. The end (Ref.C) should be returned so that the joint is flush with the hub. Grease the inside of the hub liberally with Multipurpose Grease.

Refitting inner race and spacer on stub axle

Note: There are three models of spacer (See Fig.E14). Spacer (Ref.6) - 40mm. (1.575 in) dia. 11.25 mm. (0.443 in) thick to be fitted on aluminium alloy arms on which the stub axle protrusion (Ref.'d') is equal to 107 mm (4.213 in) and with a hub inner bearing of 25 x 62 x 17mm. *Important:* Spacer (Ref.9) which is 11.5mm. (0.453 in.) thick must not be fitted on a hub with ball bearings.

Spacer (Ref. 7) - 42mm (1.654 in.) dia. x 16.25mm (0.640 in). thick to be fitted on aluminium alloy arms on which the stub axle protrusion (Ref.'d') is equal to 112mm (4.409 in) and with a hub inner bearing of 25 x 64 x 17mm.

Spacer (Ref.8) - 42 mm. (1.654 in.) dia. x (0.423 in) 10.75 mm thick: to be fitted on sheet steel arms fitted in replacement of an alloy arm.

This spacer must only be fitted a steel arm with an inner bearing of 25 x 64 x 17mm.

Fit the new spacer, with the extraction groove (Ref.'a') on the inside, and inner bearing race (Ref.10) simultaneously, using puller tube 8.0518EY as a drift.

Refitting Hubs

As there are three types of hub with ball bearings, care should be taken that the correct assembly is made.

Hubs (Ref.1 and 2. Fig.E15) with an inner bearing of 62mm (2.441 in) diameter must be fitted on alloy arms (Ref.4) which are identifiable by the 7mm (0.2761 in) thick mounting flange for the brake back plate. The hub (Ref.1) with an outer diameter of 70mm (2.756 in) can be replaced by hub (Ref.2) with an outer diameter of 72mm. (2.835 in) on condition that the 72mm (2.835 in) diameter oil thrower plate is replaced by one of 74mm. (2.913 in) diameter. The 70mm. dia. hub is no longer available as a spare.

Hub (Ref.3) with a 64mm. (2.520 in) diameter inner bearing must be used on an alloy arm (Ref.5) identifiable by the 12mm. (0.472in) thick mounting flange for the brake back plate, and on a sheet steel arm (Ref. 6) when it is used as a replacement for the alloy one. When replacing an alloy arm with a sheet steel arm, the arm is fitted with a brake plate (Ref 7), and spacer (Ref. 8). The arms in sheet steel fitted with brake plate (Ref.9) and spacer (Ref.10), must only be fitted on hubs with taper roller bearings.

Ensure that the braking track in the drum is completely free from grease. Refit hub/drum assembly (Ref.11 Fig.E16). Place the convex face of washer (Ref.12) against bearing. (flat washer which is fitted with taper roller bearings must not be used on ball bearings), and pre-tighten new hub nut to 3mkg. (22 lb.ft.), torque while spinning the drum. Slacken the nut and retighten it to 1 mkg. (7.25 lb.ft.) torque. Lock it in the two grooves (Ref.13) on stub axle, supporting the hub/drum

from underneath.

REAR HUBS FITTED WITH TAPER ROLLER BEARINGS - Removal

Taper roller bearings are fitted only on hubs fitted on sheet steel suspension arms, except when sheet steel arms have been fitted as replacement for alloy arms.

Raise rear of vehicle, and chock under rear crossmember. Remove wheel. Remove hub/drum assembly using an extractor. Remove the spacer (Ref. 3, Fig.E17) and inner race (Ref.4) as an assembly, from stub axle with the aid of special extractor 8.0518EY or similar.

Remove inner bearing using extractor in tool chest 8.0518Y or similar. Tighten bolt (Ref.A, Fig.E.18), until race (Ref. 5), and oil seal (Ref. 6), are completely extracted.

Remove outer bearing using extractor in tool chest 8.0518Y or similar.

Tighten bolt (Ref.A, Fig.E19), until race (Ref.7), is completely extracted.

HUBS WITH TAPER ROLLER BEARINGS - Refitting

The components of a bearing are paired, and must never be interchanged. Fit new bearings without degreasing.

Refit inner bearing using extractor in tool chest 8.0518Y or similar. Screw bolt (Ref.A, Fig.E20), until race (Ref.5), is installed as far as it will go. Tighten bolt to 6mkg. (43.5 lb.ft.) torque to perfect the fitting. Fit inner race of bearing, greased with Multi-purpose Grease in the hub. Fit new oil seal (ref.6 Fig.E21) with lip (Ref.'a') towards the inside, using the plate (Ref.C) until the roller (Ref.'b') rests on the hub.

Refit outer bearing using extractor in tool chest 8.0518Y or similar. Screw bolt (Ref.A Fig.E22) until the race is installed as far as it will go. Tighten bolt to 6 mkg. (43.5 lb.ft.) torque to perfect the fitting.

A hub fitted with taper roller bearings (Ref.1 Fig.E23) must only be fitted on a steel arm (Ref. 2) fitted with brake plate (Ref. 3) having a 62mm. (2.441 in.) bore, and only one brake cable hole (Ref. a). The steel arm fitted with a brake plate (Ref. 4) having a 82mm (3.228 in). bore, and two handbrake cable holes must only be used with ball hub bearings (see refitting a hub with ball bearings).

Fit a seal plate (Ref. 5 Fig.E24) and paper gasket on arms not so originally equipped, taking care to remove the brake plate without disconnecting the piping (Ref. 7) so as to avoid bleeding, and to tighten the brake plate screws to 4.5 mkg. (33 lb.ft.) torque. Using puller tube of extractor 8.0518Y, or similar as a drift, fit a new spacer (Ref. 8 Fig.E25) with the extractor groove (Ref. a) towards the arm.

Ensure that the bearing race slides freely on the stub axle. Lightly smooth the bearing suface, if necessary, and carefully clean it.

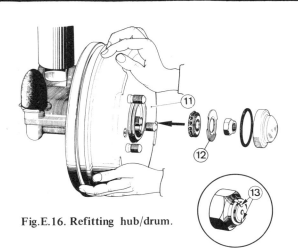

Fig.E.16. Refitting hub/drum.

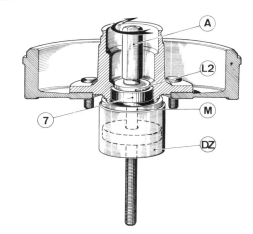

Fig.E.19. Removing outer bearing.

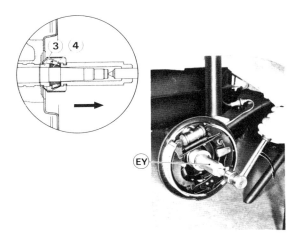

Fig.E.17. Removing inner race and spacer from stub axle.

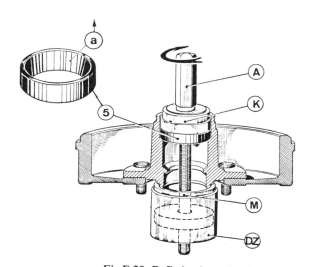

Fig.E.20. Refitting inner bearing.

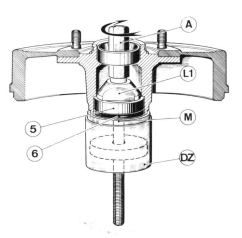

Fig.E.18. Removing inner bearing.

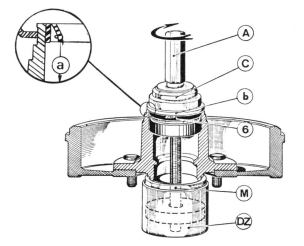

Fig.E.21. Refitting oil seal.

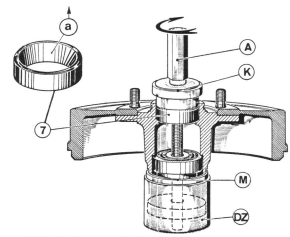

Fig.E.22. Refitting outer bearing.

Fig.E.25. Fitting spacer.

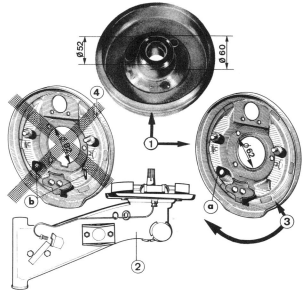

Fig.E.23. Hub assembly - taper roller bearings.

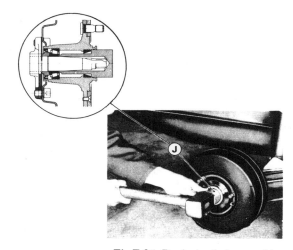

Fig.E.26. Replacing hub assembly.

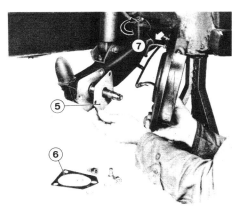

Fig.E.24. Fitting seal plate.

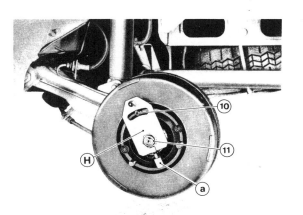

Fig.E.27. Adjustment of bearings.

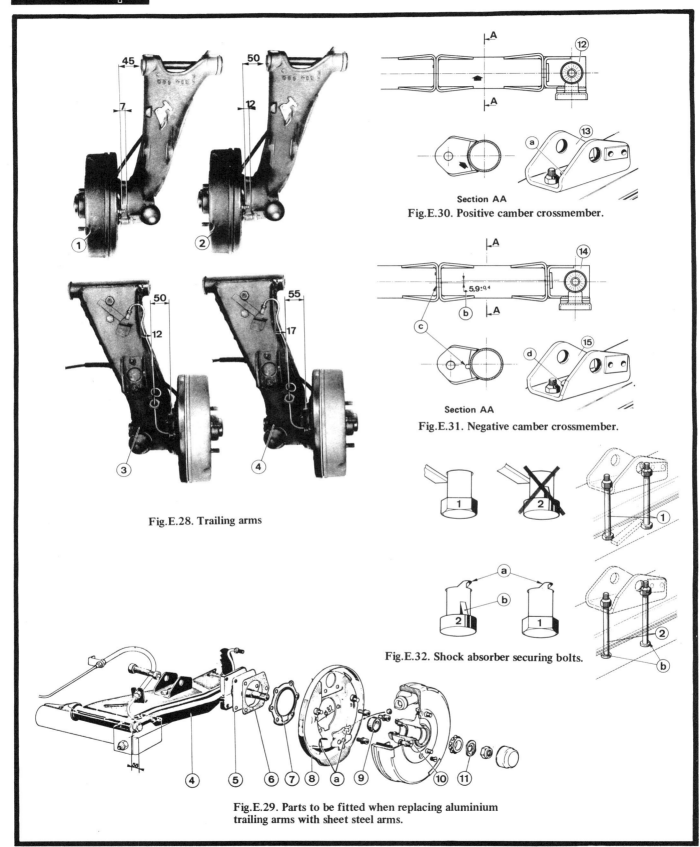

Fig.E.30. Positive camber crossmember.

Fig.E.31. Negative camber crossmember.

Section AA

Section AA

Fig.E.28. Trailing arms

Fig.E.32. Shock absorber securing bolts.

Fig.E.29. Parts to be fitted when replacing aluminium trailing arms with sheet steel arms.

Insert special drift from tool set 8.0518Y (Ref.J, Fig.E26) right into the hub. Engage the assembly until the bearing touches the spacer. Put at least 80g. of Multi-purpose Grease into the hub. Fit the bearing race, safety washer, and a new nut. Turning the drum, adjust the bearings by tightening the hub nut to 3mkg (22 lb.ft.) torque, slacken it off and retighten to 0.5mkg (3.5 lb. ft) torque. Place special gauge 8.0518H so that a wheel stud (Ref.10, Fig.E27) is in the elongated hole. Tighten bolt (Ref.'a'). by hand on the hub nut (Ref.11). Bring the wheel stud (Ref.10), in contact with the left hand extremity of the elongated hole, without slackening the hub nut (Ref.11), by turning the drum clockwise. Fit the gauge onto the wheel stud (Ref.10), and tighten. Tighten hand brake. Slacken the gauge nut and pivot gauge (Ref. H), until wheel stud touches right hand extremity of elongaged hole.

Tighten gauge nut to 0.5mkg. (3.5 lb.ft.) torque. Ensure that the screw (Ref.'a') remains tight throughout the operation. With the wheel stud touching the extreme right-hand end of the elongated hole, stake the hub nut (Ref.11) in the two grooves of the stub axle. Remove the gauge (Ref.H). Replace dust cap and 'O'-ring. Replace wheel, and tighten wheel nuts to 6 mkg. (43.5 lb.f.t) torque.

TRAILING ARM - Removal

Proceed as for 'removal of rear axle' up to 'removal of the pivot', and then remove the trailing arm. There are four types of trailing arms (See Fig.E28). Types 1 and 2 are aluminium arms, and types 3 and 4 are sheet steel arms.

TRAILING ARM - Refitting

The trailing arms fitted to the vehicle must both be of the same type, and both fitted with identical components. The aluminium arms (Type 1, Fig.E28) must not be fitted in place of types 2,3 or 4. Trailing arms types 2 and 3 are no longer

supplied as spare parts. Type 4 trailing arms may replace type 3 arms without particular conditions. Type 4 trailing arms may replace type 1 and 2 arms on condition that both arms are replaced, and that both are fitted with a sealing plate (Ref.5, Fig.E29), gasket (Ref,6), and oil thrower plate (Ref.,7) a special brake back plate (Ref.8) with an 82 mm diameter bore, and two cable holes (Ref.a), a spacer (Ref.9) of 42mm. diameter, and 10.75 mm. thick, a hub with ball bearings (Ref.10), identical to those fitted on the type 2 arm, and a domed washer (Ref.11) for hubs with roller bearings. *Reminder:* The arms in sheet steel, fitted in production, are fitted with taper roller hub bearings.

Steel arms (type 3 or 4) may be fitted on a crossmember which gives positive camber (Ref.12, Fig.E30), without vertical offset of the pivot holes, and with no notch on the inner flange, but must have the corresponding shock absorber yokes (Ref.13) with rounded corners (Ref.a).

A crossmember which gives negative camber (Ref.14, Fig. E31), having vertical offset (Ref.b) of the pivot holes and notch (Ref.c) on inner flange, must be fitted with steel arms type 4 with the corresponding shock absorber yokes (Ref. 15), having chamfered corners (Ref.d).

Type 3 trailing arms must not be fitted on a crossmember which gives negative camber.

Ensure that the shock absorber yokes are of the correct type, and that they are secured on the arms. Two types of securing bolts are available (See Fig.E32). The Hex. head bolts (Ref.1), can be used on either crossmember, whereas the cheese head bolts (Ref.2) with retaining boss (Ref.b),can only be used on crossmember with the notch (Ref.a). Insert the bolts with the head downwards, and ensure that the boss engages in the notch, (Ref.a), where applicable. Fit new Nyloc nuts, and tighten to 1.7 mkg (13 lb.ft.) torque. Proceed from appropriate point as for refitting rear axle.

Fig.F.1. Front axle assembly.

Fig.F.3. Support bar in position over mechanical assembly.

Fig.F.2. Raising front end of vehicle.

Fig.F.4. Installing support brace.

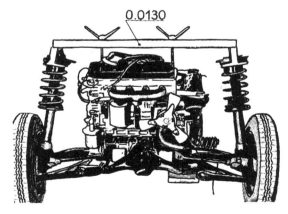

Fig.F.5. Mechanical assembly and support bar.

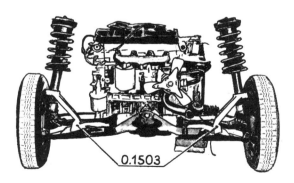

Fig.F.6. Mechanical assembly and support braces.

Front Axle

FRONT MECHANICAL ASSEMBLY - Removal

Remove or disconnect all power unit accessories and ancillaries, as described under heading ENGINE - Removal. With vehicle over pit or on car lift, disconnect steering column as described under section on steering gear. Remove complete exhaust pipe assembly. Remove brake and fuel line holding clamp from engine cradle.

Lift front end of vehicle using hoisting bar 8.1501 (See Fig.F2). If using support bar 0.0130, place chocks under engine cradle at three locations, in order to hold the assembly in position with wheels just clear of the ground, ensuring that engine cradle-to-framework attachment points are accessible. Remove wheels. On vehicles equipped with front brakes incorporating three-piston type brake callipers, remove brake calliper attachment screws, and hang callipers to wing valances without disconnecting the corresponding hoses. On vehicles equipped with front brakes incorporating two-piston type brake callipers, loosen compensation pipe couplings at the left and right-hand brake hoses, and disconnect brake hoses from corresponding attachment lugs on the wing valance. *Using support bar 0.0130:* Lift front end of body shell until mechanical assembly is fully cleared. Take body shell away from mechanical assembly, resting on chocks. Bring support bar 0.0130 over mechanical assembly (See Fig.F3). Cap shock absorber upper nuts with the support bar tubular rests, and hook both tie-bars onto the engine. Screw in both tie-bars so as to lift the engine, and release the chocks. The mechanical assembly can now be moved on its wheels

Using braces 0.1503: Hook up engine with hoist beam 8.0121, and operate chain hoist until chain is taut. Remove shock absorber upper attachment screws at wing valances. Install both flanges of support braces 0.1503 in position, so as to hold cantilevers, and engine cradle together (See Fig.F4). Remove the eleven screws used to secure engine cradle to body shell. Release chain hoist, and remove hoist beam 8.0121. Install shock absorber body support yokes on brace flanges. Place chocks under engine cradle to avoid any swinging movement of mechanical assembly on its wheels. Using hoisting bar 8.1501 attached to chain hoist, lift front end of body shell until mechanical assembly is fully cleared. The mechanical assembly can now be moved on its wheels.

FRONT MECHANICAL ASSEMBLY - Refitting

Bring mechanical assembly, firmly held by support bar 0.0130 or cantilever lower support braces 0.1503 (See Figs. F5 and F6) over pit or on car lift.

Chock mechanical assembly in horizontal position, maintaining it at the same level. Remove support bar 0.0130, where applicable. Bring body shell into position, the front end of body shell being held by chain hoist through hoisting bar 8.1501. Install body shell on shock absorber upper rests. Secure shock absorbers to wing valances, making sure upper cup reference holes are facing the engine. Use new 'DD' washers, and tighten screws to 1mkg. (7.25 lb.ft.) torque. If using support braces 0.1503, remove braces yokes (Ref.2) Fig.F7) from shock absorber bodies, and remove hoisting bar 8.1501. Hook up engine with hoist beam 8.0121 and lift assembly using chain hoist to bring engine cradle into contact with body shell. Either

method, secure engine cradle using new 'Blocfor' washers. Do not forget to re-install the backing plates at cradle front attachment points. The centre front plate is threaded. Tighten attachment screws and nuts to 3.25 mkg. (23.5 lb.ft.) torque. If using support braces 0.1503, remove both cantilever brace flanges (Ref.1 Fig.F7), release chain hoist, remove hoist beam 8.0121. Either method, raise front end of vehicle, and remove wheels. On vehicles with front brakes incorporating three-piston type brake callipers, re-install brake callipers, and tighten attachment screws to 7mkg. (5 lb.ft.) torque. On vehicles with front brakes incorporating two-piston type brake callipers, reconnect brake hoses to attachment lugs attached on wing valances, engage left and right hand brake hoses onto compensator pipe connectors, and tighten. Bleed brake systems. Lift front end of vehicle, and remove chocks from under engine cradle. Refit wheels, and tighten wheel nuts to 6mkg. (43.5 lb.ft.) torque. Refit all accessories and miscellaneous ancillaries in reverse of removal procedure.

FRONT HUB - Removal

Lift vehicle, through front frame upper crossbar using hoisting bar 8.1501, or using a trolley jack under front frame lower crossbar. Place chocks under rear end of engine cradle. Remove wheel. Loosen front hub nut while holding front hub with special tool 8.0606A. Remove front hub nut and washer. Remove tool 8.0606A. Remove brake calliper. Three-piston type callipers. Remove both attachment screws, and place callipers on cradle, without disconnecting brake feed hose. Two-piston type callipers. Disconnect brake connection pipe at hose coupling, and remove both attachment screws. Secure special holding clamp 8.0407 to drive shaft. Remove the four attachment screws for the hub and steering knuckle assembly, using an 8mm. socket wrench fitted with an extension (See Fig.F8). Remove the hub and steering knuckle assembly, and brake disc shield.

FRONT HUB - Refitting

Smear drive shaft splines with Molykote. Pack recess between steering knuckle seal lips with tallow or grease. Re-install brake disc shield, front hub and steering knuckle assembly. Install new 'Blocfor' washers on the four attachment screws, and tighten screws to 3.5 mkg. (25 lb.ft.) torque. Remove holding clamp 8.0407 from drive shaft. Clean brake disc, using a rag soaked in trichlorethylene to remove grease, if required. Re-install brake calliper. Three-piston type callipers. Tighten attachment screws to 7 mkg. (51 lb.ft.) torque. Two-piston type callipers. Tighten attachment screws to 5mkg (36 lb.ft.) torque. Engage and tighten both connectors on brake hose. Install the washer and a new nut on front hub. Tighten to 25 mkg. (180 lb.ft.) torque, using Facom SJ214 extension, or similar, and holding hub with locking tool 8.0606A. Remove tool 8.0606A. Stake hub nut by peening metal in corresponding shaft nut grooves, using staking tool 8.0606D or similar. Bleed brake system if front brakes have two-piston type brake callipers. Refit wheel, and tighten wheel nuts to 6mkg. (43.5 lb.ft.). torque.

FRONT HUB - Dismantling

Hold front hub and steering knuckle assembly in a vice

Fig.F.7. Brace yoke and cantilever brace flange.

Fig.F.8. Removing hub and steering knuckle assembly.

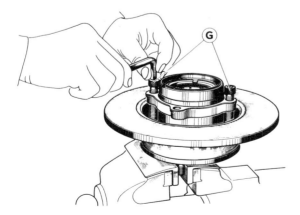

Fig.F.9. Taking front hub and steering knuckle apart.

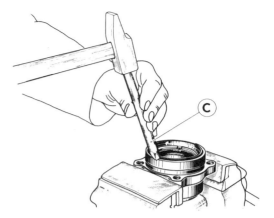

Fig.F.10. Unstaking steering knuckle nut.

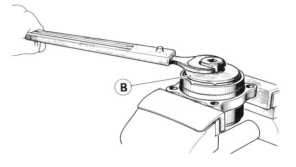

Fig.F.11. Removing steering knuckle nut.

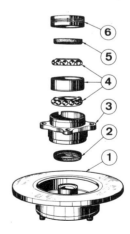

1. Front brake disc
2. Outer seal ring (55 x 70 x 10 mm.)
3. Steering knuckle
4. Ball bearing twin row
5. Inner seal-ring (54 x 72 x 10 mm.)
6. Steering knuckle nut

Fig.F.12. Front hub and steering knuckle assembly - exploded view.

fitted with lead jaws. Take front hub and steering knuckle apart from each other, by tightening each of the two removing screws 8.0606G alternately (See Fig.F9). Unstake steering knuckle nut using tool 8.0606C (see Fig.F10). Loosen and remove steering knuckle nut, using pin wrench 8.0606B (See Fig.F11). Remove bearing, resting on a drift if necessry. Remove steering knuckle outer seal ring.

FRONT HUB - Re-assembly

Clean and dry all components. Use new outer seal-ring (Ref.2, Fig.F12), inner seal ring (Ref.5), and steering knuckle nut (Ref.6). Check ball paths on bearing race. Pack bearing with Multi-purpose Grease. *Caution:* New bearings (Ref.4) are supplied with a nylon sleeve to hold both bearing parts together during handling. Remove this sleeve before assembling steering knuckle and hub.

Insert outer seal ring into steering knuckle, using block 8.0606E (See Fig.E13). Install inner seal ring into steering knuckle nut, using block 8.0606E (See Fig.F14). Insert bearing fitted with its inner cages, into steering knuckle. Install nut on steering knuckle, and tighten to 18 mkg. (130 lb.ft.) torque, using pin wrench 8.0606B. Stake steering knuckle nut at staking groove provided, using staking tool 8.0606D or similar. Clamp body 8.0606F2, of fixture 8.0606F, across both flats, in a vice. Assemble steering knuckle with hub using special screw 8.0606F1 (See Fig.F15).

FRONT HUB WITH ONE PIECE STEERING KNUCKLE PIVOTS - Removal

Lift vehicle, through front frame upper crossbar using hoisting bar 8.01501 or using a trolley jack under front frame lower crossbar. Place chocks under rear part of engine cradle. Remove wheel. Loosen front hub nut while holding front hub with tool 8.0606A.

Remove front hub nut and washer. Remove tool 8.0606A. Remove connection pipe on brake feed pipe. Loosen both attachment screws of the brake calliper, and remove calliper. Attach holding clamp 8.0407 to drive shaft. Remove elastic bushing pivot pins from cantilever. Pull suspension element towards oneself in order to release drive shaft from hub (See Fig.F16). Put aside drive shaft. Temporarily assemble cantilever to cradle by inserting pivot pins into the forks and elastic bushings. Unstake steering knuckle nut using special tool 8.0606C or similar. Remove steering knuckle nut. Place end pad 8.0606F4 on hub sleeve (See Fig. F17). Screw up puller 8.0606F3 in place of the steering knuckle nut. Using screw 8.0606F1, pull out hub/disc assembly. Remove bearing and sealing ring from steering knuckle pivot.

FRONT HUB WITH ONE PIECE STEERING KNUCKLE PIVOTS - Refitting

Insert outer seal ring into steering knuckle, using block 8.0606E. Check ball paths on bearing race. Pack bearing with Multipurpose Grease. Insert bearing fitted with its inner cages into steering knuckle. Tighten new steering knuckle nut with its sealing ring. Fit hub/disc assembly in place using nut 8.0606F2 and screw 8.0606F1 (See Fig.F18). Remove nylon ring, used to hold new bearings together, before assembling steering knuckle and hub. Remove screw 8.0606F1 and nut 8.0606F2. Tighten steering knuckle nut to 18 mkg. (129 lb.ft.) torque. Remove

pins from cantilever elastic bushings. Stake steering knuckle nut in the two grooves provided on the steering knuckle pivot, using staking tool 8.0606D or similar. Smear drive shaft splines with Molykote. Pack recess between steering knuckle seal lips with tallow or grease. Engage drive shaft in hub. Bring cantilever in position for assembly on engine cradle, placing new 'Vulkollan' washers between elastic bushings and cantilever forks. Smear elastic bushing pivot pins with tallow and insert them. Install new Nyloc nuts without tightening. Remove holding clamp 8.0407.

Clean brake disc, removing grease with a rag soaked in trichoethylene if required. Re-install brake calliper, and tighten both attachment screws to 5mkg. (36 lb.ft.) torque. Engage, and tighten both couplings on brake hose connection. Install washer and new nut on front hub. Tighten nut to 25mkg. (180 lb.ft.) torque, using Facom SJ214 extension, or similar, and holding hub with tool 8.0606A. Remove tool 8.0606A. Stake hub nut in the two grooves provided on the extremity of the drive shaft, using staking tool 8.0606D or similar. Bleed braking system. Remove chocks and rest vehicle on its wheels. Tighten wheel nuts to 6mkg. (43.5 lb.ft.) torque. Manœuvre vehicle so that it resumes its correct height position. Tighten cantilever elastic bushing pivot pins Nyloc nuts to 3.5 mkg (25 lb.ft.) torque. Ensure that shock absorber upper support attachment screws on wing valance are properly tightened to 1mkg. (7.25 lb.ft.). torque.

ELASTIC BUSHING ON FRONT CRADLE - Removal

Lift vehicle and place chocks under rear end of cradle. Remove wheel and install locking wrench 8.0606A. Loosen and remove hub nut. Lock drive shaft using clamp 8.0407. Remove cantilever pivot pins. Pull suspension element towards oneself to release cantilever forks. Remove the four 'Vulkollan' washers. Remove elastic bushings using tool B in tool kit 8.0904Z as shown in Fig.F19.

ELASTIC BUSHING ON FRONT CRADLE - Refitting

Smear the new elastic bushing outer sleeve with tallow. Assemble elastic bushing and special tool 8.0904B, as shown in Fig.F20. Tighten screw so as to engage elastic bushing into cradle eye. The bushing should not protrude either side of the eye. Remove tool 8.0904B. Replace other cradle elastic bushings in same manner. Bring cantilever in position for assembly on cradle, installing new 'Vulkollan' washers between elastic bushings and cantilever forks. Smear elastic bushings pivot pins with tallow, and insert them in position. Install new Nyloc nuts, without tightening. Remove clamp 8.0407. Install washer and a new hub nut, and tighten to 25 mkg. (180 lb.ft.) torque, using Facom extension SJ214 or similar, and holding hub with special tool 8.0606A. Remove tool 8.0606A. Stake hub nut into corresponding grooves of drive shaft end, using staking tool 8.0606D or similar. Refit wheel. Remove chocks, and rest vehicle on its wheels. Tighten wheel nuts to 6mkg. (43.5 lb.ft.) torque. Manœuvre vehicle to re-establish its correct height position. Tighten cantilever elastic bushing pivot pin Nyloc nuts to 3.5 mkg. (25 lb.ft.) torque.

1st INSTALLATION CANTILEVER - Removal

The 1st installation cantilever has a lower ball joint housing fitted with Belleville washers, and one locking washer, secured by a snap ring.

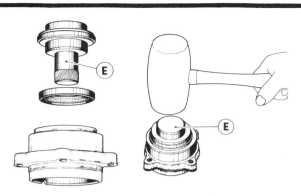

Fig.F.13. Installing outer seal ring.

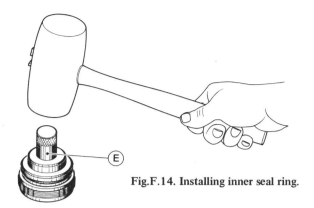

Fig.F.14. Installing inner seal ring.

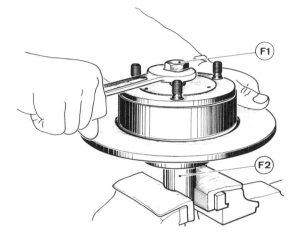

Fig.F.15. Assembling steering knuckle with hub.

Fig.F.16. Releasing drive shaft from hub.

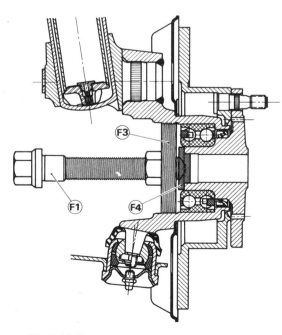

Fig.F.17. Pulling out hub/disc assembly.

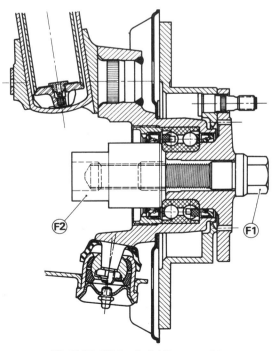

Fig.F.18. Fitting hub/disc assembly.

Fig.F.19. Removing elastic bushings.

Fig.F.20. Refitting elastic bushings.

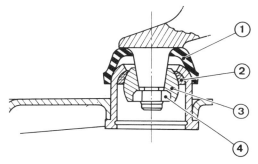

Fig.F.21. Detail of ball-joint assembly-
1st installation.

Fig.F.23. 1st installation cantilever.

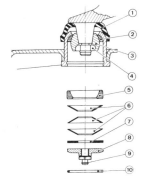

Fig.F.22. Ball joint assembly -
1st installation.

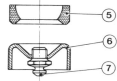

Fig.F.25. Lower half bearing and ball-
joint housing locking nut.

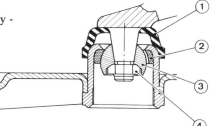

Fig.F.24. Detail of ball joint assembly-
2nd installation.

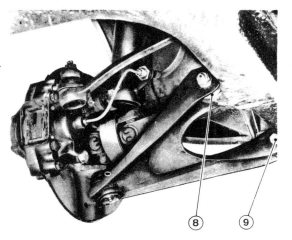

Fig.F.26. 2nd installation cantilever.

Raise front end of vehicle, using a trolley jack under front frame lower crossbar, or using hoisting bar 8.1501 and the front frame upper crossbar. Place chocks under front part of engine cradle. Remove wheel. Install locking clamp 8.0407 on drive shaft. Push back ball joint housing locking washer snap-ring, using a 2.5mm. (0.098 in.) dia. punch inserted through the hole provided for this purpose. Remove snap-ring by prising off with a screw-driver. Remove the locking washer, rubber sealing washer, and the three Belleville washers from the ball joint housing. Remove the pivot pins from the cantilever elastic bushings. Remove steering knuckle arm ball-joint nut, using serrated wrench 8.0903AZ or similar. Install special remover 8.0903H in lieu of ball-joint locking washer. Insert snap-ring into ball-joint housing groove, using special clamp 8.0903B or similar. Hold cantilever perpendicular to ball-joint housing shank axis, and dismantle cantilever from steering knuckle pivot by tightening the remover screw. Remove cantilever and ball headed rubber protector. Remove the snap-ring, remover, lower Nylon half-bearing, ball joint, and upper Nylon half-bearing from the cantilever.

1st INSTALLATION CANTILEVER - Refitting

Assemble the rubber protector (Ref.1, Fig.F21), cantilever with half-bearing (Ref.2 - the thinner one), ball head (Ref.3, on the ball joint shank, and screw in a new serrated nut (Ref.4). Tighten ball-joint nut to 2.75 mkg (20 lb.ft.) torque, using special wrench 8.0903AZ or similar. Temporarily secure cantilever to cradle by inserting pins into forks and elastic bushings. Stake ball-joint nut into the two grooves provided in the shank, using staking tool 8.0903JZ or similar. Remove pins from cantilever elastic bushings. Install lower half-bearing (Ref.5, Fig. F22 - the thicker one), the three Belleville washers (Ref.6), ensuring that they are correctly positioned, rubber sealing washer (Ref.7), and ball-joint housing locking washer (Ref.8), fitted with a grease nipple (Ref.9). Install a new snap-ring (Ref.10), in the centre groove of special tool 8.0903B with snap-ring gap facing away from tool hinge. Squeeze snap-ring, by compressing both handles of tool until tool is fully closed. Hold cantilever perpendicular to axis of ball-joint housing shank. Fully engage lower centring section of tool into ball-joint housing, and release tool handles. The tool will be held in position by snap-ring pressure. Place driving plug of tool against snap-ring, strike a sharp blow to squeeze Belleville washers, and engage snap-ring into its groove. Position one end of snap-ring in line with hole provided for its removal. Remove holding clamp 8.0407.

Bring cantilever into position for assembly on engine cradle, placing new Vulkollan washers (Ref.11, Fig.F23) between elastic bushings and cantilever forks. Smear elastic bushing pivot pins (Ref.12) with tallows, and insert them. Install new Nyloc nuts,

without tightening, and refit wheel. Remove chocks, and lower vehicle onto its wheels. Tighten wheel nuts to 6mkg (43.5 lb.ft) torque. Manoeuvre vehicle to 'bed in' parts. Tighten Nyloc nuts on cantilever elastic bushing pivot pins to 3.5mkg. (2.5lb.ft.) torque. Lubricate lower ball-joint with Multi-purpose Grease.

2nd INSTALLATION CANTILEVER - Removal

The 2nd. installation cantilever has a lower ball-joint housing fitted with one locking nut.

Raise front end of vehicle using a trolley jack under front frame lower crossbar, or using hoisting bar 8.1501 and the front frame upper crossbar. Place chocks under front part of engine cradle, and remove wheel. Install locking clamp 8.0407 on drive shaft. Remove locking nut from ball-joint housing. Remove pins from cantilever elastic bushings. Remove steering knuckle arm ball-joint nut, using serrated wrench 8.0903AZ or similar. Take cantilever apart from steering knuckle pivot by installing special remover 8.0903L in lieu of ball-joint housing locking nut, and holding cantilever perpendicular to ball-joint shank axis. Remove cantilever and ball-head rubber protector. Remove special remover, lower half-bushing and ball-head from cantilever.

2nd INSTALLATION CANTILEVER - Refitting

Assemble rubber protector (Ref.1 Fig.F24), cantilever fitted with upper half bearing (Ref.2 the thinner one), and ball-head (Ref.3) onto the ball-joint shank. Screw in a new serrated nut (Ref.4) and tighten to 3.75 mkg (27 lb.ft.) torque. Temporarily secure cantilever to cradle by inserting pivot pins into forks and elastic bushings. Stake ball-joint nut into the two grooves provided in the shank, using staking tool 8.0903JZ or similar. Remove pins from cantilever elastic bushings. Install lower half-bearing (Ref.5, Fig.F25 - the thicker one), and ball-joint housing locking nut (Ref.6) fitted with grease nipple (Ref.7). Tighten locking nut to 0.75 mkg (5.4 lb.ft.) torque, while holding cantilever perpendicular to ball-joint shank axis. Remove holding clamp 8.0407. Bring cantilever into position for assembly onto engine cradle, placing new Vulkollan washers (Ref.8 Fig.F:26) between elastic bushings and cantilever forks. Smear elastic bushing pivot pins (Ref.9) with tallow, and insert them. Install new Nyloc nuts, without tightening. Stake locking nut (Ref.6 Fig.F25) in the two grooves provided on ball-joint housing, using staking tool 8.0606D or similar. Refit wheel, remove chocks, and lower vehicle onto its wheels. Tighten wheel nuts to 6mkg. (43.5 lb.ft.) torque. Manoeuvre vehicle to 'bed in' parts. Tighten Nyloc nuts on cantilever elastic bushing pivot pins to 3.5 mkg (25 lb.ft.) torque. Lubricate lower ball-joint with Multipurpose Grease.

Steering

STEERING GEAR WITH CONNECTING ROD - Removal
(204 Only)

Three point engine mounting: Place vehicle over pit or on car lift. Disconnect battery. Chock vehicle under lower front crossmember to raise front wheels 10-20mm. (0.4 - 0.8 in.). Remove front wheel on steering wheel side. Remove bolts from column protector (Ref.1 Fig.G3), and raise protector above the pedals. Remove bolt securing flector to steering column. Carefully raise steering wheel, and place a 40mm. (1.61 in) thick block of wood (Ref.2) between steering wheel and column cover plates.

Position support bar 0.0130 (see Fig.G4). Tighten support bolts to free power unit mounting blocks. Remove nuts from the two blocks on steering box. Disconnect exhaust pipe from manifold. Unlock and remove track rod bolts (Ref.3, Fig.G5) from connecting rod. Remove bolt (Ref.4) securing exhaust pipe to gearbox housing. Remove bolts securing steering box to engine cradle. Remove clamp retaining brake and fuel lines on engine cradle. Slacken the seven nuts securing front of engine cradle. Remove the four nuts securing rear of engine cradle. Lower power unit 20-30mm. (0.8 - 1.2 in) by slackening support bolts in support bar 0.0130, to facilitate removal of steering box. Withdraw steering box from steering wheel side.

Four point engine mounting: Disconnect battery. Separate exhaust pipe from manifold. Remove flector bolt (Ref.1, Fig.G6). Insert a 40mm (1.6in) thick block of wood (Ref.2) between steering wheel and column cover plates. Chock under front crossmember (Ref.3 Fig.G7). Remove wheel on steering wheel side (Ref.4). Disconnect track rods (Ref.5). Remove exhaust clamp bolt (Ref.6), steering box bolts (Ref.7), the four-way union bolt (Ref.8), and the four rear cradle nuts (Ref.9). Slacken the seven front cradle bolts (Ref.10), and the two nuts (Ref.11) securing power unit to lower rubber blocks. The engine cradle should rest on the lower blocks (Ref.12). Remove steering box.

STEERING GEAR WITH CONNECTING ROD - Refitting

Three point engine mounting: Engage steering box from steering wheel side. Raise power unit 20-30mm (0.8 - 1.2 in). Secure engine cradle at rear, checking that the brake and fuel line clamp bolt engages. Tighten the eleven cradle securing nuts to 3.5 mkg (25 lb.ft.) torque, holding bolt heads from inside if necessary. Tighten down brake and fuel line clamp. Secure steering box, fitting new DE washers under bolts. Tighten the four bolts to 3.5 mkg (25 lb.ft.) torque. Lower power unit onto supports on steering box, inserting a flat washer between each support and rubber block. Use new Blocfor washers and tighten the nuts to 3.5 mkg (25 lb.ft.) torque. Remove support bar 0.0130. Reconnect exhaust pipe to manifold, fitting a new gasket. Fit and tighten exhaust pipe clamp bolt in gearbox. Refit track rods. Screw down securing bolts, fitted with new lock washers, without tightening them. Engage steering column in flector. Fit a new bolt (Part No. 4043.03), and tighten to 1mkg. (7.25 lb.ft.) torque. Lock it by spreading the protruding end. Position steering column protector, and tighten the three bolt. Refit wheel, and lower vehicle. Tighten wheel nuts to 6mkg (43.5 lb.ft.) torque. Reconnect battery, and reset clock. Manoeuvre vehicle to re-establish correct riding position. Check the toe-out, which should be 2 ±1mm. (0.079 ± 0.039 in.)

One half turn of the connecting rod eye alters the parallelism by 1.7mm (0.067 in). if the thread is 1.5 mm pitch, and by 1.15mm (0.045 in) if the thread is 1.0mm pitch. If the adjustment of the parallelism requires altering the position of the eye by more than half a turn, the adjustment must be effected on both left and right eyes, so as not to alter the steering lock angles. To keep position of the eyes, insert a 10mm. (0.394 in.) dia. rod in the rubber bushes, align them parallel to the cradle, and retighten lock nut to 2.5 mkg. (18 lb.ft.) torque. Tighten track rod bolts to 3.5mkg. (25 lb.ft.). Bend tabs up around bolt heads. Refit connecting rod gaiters of the 'eyes' and tighten clamps.

Four Point engine mounting: Place steering box, from steering wheel side, on cradle. Tighten the four rear cradle bolts (Ref.9 Fig.G7), holding the nuts inside vehicle, to 3.5mkg. (25 lb.ft.) torque. Tighten the seven cradle bolts (Ref.10), the four steering box bolts (Ref.7) fitted with new star washers, and the two lower block nuts (Ref.11) to 3.5mkg (25 lb.ft.) torque. Reconnect exhaust pipe to manifold, fitting a new gasket. Refit exhaust pipe clamp bolt (Ref.6), and the four way union bolt (Ref.8). Connect up track rods, fitting new lock washers, without tightening bolts. Fit a new flector bolt. *Note:* There are two types of flector bolt, a hollow bolt, and a solid bolt. The hollow bolt should be fitted with an internally toothed washer, and a normal nut, tightened to 1mkg (7.25 lb.ft.) torque. The hollow end of the bolt should be spread after tightening the bolt. The solid bolt should be fitted with a Nyloc nut (without a washer) tightened to 1.5mkg (11 lb.ft.) torque. Refit wheel, and lower vehicle. Tighten wheel nuts to 6mkg. (43.5 lb.ft.) torque.

Reconnect battery, and reset clock. Manoeuvre vehicle to re-establish correct riding position. Check toe-out, which should be 2 ± 1mm. (0.79 ± 0.039 in). One half turn of connecting rod eye alters the parallelism by 1.15 mm. (0.045 in.). If more adjustment is required, it must be effected to both left and right eyes, so as not to alter the steering lock angles. To position eyes correctly on vehicle, insert a 10mm. (0.394 in.) dia. rod in the rubber bush, align them parallel to engine cradle, and retighten lock nut to 2.5 mkg. (18 lb.ft.) torque. Tighten track rod bolts to 3.5 mkg. (25 lb.ft.) torque, and bend tab washers up around the heads. Position gaiters on track rods, and on sealing plate at base of steering column.

SINGLE ROD STEERING GEAR - Removal

Disconnect track rods (Ref.1, Fig.G8). Remove lower flector bolt (Ref.2 Fig.G9). Remove the two bolts (Ref.3 Fig. G10) securing steering box to engine cradle. Disengage pinion from flector and withdraw it from steering wheel side. Check condition of flector, replacing it if damaged in any way.

SINGLE ROD STEERING GEAR - Refitting

Carefully grease bearing face (Ref.1 Fig.G11) for oil seal (Ref.2). Position seal (Ref.2) as shown in Fig.G11 (do not crush joint). Position flector (long collar - ref. a Fig.G12 - towards column), and fit a new bolt (Ref.3) without tightening. Engage steering box from steering wheel side, and connect it to flector. Fit a new bolt (Ref.4), without tightening. Secure steering box to engine cradle (Ref.5), fitting new star washers,

Fig.G.1. 204 Steering gear with connecting rod.

1. Steering box
2. Pinion (8 teeth)
3. Rack (30 teeth)
4. Connecting rod
5. Connecting rod link
6. Connecting rod link bolt
7. Flexible bush
8. Steering box plug filter
9. Lower steering box plug
10. Rack plunger
11. Connecting rod gaiter
12. Fixed protector on steering box
13. Rack gaiter
14. Track rod adjuster
15. Track rod
16. Ball joint
17. Flector
18. Steering column
19. Gear change control rod
20. Ignition switch on anti-theft lock
21. Steering wheel

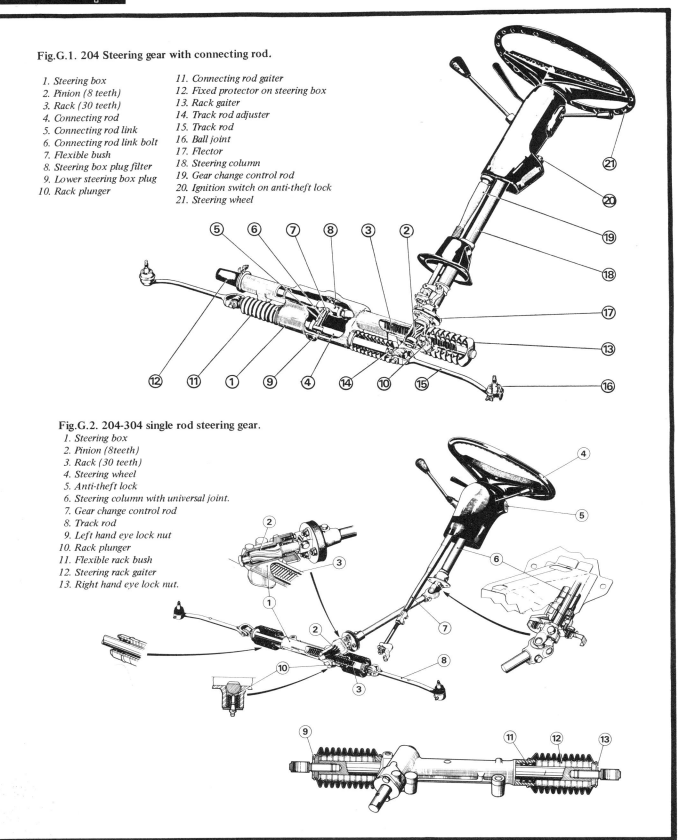

Fig.G.2. 204-304 single rod steering gear.

1. Steering box
2. Pinion (8teeth)
3. Rack (30 teeth)
4. Steering wheel
5. Anti-theft lock
6. Steering column with universal joint.
7. Gear change control rod
8. Track rod
9. Left hand eye lock nut
10. Rack plunger
11. Flexible rack bush
12. Steering rack gaiter
13. Right hand eye lock nut.

Fig.G.3. Removing column protector.

Fig.G.4. Supporting power unit.

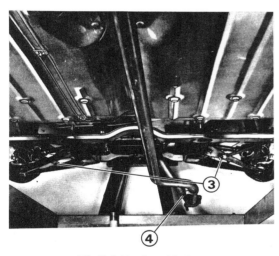

Fig.G.5. Track rod bolts.

Fig.G.6. Removing flector bolt.

Fig.G.7. Steering gear from underside of vehicle.

95

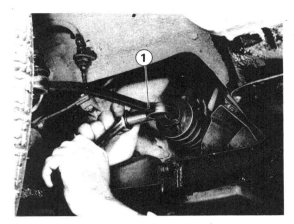

Fig.G.8. Disconnecting track rods single rod steering gear.

Fig.G.9. Removing lower flector bolt.

Fig.G.10. Removing steering box securing bolts.

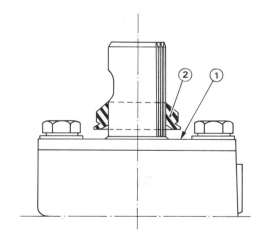

Fig.G.11. Positioning oil seal.

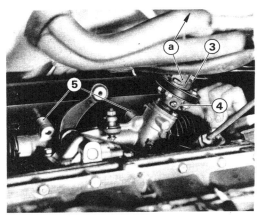

Fig.G.12. Steering box in position.

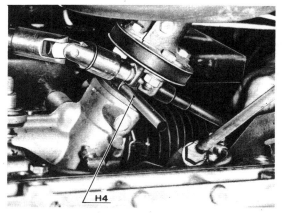

Fig.G.13. Tightening lower flector bolt.

Fig.G.14. Slackening eye lock nut.

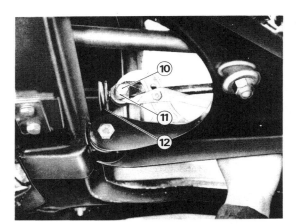

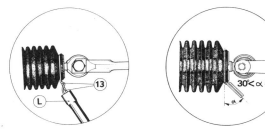

Fig.G.15. Track rod pivot.

without tightening bolts. *Note:* There are two types of flector bolt, a hollow bolt and solid bolt. The hollow bolt should be fitted with an internally toothed washers and a normal nut. The solid bolt should be fitted with a Nyloc nut (without a washer). Insert special rod 8.0704 H4, (See Fig.G13) and tighten lower flector bolt. Tighten bolt with normal nut to 1mkg (7.25 lb.ft.) torque, and lock it by spreading hollow end of bolt. Tighten bolt with Nyloc nut to 1.5 mkg (11 lb.ft.) torque. Tighten the two bolts securing steering box to engine cradle to 3.5 mkg (25 lb.ft.) torque. Connect up track rod arms without tightening bolt. Manœuvre vehicle to re-establish correct riding position, and place steering wheel in straight ahead position. Check toe-out, which should be 2 ± 1mm. (0.079 ± 0.039in). To adjust the parallelism, disconnect track rods, slacken lock nut (ref. 8, Fig.G14), and screw the eye in or out to obtain the correct toe-out. Half a turn of the eye alters the parallelism by 1.15mm. (0.045 in.). If more adjustment is required both left and right eyes should be adjusted so as not to alter the steering lock angles. Insert a 10mm. (0.394 in.) dia. rod into the eye, and align it parallel to the engine cradle. Tighten lock nut to 2.5 mkg (18 lb. ft) torque. Proceed in same manner for other eye. Recheck parallelism. Tighten pivot bolts (Ref.10, Fig.G15) to 3.5 mkg (25 lb.ft.) torque. Bend tabs (Ref.11) up around heads. Clean grease from lock nut grooves (Ref.12). Smear a little Colfix (Part No. 9724.29) in the grooves. Close rubber gaiters .
Note: The legs of the outer clamps (Ref.13) must be placed downwards and facing outwards. Do not distort the legs from their original shape. Bend the legs out to an angle of 30º to 45º from vertical.

Technical Data

STEERING

Type	Rack and pinion, ratio 18.6 : 1
Camber angle	0º 30' ± 45'
Castor angle	0º 30' ± 30'
King-pin inclination	9º 30'
Toe-out	2 ± 1 mm (0.08 in. ± 0.04)

Front Suspension

SUSPENSION UNIT - Removal

Raise front end of vehicle using trolley jack under front frame lower crossbar, or using hoisting bar 8.1501 under front frame upper crossbar. Chock under rear of engine cradle. Remove wheel. *204 with three-piston brake callipers:* Remove the two attachment screws of calliper on wing valance without disconnecting brake hose.

204-304 with two-piston brake calliper: Unscrew hose nut (Ref.2, Fig.H1). Remove the two attachment screws of brake calliper (Ref.3), and hang calliper on wing valance without disconnecting brake hose. *Note:* On the first 204's fitted with two-piston brake callipers, the hose support lug welded to the shock absorber body is not split, and removal of the support element therefore necessitates opening the hydraulic system. In this case, disconnect the hose at the supportplug (Ref. 4) level, and leave calliper on knuckle.

Unscrew hub nut, holding hub with special tool 8.0606A. Remove hub nut and washer. Remove tool 8.0606A. Remove connecting link bearing nut, and uncouple connecting link using special extractor 8.0704C (see Fig.H2). Remove triangle bushing pins. Uncouple link rod (Ref.5) from anti-roll bar, where applicable. Separate grooved end (Ref.6, Fig.H3) of the hub, carefully holding the drive shaft to prevent it coming out axle side and risk draining engine sump and damaging oil seal ring. Place drive shaft towards front of sub-frame on anti-roll bar. Remove upper support attachment bolt on wing valance while holding support element. Remove support element.

SUSPENSION UNIT - Refitting

Bring support element under wing valance so that the hole (Ref.1 Fig.H4) on the upper cup is towards the engine on vehicles with 'fixed' spring front suspension units, or that the limit cup (Ref.2 Fig.H5) is parallel to the car axle on vehicles fitted with 'rotating' spring front suspension units. Fit support element on wing valance, with three new bolts fitted with double tooth washers. Tighten the three bolts to 1mkg (7.25 lb.ft.) torque. Apply Molykote to grooved end of drive shaft. Engage hub on grooved end, carefully holding drive shaft to prevent it coming out at axle end. Engage anti-roll bar link rod in corresponding hole on triangle , where appropriate. Position triangle, fitting new Vulkollan washers (Ref.3 Fig.H6). Tallow and fit elastic bushing pins (Ref.4). Screw on new Nyloc nuts without tightening. Clean brake disc, using rag dipped in trichlorethylene to clean off grease. Fit brake calliper. Connect link rod to steering knuckle lever with the split pin hole (Ref.5) parallel to brake disc. Fit a new internal tooth washer. Fit and tighten bearing nut to 4.25 mkg (31 lb.ft.) torque. Pin the end of the bearing.

204 with three-piston brake callipers: Tighten the two calliper attachment bolts to 7 mkg (51 lb.ft.) torque.

204-304 with two-piston brake callipers: Tighten the two calliper attachment bolts to 5mkg (36 lb.ft.) torque. Tighten hose attachment nut on support lug.

Fit a new hub nut and washer. Tighten hub nut to 25 mkg (181 lb. ft). torque, using Facom extension SJ214 or similar, and holding hub with special tool 8.0606A. *Note:* The Facom extension SJ214 doubles the torque, so adjust torque wrench to 12.5 mkg (90.5 lb.ft.) torque. Remove tool 8.0606A. Lock hub nut in the grooves on the end of the drive shaft with staking tool 8.0606D or similar. Bleed hydraulic system on 204's with normal hose support lug which necessitated opening hydraulic system during removal procedure. Refit wheel, and lower vehicle onto its wheels. Ensure that anti-roll bar link rod is correctly fitted, and that spacer (Ref.a Fig.H7) is in place. Fit a new Nyloc nut without tightening. Tighten wheel nuts to 6mkg (43.5 lb.ft.) torque. Manœuvre vehicle to re-establish correct riding position. Tighten triangle pin nuts to 2.75 mkg (20 lb.ft.) torque. Tighten anti-roll bar link lever lower nut (Ref. 6, Fig.H7) to 1.25 mkg. (9lb.ft.) torque.

FRONT ANTI-ROLL BAR - Removal

Place vehicle on car lift or over a pit. Remove the link rod lower Nyloc nuts (remove the lower attachment cups and rubber), the Nyloc nuts and washers (ref.1 Fig.H8), and the bushing clamps (Ref.2). Pull away, in an upwards direction, the anti-roll bar and its rubber bushings. Remove link rods, including cups, upper rubber attachments, and spacer tubes. Remove one front wheel. Remove anti-roll bar from side that wheel has been removed, passing it behind shock absorber body.

FRONT ANTI-ROLL BAR - Refitting

Proceed in opposite order to remove tightening nuts after assembly is complete, and with the vehicle in its natural riding position. When assembling, certain special precautions need to be taken. Fit the rubber bushings (Ref.3 Fig.H8) between the ends of the supports (Ref.4) on the sub-frame. Do not forget the spacer (Ref.5). Fit the cups on either side of the lower triangle. Use two new Nyloc nuts (Part No. 6939.06), two new Nyloc nuts (Part No. 6939.34), and four new Serpress nuts/Part No. 6935.13). Tighten bushing clamps to 1mkg (7.25 lb.ft.) torque, link rods on the bar to 4.5 mkg (33 lb.ft.) torque, link rods on triangles to 1.25 mkg (9 lb.ft.) torque, and wheel nuts to 6mkg (43.5 lb.ft.) torque.

Fig.H.1. Two-piston brake calliper and hydraulic connections.

Fig.H.2. Uncoupling connecting link.

8.0704 C

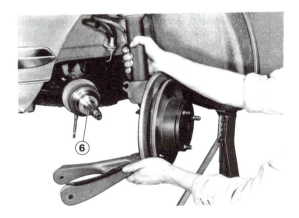

Fig.H.3. Separating hub and drive shaft.

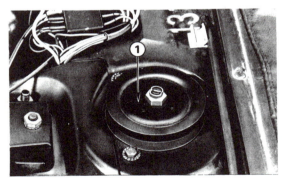

Fig.H.4. Positioning of front suspension with 'fixed' springs.

Fig.H.5. Positioning of front suspension with 'rotating' springs.

Fig.H.6. Refitting hub and link rod.

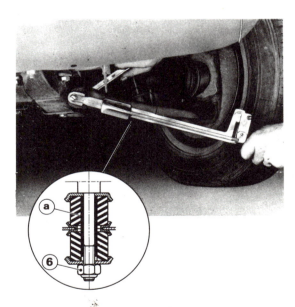

Fig.H.7. Correct fitting of anti-roll bar link rod.

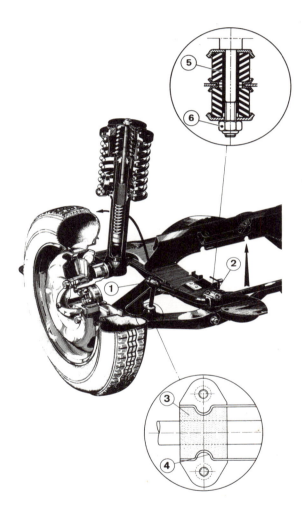

Fig.H.8. Front anti-roll bar details.

Technical Data

FRONT SUSPENSION

ROTATING SPRING SUSPENSION

TYPES	ANTI-ROLL BAR Dia. in mm	P.N.	Flexibility mm/100 kg	Free height in mm	SPRINGS Height in mm under charge	Reference Marks	P.N.	SHOCK ABSORBERS Reference Marks	P.N.
204 Luxe	without	-	60	417	190.5 to 195.5 / 195.5 to 200.5 (1)	1 blue / 1 yellow	5001.91 / 5001.92	Orange on rod	
204 GL / 204 BD				507	185 to 190 (1) / 190 to 195 (1)	1 green/1.red / 1 green	5001.87 / 5001.88		
204 B / 204 U4	19	5081.07	85	491	168 to 173 (1) / 173 to 178 (1)	2 red / 2 blue	5001.93 / 5001.94	without reference marks	5201.44
204 Coupe				468	204.5 to 209.5 / 209.5 to 214.5 (2)	1 red / 1 white	5001.89 / 5001.20		
204 Conv.	16	5081.05							

(1) Height under charge of 318 kg
(2) Height under charge of 260 kg

FIXED SPRING SUSPENSION

	TYPES	ANTI-ROLL Dia. in mm	P.N.	Flexibility mm/100 Kg	Free height in mm	SPRINGS Height in mm under charge	Reference Marks	P.N.	SHOCK ABSORBERS Reference Marks	P.N.
Without anti-roll bar	204 Luxe / 204 GL / 204 B / 204 BD / 204 U4	—	—	60	366.5	170.7 to 175.7 / 175.7 to 180.7 (1)	1 blue / 1 yellow	5001.57 / 5001.58	None or orange on the rod (3)	5201.28
	204 Coupe / 204 Conv.	—	—	40	288.5	156.3 to 161.3 / 161.3 to 166.3 (1)	2 white / 1 white	5001.59		
With anti-roll bar	204 GL / 204 BD / 304 AO1	18 / 19 (4)	5081.06 / 5081.07		455	170 to 175 / 175 to 180 (1)	1 green 1 red / 1 green	5001.71 / 5001.72		
	204 Coupe	18 / 19 (4)	5081.06 / 5081.07	85	415.5	189.5 to 194.5 / 194.5 to 199.5 (2)	1 red / 1 white	5001.73 / 5001.74	Green on rod without mark (3)	5201.38 / 5201.42 (3)
	204 Conv.	16	5081.05							
	204 B / 204 U4	18 / 19 (4)	5081.06 / 5081.07		438	153 to 158 / 158 to 163 (1)	2 red / 2 blue	5001.81 / 5001.82		

(1) Height under charge of 318 kg.
(2) Height under charge of 260 kg.
(3) As from 1969 Motor show
(4) The 19mm. dia. anti-roll has been fitted instead of the 18 mm one since the beginning of the series.

204 Gl	-	8 760 358	204 B -	6 794 619
204 Co	-	6 488 003	204 BD	6 642 332
204 U4	-	6 503 625		

NOTE - The 19 mm dia. anti-roll bar has equipped the 304 front suspension since the beginning of the series.

Rear Suspension

SUSPENSION UNIT - Removal

Saloons: Remove rear seat, rear back rest, and upholstery panel of rear shelf. Raise end of rear shelf sound proofing.
Breaks: Strip the upper part of shock absorber attachment.
Coupes: Remove the upper upholstery of rear side. Unscrew and remove the three shock absorber attachment nuts (Ref.1 Fig.J1). Raise vehicle, using a trolley jack fitted with an adjustable cross-bar 8.1502AZ (see Fig.J2), or similar. Chock ends of rear cross-member (Ref.2). Remove wheel. Remove shaft (Ref.3 Fig.J3) On 204's fitted with an aluminium alloy arm, drive out the shaft with a hammer and drift. Remove suspension unit.

SUSPENSION UNIT - Refitting

Put shock absorber on the arm. Engage the shaft from the inside to the outside and refit nut (See Fig.J4). On 204's with aluminium alloy arms, insert the shaft with the spline showing. Raise the arm with the trolley jack to apply the upper attachment. Tighten the three attachment nuts to 1mkg (7.25 lb.ft.) torque. Continue raising vehicle with jack until raised high enough to compress the spring. Tighten the shock absorber shaft new Nyloc nut to 5.5 mkg (40 lb.ft.) torque. Bring the arm to the maximum relaxed position. Refit wheel, and lower vehicle to its normal riding position. Tighten wheel nuts to 6mkg (43.5 lb.ft.) torque.

Saloons: Refit rear shelf upholstery panel, rear back rest, and rear seat cushion.
Breaks: Re-upholster the upper part of the shock absorber attachment.
Coupes: Refit the upper upholstery of rear side.

REAR SUSPENSION RUBBER BUSHINGS - Replacement

With the suspension unit removed from vehicle, extract the rubber bushing with special tool 8.0904A (see Fig.J5 and J6). Refit by introducing the new rubber bushing with special tool 8.0904A (See Fig.J7), ensuring that the protrusion on either side of the shock absorber eye is equal at completion of the operation.

REAR ANTI-ROLL BAR - Removal

Unhook hand-brake cable at Ref.1 (Fig.J.8). Remove anti-roll bar clamps, and re-inforcement plates (Ref.2). Make a reference mark at the left-hand end of the anti-roll bar if the paint mark (Ref.3) is no longer visible. Remove anti-roll bar.

REAR ANTI-ROLL BAR - Refitting

Pass anti-roll bar above hand-brake cable and exhaust pipe, and fit correctly with the reference mark on the left hand side. If badly fitted the anti-roll bar risks touching the rear brake cables (Ref. 6 Fig.J8). Place each six-sided end of the anti-roll bar between the clamp and plate. Line up the central straight part (Ref.4) of the anti-roll bar with the arm bushing shafts (Ref.5). Tighten the four new Nyloc nuts to 3.25 mkg (23.5 lb. ft) torque. Clip on the hand brake cables.

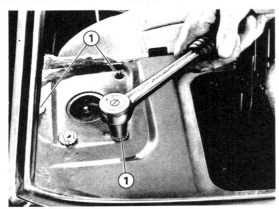

Fig.J.1. Removing shock absorber attachment nuts.

Fig.J.2. Raising rear end of vehicle.

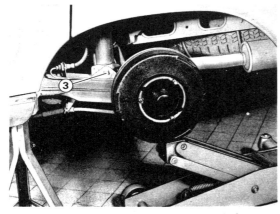

Fig.J.3. Removing suspension unit shaft.

Fig.J.5. Special tool 8.0904A.

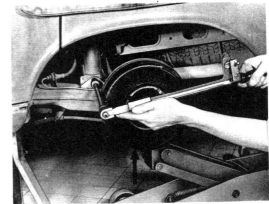

Fig.J.4. Refitting suspension unit shaft.

Fig.J.6. Removing rubber bushing.

Fig.J.7. Refitting rubber bushing.

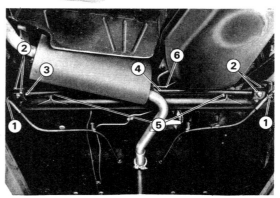

Fig.J.8. Rear anti-roll bar.

Technical Data

REAR SUSPENSION

Type: Independent, single trailing arms, telescopic struts with coil springs and co-axial dampers.

		ANTI-ROLL BARS			SPRINGS				SHOCK ABSORBERS	
TYPES		Dia. in mm	P.N.	Flexibility mm/100 Kg	Free height in mm	Height in mm under charge	Reference Marks	P.N.	Reference Marks	P.N.
Without anti-roll bar	204 Luxe 204 GL	—	—	22.5	303	226 to 231 231 to 236 (1)	1 blue 1 yellow	5101.78 5101.79	none	5205.62
	204 B 204 U4 204 BD	—	—	16	288.5	232.5 to 237.5 237.5 to 242.5	1 green 1 red	5101.83 5101.84	Yellow or orange on rod and cup	5205.63
	204 Coupe					200.6 to 205.6	2 white	5101.85	Green on cup white on rod	5205.64
	204 Conv.			18	263	205.6 to 210.6 (1)	1 white	5101.86	Blue on cup Blue & white on rod	5 205.65
With anti-roll bar	204 GL	15	5170.15	22.5	303	226 to 231	1 blue	5101.78	Red on cup and without mark on rod Yellow on end of rod (3)	5 205.69
	204 Coupe up to n° 6 488 321					231 to 236	1 yellow	5101.79		
	204 Coupe as from no. 6 488 231				293	218 to 223 223 to 228	2 red 1 white	5102.01 5102.02		
	204 Conv.	13	5170.17	22.5	286.5	210 to 215 215 to 220 (1)	2 yellow or 2 white 2 green or 1 white	5101.91 5101.92	Red on cup and blue on rod (3)	5205.70
	204 B - BD &U4	15	5170.15		322.5	214 to 219 219 to 224 (1)	1 red 1 blue 1 green 1 red	5102.05 5102.06	Yellow on rod (3)	5205.69
	304 AO1				312.5	204 to 209 209 to 214	1 white 1 red 2 blue	5102.04		

(1) Height under charge of 318 kg
(2) Height under charge of 460 kg
(3) As from "1969" Motor Show models.

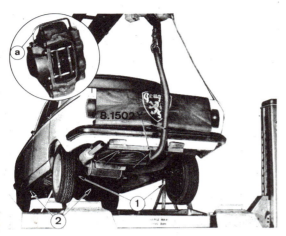

Fig.K.1. Raising vehicle and identification of three-piston calliper.

Fig.K.2. Setting rear brake shoes to minimum effective position.

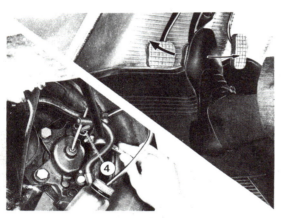

Fig.K.3. Bleeding front brakes.

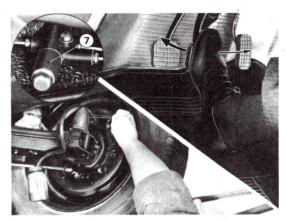

Fig.K.4. Bleeding rear brakes of vehicle with compensator under rear floor.

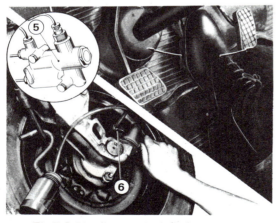

Fig.K.5. Bleeding rear brakes of vehicle with compensator on front left-hand wing valance.

Fig.K.6. Closing shoes against drums.

Braking System

BRAKES - Bleeding

Raise rear of vehicle, and chock under extremities of rear cross-member (Ref.1 Fig.K1). On 204 vehicles fitted with three-piston callipers (identifiable by the exterior brake pipe - Ref. a), chock under front sub-frame (Ref.2), and remove front wheels. Set rear brakes so that the shoes are as far as possible from the drums, using the adjusted (Ref. 3 Fig.K2). This position is in the centre of the total rotational curve (Ref.a). While bleeding, maintain fluid level in master cylinder. Use only Lockheed 55, Nafic FN 3 or Peugeot brake fluid. These fluids can be inter-mixed in any proportions.

Front brakes: Connect a tube to the front right-hand calliper bleed nipple, and place other end in a jar containing a small quantity of clean brake fluid. Release handbrake, and depress brake pedal fully. Slacken calliper bleed nipple (Ref.4, Fig.K3). Hold brake pedal fully down, and re-tighten bleed nipple. Release brake pedal slowly. Repeat this operation until the brake fluid flowing down tube is free from air bubbles. Finally tighten bleed nipple to 1.25 mkg. (lb.ft.) torque. Perform same operation on front left-hand calliper. *Note:* Some Girling 14 LF callipers have two bleed nipples. In this case bleed the lower one first, and then the upper one.

Rear brakes: There are two fittings of rear brakes. On 204 vehicles with a compensator under the rear floor (Ref.7 Fig.K4), and on 304 vehicles perform the bleeding operation in the same manner as for the front brakes.

On 204 vehicles with a compensator on the front left-hand wing valance (Ref.5), connect a tube to the rear righthand wheel bleed nipple, and place other end in a jar containing a small quantity of clean brake fluid. Apply the handbrake, and the brake pedal slowly. Slacken the right-hand wheel bleed nipple (Ref.6). Hold brake pedal fully depressed, and re-tighten bleed nipple. Release brake pedal slowly. Repeat this operation until the brake fluid flowing down tube is free from air bubbles. Finally tighten bleed nipple to 1.25 mkg (9 lb.ft.) torque. *Note:* If the brake pedal action suddenly becomes hard, the compensator has operated due to too rapid a pedal movement. To clear this, press the brake pedal down, close bleed screw, release handbrake, release brake pedal sharply, apply handbrake, and continue with bleeding operation. Perform bleeding operation in same manner for the rear left hand wheel.

REAR BRAKES - Adjusting

On both rear wheels, close the brake shoes up against the drums by turning adjusters as far as possible towards the bottom of the wheel (See Fig.K6). Take up the play by applying brake pedal hard two or three times. *Warning:* The pedal action must be hard, if not check brake lines and. hoses under pressure (swelling of hoses), and replace if necessary, bleed brakes carefully, and check operation of compensator. If the pedal action is still not hard, check for leaks. Release trailing shoes by turning adjuster towards top of wheel (Ref. 3 Fig.K7). Release leading shoes progressively by turning adjuster towards top of wheel (Ref.4 Fig.K8) until the wheel just turn freely with the shoes just touching the drums. Apply the trailing shoes to the drums. Slacken off trailing shoes until they are just touching the drums.

HANDBRAKE - Adjusting

Position handbrake lever on sixth notch (See Fig.K9). Slacken the lock nuts, and unscrew the adjusters (Ref. 1 Fig.K10 or Ref.2 Fig.K11), until the rear brake begin to bind. Balance the tension of the left and right-hand cables so that the jack lever (Ref. 3 or 4, Fig.K12, as appropriate) is in the normal "applied" position. Re-tighten the lock nuts. Check the stroke of the pedal, the handbrake lever operating position (six to eight notches), the oil tightness of the brake lines, the fluid level in the reservoir, that the breather hole in the reservoir cap is clear, and the brake operation with the vehicle in use.

BRAKE PLATES

There are three types of brake plates fitted to vehicles (see Fig.K13). In all three cases, the only difference between the left and right brake plate is the symmetry of the holes.

On 204 vehicles with aluminium alloy arms: Fit an oil thrower cup (Ref.4) and a brake plate (Ref.1 or 2).

On 204 vehicles with sheet steel arms and wheel ball bearings: (sheet steel arms adapted to 204 vehicles in place of aluminium alloy ones). Fit a sealing plate (Ref.5), a paper gasket (Ref.6), an oil thrower cup (Ref.4), and a brake plate (Ref.2).

On 204 and 304 vehicles with sheet steel arms and taper roller wheel bearings: Fit a sealing plate (Ref.5), a paper gasket (Ref.6), and a brake plate (Ref.3).

All vehicles: Tighten the brake plate retaining screws (Ref.7 Fig.K 14) to 4.5 mkg (33. lb.ft.) torque. The wheel brake cylinder (Ref.8) should be 19mm (0.748 in) diameter. The leading brake shoe (Ref.9), should have Ferodo 4Z lining of length 231 mm (9.094 in.) and width 40mm (1.575 in.). The trailing brake shoe (Ref.10) should have Ferodo 4Z lining of length 176 mm (6.929 in.) and width 40 mm (1.575 in). The handbrake cable (Ref.11) should be hooked up, passing across lug (Ref. a). The retaining spring (Ref.12) should be hooked on from above (at Ref.b), and passing under lug (Ref.'c'). The shoe retaining spring (Ref.13) should have the tab (Ref.'d') engaged in the plate, and then be sealed off with filter (Ref.'e'). All Assemblies should have a handbrake link plate (Ref.14). The return spring (Ref.15) should have the hook (Ref.'f') passed under the trailing shoe, and the other hook (Ref.'g') passed over the leading shoe.

BRAKE PADS - Replacement

All four brake pads must be replaced when any one of them is down to 2mm (0.079 in) thickness. Raise front end of vehicle, and chock under the left and right extremities of the front sub frame. Remove front wheels. Drain reservoir down to minimum level mark. Remove brake pads. Push pistons back into the callipers, using a piece of wood as a lever. Check that no fluid leaks past the pistons, that the rubber protectors are in good condition, and that the disc is not excessively worn. The brake pads and disc must be free from all traces of oil grease, etc. Install the new pads.

Fig.K.7. Slackening trailing shoe.

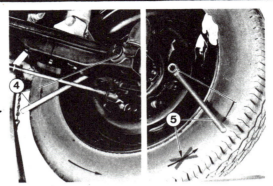

Fig.K.8. Slackening leading shoe.

Fig.K.9. Handbrake lever on sixth notch.

Fig.K.11. Handbrake adjuster - 2nd fitting.

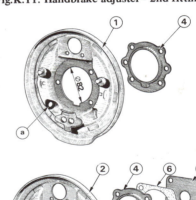

Fig.K.10. Handbrake adjuster - 1st fitting.

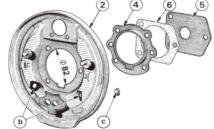

1st fitting

2nd fitting

Fig.K.12. Balancing tension of handbrake cables .

Fig.K.13. Brake plates.

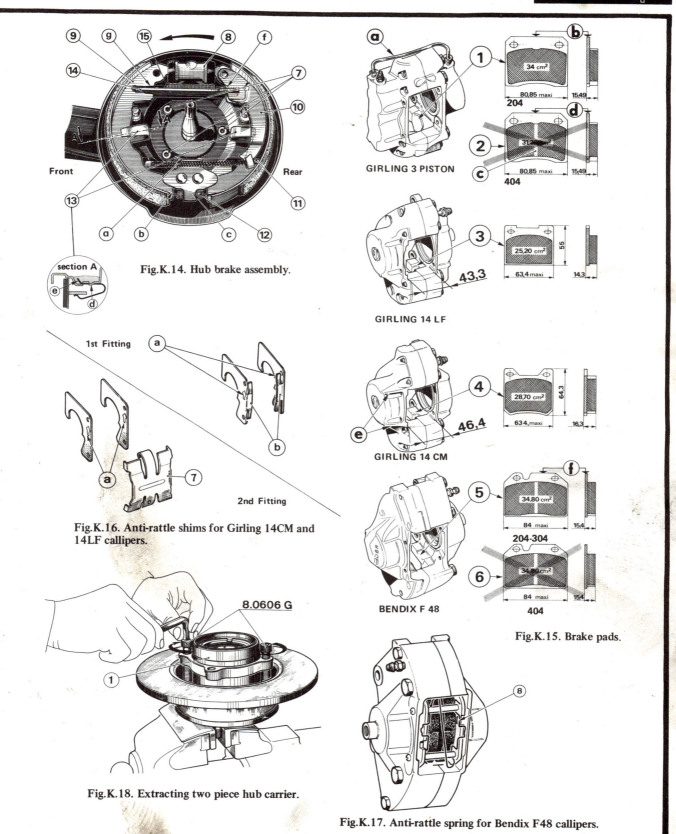

Fig.K.14. Hub brake assembly.

section A

Front

Rear

GIRLING 3 PISTON

204

404

GIRLING 14 LF

43,3

GIRLING 14 CM

46,4

BENDIX F 48

204-304

404

Fig.K.15. Brake pads.

1st Fitting

2nd Fitting

Fig.K.16. Anti-rattle shims for Girling 14CM and 14LF callipers.

8.0606 G

Fig.K.18. Extracting two piece hub carrier.

Fig.K.17. Anti-rattle spring for Bendix F48 callipers.

109

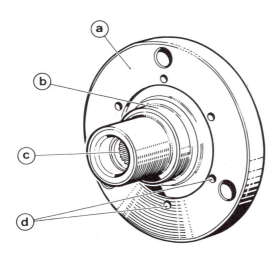

Fig.K.19. Check points on hub.

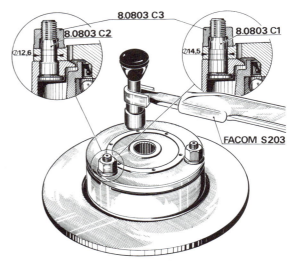

Fig.K.21. Inserting guides for disc/hub assembly.

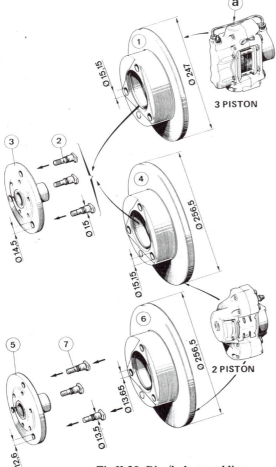

Fig.K.20. Disc/hub assemblies.

Fig.K.23. Mounting hub/disc on support.

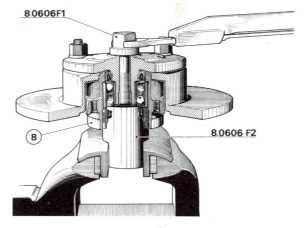

Fig.K.22. Fitting hub/disc assembly on hub carrier.

Warning: There are four sets of pads which are not interchangeable.

On 204 vehicles with three-piston callipers (identifiable by external gallery, Ref.'a' Fig.K15), fit pads (Ref.1) type Fadil L113 without groove having one green and one white reference on the pad back plate (Ref.'b'). The pads (Ref.2) type Abex NS 414 with groove (Ref.'c'), and with one green and two white reference marks (Ref.'d') must never be fitted on 204 vehicles.

On 204 with Girling 14 LF2 piston Callipers (identifiable by no external gallery and a G marked on the calliper), fit the pads (Ref.3).

On 204 and 304 with Girling 14 CA12 piston callipers identifiable by no external gallery and G marked on calliper ribbing (Ref.'e') on the calliper, fit the pads (Ref.4).

On 204 and 304 with Bendix F48 callipers, fit pads (Ref.5) type Abex NS 413 with one white and one green reference on the back plate (Ref.'f'). The pads (Ref.6) type Abex NS 414 with no reference must not be fitted to 204 or 304 vehicles.

On grinding 14CM and 14LF callipers fit anti-rattle shims between pads and pistons with the arrow pointing upwards. There are two types of shim which are not interchangeable separately. When replacing shims on 14CM callipers fit the shims with no tabs, and fit spring plate (Ref.7 Fig.K.16), and on 14LF callipers fit shims with tabs (Ref.'b').

On Bendix F48 callipers use the anti-roll rattle spring (Ref.8 Fig.K17).

Insert the brake pad retaining pins with the heads on the pins towards the inside of the calliper. Fit new clips in such a way that the rubber cups cannot be damaged by them. Each calliper type has a different type of retaining pin and clip. These pins and clips are not interchangeable. Replace wheel, and lower vehicle onto its wheels. Tighten wheel nuts to 6mkg (43.5 lb.ft.) torque. Top up brake fluid in reservoir. Apply brakes a few times, and recheck brake fluid level in reservoir before driving the vehicle.

DISC - Removal

Remove hub/disc assembly as previously described. If a two piece hub carrier is fitted, extract it by screwing in the two screws 8.0606G or similar. Alternately (see Fig.K18), Withdraw the three wheel studs using a press. Ensure that there are no burrs or chips on the disc mating face (Ref.a Fig.K19) of the hub. Ensure that there are no scratches or grooves on the oil bearing face (Ref.'b'). Make sure that the splines (Ref.'c') are note flattened or worn. Make sure that the drainage holes (Ref. 'd') are free.

DISC - Removal

There are three types of disc, and only the following assemblies are to be realised.

On 204 vehicles with three-piston callipers (identifiable by exterior fluid line - (Ref.a Fig.K.20), fit disc (Ref.1) of 247mm (9.724 in). diameter, wheel studs (Ref.2) of 15mm (0.591 in) diameter, and hub (Ref.3) with holes of 14.5 mm (0.0571 in.)

diameter.

On 204 vehicles with two-piston callipers (no external fluid line), and hubs (Ref.3) with holes of 14.5 mm (0.571 in). diameter fit disc (Ref.4) of 256.5mm (10.098 in) diameter with 15.5 mm (0.596 in) diameter holes, and wheel studs (Ref.2) of 15mm (0.591 in) diameter.

On 204 and 304 vehicles with two-piston callipers (no external fluid line), and hubs (Ref.5) with holes of 12.6mm (0.496 in.) diameter, fit disc (Ref.6), of 256.5mm (10.098in) diameter with holes of 13.65mm (0.537 in) diameter, and wheel studs (Ref.7) of 13.5mm (0.531 in) diameter.

To find the correct disc/hub position, assemble the new or skimmed disc on the hub using the guides from tool chest 8.0803Z (Ref. 8.0803C1 or C2 Fig.K21, according to hole size). Tighten the nuts (Ref. 8.0803 C3) to 6 mkg. (43.5 lb.ft.) torque. Fit the hub/disc assembly on the hub carrier (Ref.8 Fig.K22), and tighten bolt (Ref. 8.0606F1 to 3 mkg (22 lb.ft.) torque. Mount the assembly on the support (Ref. 8.0803D1, Fig.K23) using the Allen screws (Ref.8.083D2). Install dial indicator with the feeler at 22mm (0.866 in) from the edge of the disc. Rotate the disc slowly one complete revolution. The maximum run-out must not exceed 0.05mm (0.002 in). If it does exceed this figure, move the disc through one third of a revolution on the hub without removing hub carrier. Repeat the run-out check. If, after trying the three possible positions, the run-out exceeds 0.05mm (0.002 in.) fit a new hub/disc assembly.

Mark the position of the disc in relation to the hub. Remove hub carrier and guides from tool chest 8.083Z. Fit new wheel studs of the correct type, using a press with a pressure of 10 tons for each stud, aligning the reference marks. Ensure that the bearings and seals are in perfect condition. On 204's with a two-piece strut/hub carrier, re-assemble the two parts using special tools 8.0606F1 and F2. Refit unit to vehicle. Before refitting calliper, check run-out of disc. The maximum allowable run-out with the disc in place on the vehicle is 0.07mm (0.0027 in.).

BRAKE CALLIPER - Removal

Raise front end of vehicle, and chock under left and right-hand ends of engine cradle. Remove front wheels. Seal off master cylinder inlet. Disconnect brake line at entry to calliper (Ref.2 or 3 Fig.K.24, according to type of calliper). Slacken the union. Remove the two calliper support bolts (Ref.5), and withdraw calliper.

BRAKE CALLIPER - Refitting

On any vehicle, the callipers, discs, and protector plates, must be of the same type. There are four types of calliper (shown on Figs. K25, K26, K27 and K28).

The swivel (Ref.2 Fig.K25) is no longer available from the spare parts department, but swivel (Ref.2a) is available from spare parts department. Either protector (Ref.4 or 4a) may be fitted to assembly.

The Girling two-piston 14 LF calliper is fitted in production with a disc (Ref.7 Fig.K26), either on a swivel (Ref.8) with a protector plate (Ref.9), or on a monobloc swivel (Ref.10) with a protector plate and strengthener (Ref.11), or a protector plate

Fig.K.24. Brake callipers.

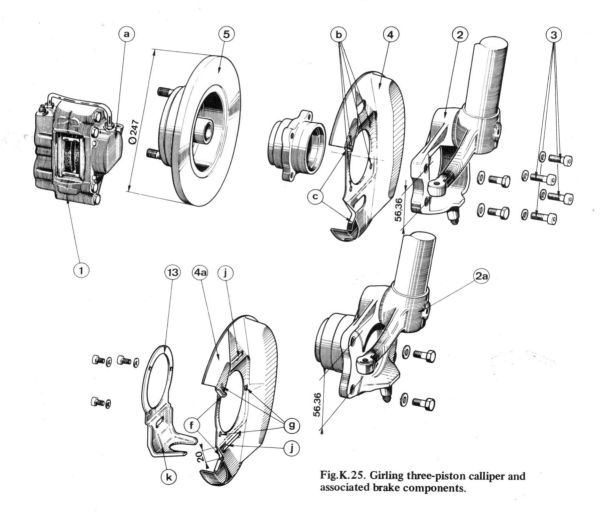

Fig.K.25. Girling three-piston calliper and associated brake components.

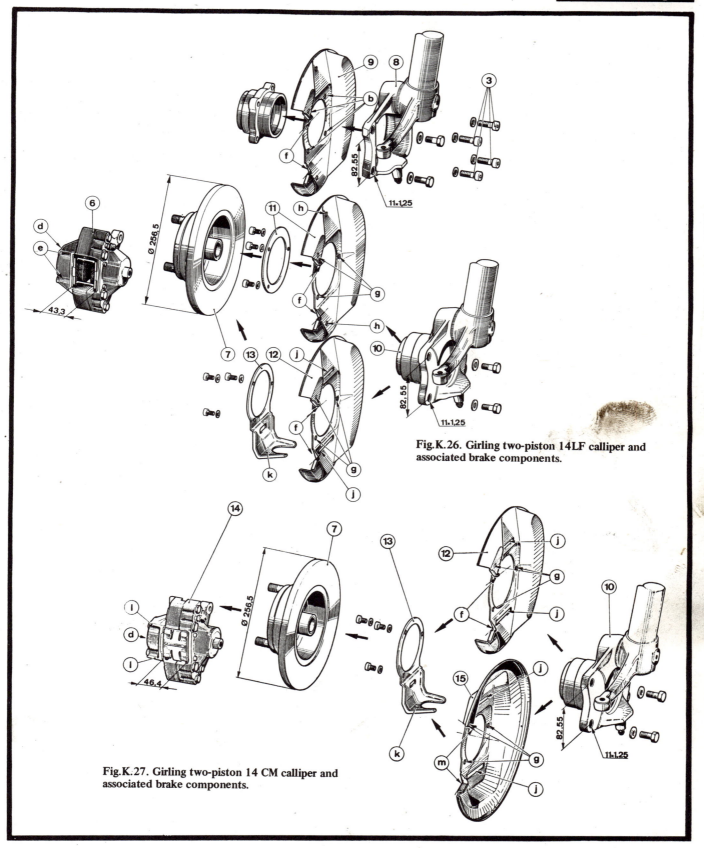

Fig.K.26. Girling two-piston 14LF calliper and associated brake components.

Fig.K.27. Girling two-piston 14 CM calliper and associated brake components.

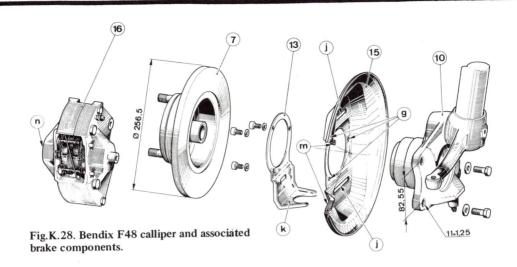

Fig.K.28. Bendix F48 calliper and associated brake components.

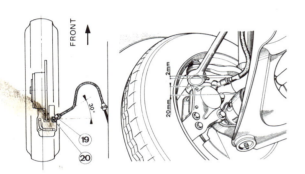

Fig.K.29. Three-piston calliper union position.

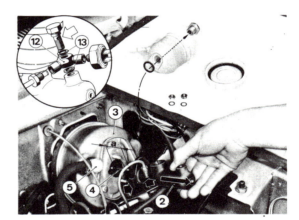

Fig.K.30. Removing master cylinder.

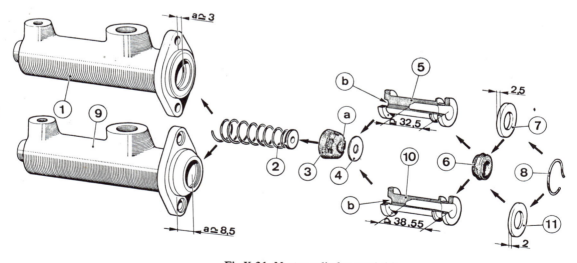

Fig.K.31. Master cylinder repair kits.

(Ref.12) and strengthener (Ref.13).

The Girling two-piston 14CM calliper is fitted in production with a disc (Ref.7 Fig.K27) on a monobloc swivel (Ref.10), with either a protector plate (Ref.12) and strengthener (Ref.13), or a protector plate (Ref. 15) and strengthener (Ref.13).

The Bendix F48 calliper is fitted in production with a disc (Ref.7, Fig K28) on a monobloc swivel (Ref.10), with a protector plate (Ref.15), and strengthener (Ref.13).

INTERCHANGEABILITY

The Girling 14LF callipers may be replaced by Girling 14 CM callipers on condition that two new or skimmed discs are also fitted. Either Girling two-piston calliper may be replaced by the Bendix F48 Callipers on condition that monobloc swivels are fitted, and also that two new or skimmed discs, two protectors (Ref.5), and two strengtheners (Ref.13), are fitted. The protectors and strengtheners (Ref.11) may be replaced by protectors (Ref.12 or 15), on condition that strengtheners (Ref.13) are also fitted. Protectors (Ref.12) may be replaced by protectors (Ref.15).

Lock the three bolts retaining the protector on the mono-bloc swivel using normal locking 'Loctite'. Tighten the two calliper mounting bolts, fitted with new star washers, and the threads smeared with 'Loctite' beforehand, to 5mkg (36 lb.ft.) torque on two-piston callipers, or 7mkg (51 lb.ft.) torque on three-piston callipers. On two-piston callipers tighten the brake line unions to approximately 1mkg (7.25 lb.ft.) torque. On three-piston callipers position the union (Ref.19, Fig.K29) at 30º to the front of the vehicle. Tighten the bolt (Ref.20) to 2.25 (16 lb.ft.) torque, ensuring that the clearances indicated are respected.
Bleed and adjust brake system.

MASTER CYLINDER - Removal

Drain reservoir and remove master cylinder (Ref.2 Fig.K. 30). *Warning:* On 204 vehicles with a servo-brake (Ref.3) (Masterval or Bosch servo); do not withdraw thrust rod (Ref.4) from servo, and check protrusion (ref.a) of rod in relation to mating face of servo unit, with the engine idling after having accelerated. The protrusion should be 36.3 - 36.5mm (1.429 - 1.437 in). If the protrusion is not within this tolerance, ensure that vacuum line is correctly fitted and in perfect condition, that the valve (Ref.5) is not defective, and that the brake pedal returns to its rest position. No action is possible on the servo unit except its replacement, replacement of the valve (Ref.5), and adjustment of thrust rod.

On 204 vehicles without servo assistance, the protrusion of the rod, with the gasket removed, must be 35.35 - 35.85mm (1.392 - 1.411 in) with an alloy pedal support or 36 - 36.55mm (1.417 - 1.439 in) with a sheet metal pedal support. To obtain this protrusion, adjust the rubber pedal stop.

MASTER CYLINDER - Dismantling

Remove hydraulic switch where fitted. Withdraw piston, cup, spring assembly, and the residual pressure valve, where fitted. Blow the main cup out using an air line or foot pump.

MASTER CYLINDER - Re-assembly

The master cylinder must be washed only in alcohol or brake fluid. Blow the parts dry to remove all traces of the liquid used.

Check master cylinder for dust, scratches, burrs, impact marks, rust, wear, or distortion at cylinder bore, threads, feed and return outlets, compensating orifices, and piston, to ensure that there is no possibility of leakage. Do not clean piston or cylinder with emery cloth, The cups, safety disc, and snap-ring, must be replaced whenever the master cylinder is repaired. The master cylinder must never be re-assembled with the residual pressure valve in place.

There are two repair bits available, which are not inter-changeable. On master cylinder (Ref.1, Fig.K31) with a protrusion (Ref,a) of approximately 3mm (0.118in) fit the spring (Ref.2), main cap (Ref.3) with anchoring nipple (Ref.'a'), security disc (Ref.4), piston (Ref.5) with recess (Ref.b), and a bore of approximately 32.5mm (1.28 in) (the pistons with no recess must be replaced), secondary cup (Ref.6), stop washer (Ref.7) 2.5mm (0.098 in) thick, and snap ring (Ref.8). On master cylinder (Ref.9) with a protrusion (Ref.a) of approximately 8.5mm (0.335 in) fit the spring (Ref.2), main cup (Ref.3), security disc (Ref,4), piston (Ref.10) with recess (Ref.'b') and a bore of approximately 38.55mm (1.518 in) secondary cup (Ref.6), stop washer (Ref.11), 2mm (0.079 in) thick, and snap ring (Ref.8).

Lubricate the components with brake fluid before assembling them. The master cylinder must be kept perfectly clean during assembly. Install safety disc (Ref.4 Fig.K32) on primary cup (Ref.3). Install secondary cup on piston with lips (Ref.a) towards the front. Insert components, without damaging the cups, with the metal spring cup (Ref.b) bearing on the main cup. Position the stop washer. Position snap ring in snap ring in recess (Ref.'c'), using a rod with rounded end to hold piston in. Fit and tighten hydraulic switch, where fitted, equipped with a new washer to 2.5mkg (18 lb.ft.) torque. Blow air through the outlet (Ref.'d'). It should pass through the return orifice (Ref.'e'), and no leakage should be apparent. Operate piston a number of times to make sure it returns against its stop.

MASTER CYLINDER - Refitting

There are four models of master cylinder (shown in Fig.K 33). In the event of a replacement being necessary, on 204 fitted with a hydraulic stop light switch fit master cylinder (Ref.2) with a horizontal outlet (Ref.'b'). On a right-hand drive 204 fitted with a hydraulic stop light switch on the banjo union (Ref.5), on all 204 vehicles fitted with a mechanical stop light switch on the pedal support (1969 Motor Show Model with sheet metal support), and on 304 vehicles, fit master cylinder (Ref.4) without the switch outlet and with a protrusion at the rear (Ref.c) of more than 8mm (0.315 in).

On 204 vehicles without a servo unit, and with a sheet metal support, fit a new gasket (Ref.6 Fig.K34). Fit two new star washers and tighten nuts (Ref.7) to 1mkg (7.25 lb.ft.) torque. Refit reservoir, installing a new rubber seal, and ensuring that the upper rim is horizontal. Tighten union bolt (Ref.8) to 1.5 mkg (9 lb.ft.) torque. Connect hydraulic line (Ref.9) to clutch. Fill up reservoir slowly with brake fluid. When the fluid appears in the outlet orifice (Ref.10), connect up the brake

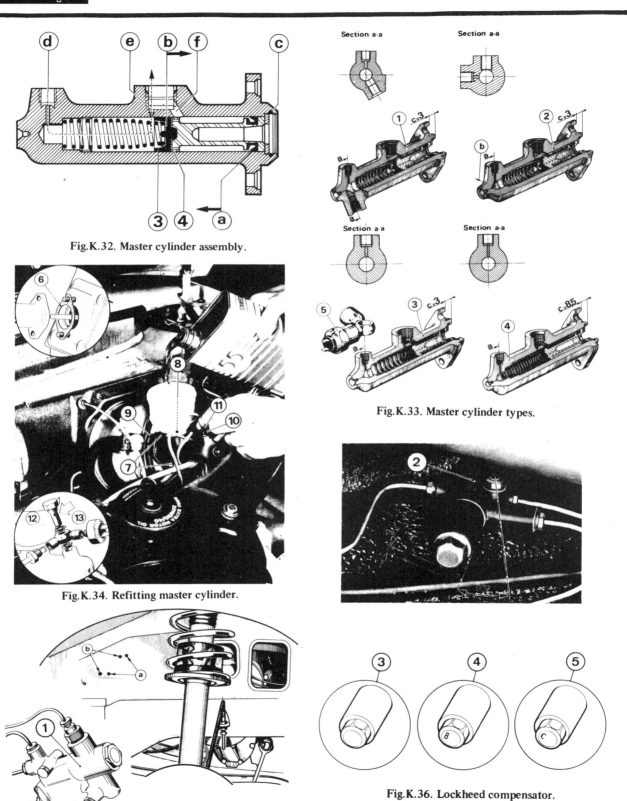

Fig.K.32. Master cylinder assembly.

Section a-a   Section a-a

Fig.K.33. Master cylinder types.

Fig.K.34. Refitting master cylinder.

Fig.K.35. Girling compensator.

Fig.K.36. Lockheed compensator.

line. Tighten union nut (Ref.11) to approximately 1.5 mkg (9 lb.ft.) torque, or the bolt for the union (Ref.12) fitted with two new washers (Ref.13) t0 2.25 mkg (16 lb.ft.) torque. Bleed one of the brake callipers. If the hydraulic system is in good condition, bleeding one calliper is sufficient. If the brakes feel 'spongy' then bleed the whole system.

COMPENSATOR

The main symptoms of abnormal compensator operation, excluding any other possible defects in the braking system, are the front wheels braking excessively (rear wheels only lock when handbrake is applied), or rear wheels braking excessively (rear wheels lock whenever brakes are applied). The vehicle must be tested with a nominal load on a dry, flat, clear road. It is not worthwhile driving vehicle in excess of 30 m.p.h. (50 km/h).

Girling compensator (Ref.1 Fig.K35) on front left-hand wing valance (up to 1968 Motor Show). The compensator must be mounted using the two holes (Ref.a , Fig.K35) on all 204 vehicles except Break and Light Van, or using the two holes (Ref.b) on 204 Break and Light Van only.

Lockheed compensator (Ref.2 Fig.K36) under rear floor (since 1968 Motor Show). The compensator must not be dismantled, only its replacement is possible. The compensator should be mounted at 37º from the vertical with a minimum gap of 14mm (0.551 in) between anti-roll bar and compensator. There are three models of Lockheed compensator. The first fitting on 204 models (Ref.3) Fig.K36), with no marking, must not be fitted in place of the later models (Ref.4 and 5). The compensator with a 'B' mark (Ref.4) must be fitted on all 204 models except Convertible and Coupe, all 304 models except Convertible and Coupe, and may be fitted in place of 1st fitting compensator (Ref.3) on all 204 models except Convertible and Coupe. The compensator with a 'C' mark (Ref.5) must be fitted on 204 and 304 Convertible and Coupe models, and may be fitted in place of 1st fitting compensator on 204 Convertible and Coupe.

Technical Data

BRAKING SYSTEM	204 (XK 4)	304 (XL 3)
Front	Girling or Bendix discs	Girling discs
Rear	H.C.S.F. drums	
Handbrake	Cable-operated, on rear wheels only	
Power assistance	Bendix Mastervac	

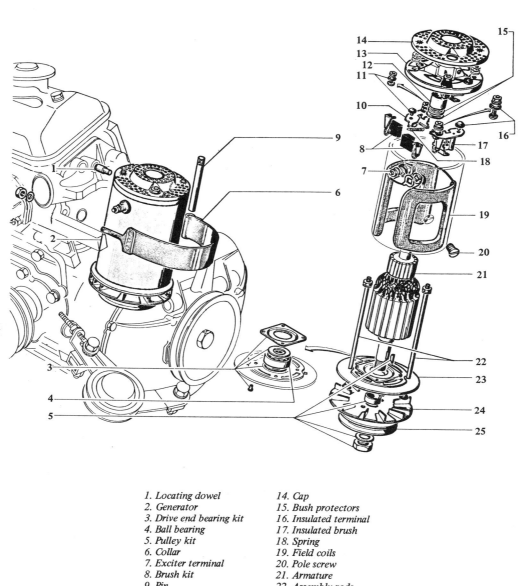

1. Locating dowel
2. Generator
3. Drive end bearing kit
4. Ball bearing
5. Pulley kit
6. Collar
7. Exciter terminal
8. Brush kit
9. Pin
10. Ground brush
11. Neutral terminal
12. Graphite bush
13. Cover

14. Cap
15. Bush protectors
16. Insulated terminal
17. Insulated brush
18. Spring
19. Field coils
20. Pole screw
21. Armature
22. Assembly rods
23. Cover
24. Vane fan
25. Driving pulley

Fig. L.1 Details of generator (Ducellier).

Electrical Equipment

SPECIAL PRECAUTIONS TO BE OBSERVED WHEN WORKING ON A VEHICLE EQUIPPED WITH AN ALTERNATOR

The following must be avoided.

Changing battery on vehicle, without having disconnected cables connecting battery to electrical circuit of vehicle.

Reversing polarity of battery, regulator , or alternator.

Disconnecting battery while alternator is running. Starting engine without connecting battery. Operating regulator without connecting it to alternator earth. Earthing field terminal on alternator, or regulator. Soldering, or unsoldering diodes without using heat sink. Applying volt-rise to diodes. Effecting electro-welding on vehicle without disconnecting alternator.

GENERATOR - Removal and Refitting

Disconnect battery. Disconnect connections on generator. Remove belt tensioner. Remove belt. Unbolt generator attaching collar. To refit, insert generator support centring dowel into corresponding hole in generator body. Tighten collar nut to 1mkg (7.25 lb.ft.) torque, maximum. Fit belt on crankshaft, generator and water pump pulleys, taking care not to twist it through more than 90º. Engage tensioner pulley on fan belt, and then secure tensioner to cylinder block. Using adjuster, tension fan belt. Make two reference marks 100mm. apart on fan belt when it is slack. When it is tensioned, the two marks should be 102 to 102.5 mm. apart when a dynamo is fitted, and 101.5 to 102 mm apart when an alternator is fitted. Tighten tensioner pivot nut to 4mkg (29 lb.ft.) torque, and the two support bolts to 1.75 mkg (13 lb.ft.) torque. Tighten tensioner puller nut.

Technical Data

ELECTRICAL EQUIPMENT

Battery earth	Negative	
Battery	12V 40 a.h.	
Generator	Ducellier 7319 or 7320 or Paris-Rhone G10C 34, C10C 46 or G10 C 50	204 Petrol Saloons, Breaks or Light Vans 204 Convertibles and Coupes up to Serial, Nos.204C-6415527 and 204Co-6478833
	Ducellier 7320 or Paris-Rhone G10 C 50	304 vehicles
Nominal voltage	12V	
Maximum power	330 W	
Output under 13 volts	25A	
Corresponding speed (cold)	2,500 RPM (Ducellier) 2,300 RPM (Paris-Rhone)	
Cut-in speed	1,800 RPM (Ducellier) 1,450 RPM (Paris-Rhone)	
Armature resistance at 20ºC	7 ± 0.5 ohms	
Crankshaft pulley dia.	118 mm (4.65 in.)	
Generator pulley dia.	75 (2.95 in.)	
Drive ratio	1.61 : 1	
Regulator	Ducellier 8343 or Paris-Rhone YD 217	All 204 and 304 vehicles except 204 Convertibles and Coupes from Serial Nos.204C - 6415 528 and 204Co - 6578 834
	Ducellier 8349 or Paris-Rhone AYA 21	204 Convertibles and Coupes from Serial Nos. 204C - 6415 528 and 204C - 6478 834

		Ducellier 7345	204 Convertibles and Coupe from Serial
Alternator		SEV/Motorola	Nos. 204C - 6415528 and 204Co -
		14V 26 656	6478834

	Ducellier Ref.	Paris-Rhone Ref.	
Starter Motor			
	6155	D8 E50	204 Petrol: Saloons, Breaks, Coupes, Convertibles and Light Vans
	6155	D8 E50	304

	DUCELLIER		PARIS-RHONE
	6155	6178	D8 E50
Nominal battery voltage		12V	
Locked torque	1 m.kg = 9.8 Nm	2 m.kg - 19.6 Nm	1.33 m.kg = 13 Nm
Corresponding consumption	400A	530A	400A
Maximum power	1 ch = 0.736 kW	1.5 ch = 1.104 KW	1.1 ch = 0.8 KW
Corresponding consumption	240A	300A	200A
Corresponding torque	0.45 m.kg = 4.41 Nm	0.5 m.kg = 4.9 Nm	0.43 m.kg = 4.2 Nm
Turning sense from pinion side		anti-clockwise	
Number of teeth		9	
Module	2.116	2.54	2.116
Pressure angle	12o	20o	12o
Spring strength on new brushes		about 1.5 g.	

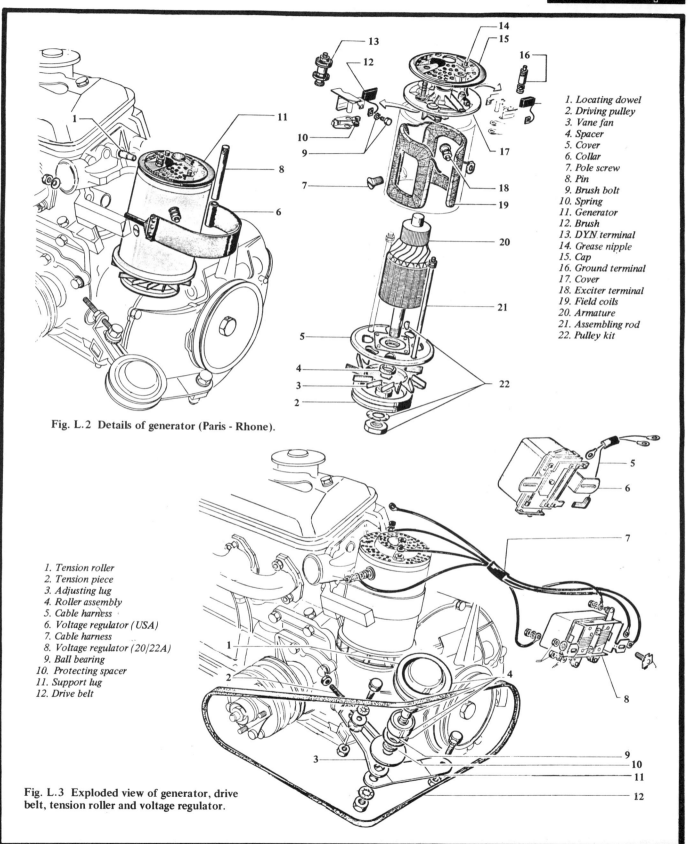

1. Locating dowel
2. Driving pulley
3. Vane fan
4. Spacer
5. Cover
6. Collar
7. Pole screw
8. Pin
9. Brush bolt
10. Spring
11. Generator
12. Brush
13. DYN. terminal
14. Grease nipple
15. Cap
16. Ground terminal
17. Cover
18. Exciter terminal
19. Field coils
20. Armature
21. Assembling rod
22. Pulley kit

Fig. L.2 Details of generator (Paris - Rhone).

1. Tension roller
2. Tension piece
3. Adjusting lug
4. Roller assembly
5. Cable harness
6. Voltage regulator (USA)
7. Cable harness
8. Voltage regulator (20/22A)
9. Ball bearing
10. Protecting spacer
11. Support lug
12. Drive belt

Fig. L.3 Exploded view of generator, drive belt, tension roller and voltage regulator.

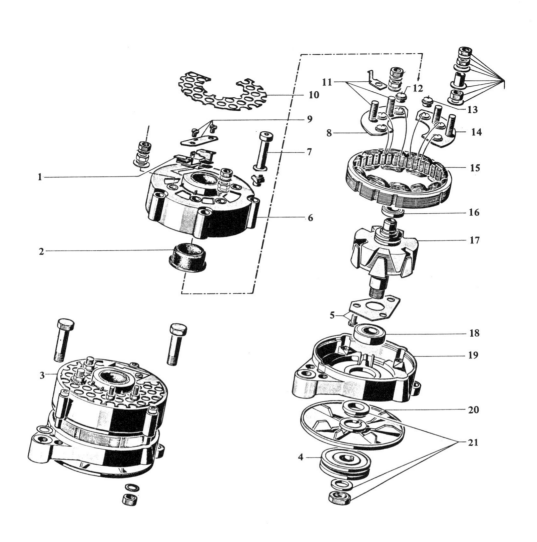

1. Brush holder assembly
2. Rubber cap
3. Alternator
4. Drive pulley
5. Front bearing retainer
6. Rear cover
7. Alternator mounting
8. Negative diode holder
9. Brush holder retainer
10. Protecting plate
11. Diode holder

12. Negative diodes
13. Positive diodes
14. Positive diode holder
15. Stator
16. Rear bearing
17. Rotor
18. Front bearing
19. Front cover
20. Vane fan
21. Pulley kit

Fig. L.4 Details of alternator (Sev).

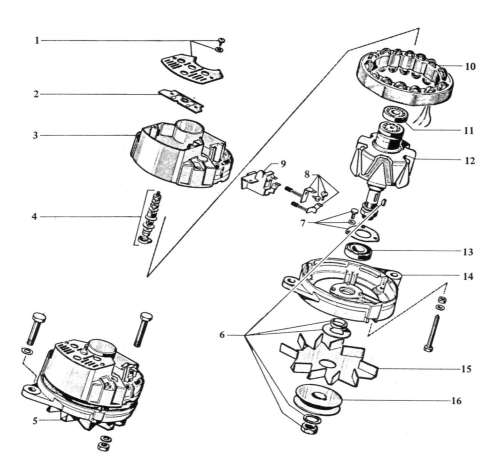

1. Rear cover
2. Fuse
3. Diode holder
4. Terminal components
5. Alternator assembly
6. Pulley attachments
7. Front bearing retainer
8. Brush retainer

9. Brush holder
10. Stator
11. Ball bearing
12. Rotor
13. Ball bearing
14. Cover
15. Vane fan
16. Pulley assembly

Fig. L.5 Details of alternator (Ducellier) -
single phase.

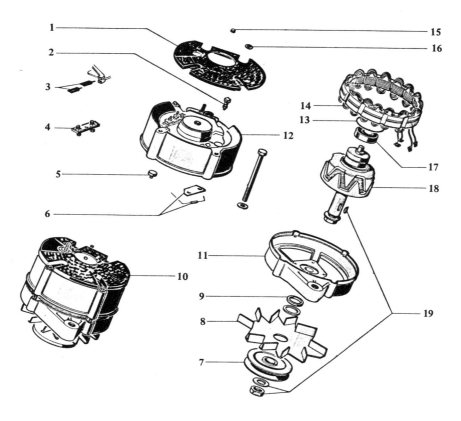

1. Cover
2. Fuse assembly
3. Alternator brush
4. Fuse holder
5. Relay terminal
6. Condensor
7. Pulley
8. Vane fan
9. Spacer
10. Alternator assembly

11. Cover (drive end)
12. Cover (commutator end)
13. Gasket
14. Stator
15. Plastic plug
16. Attaching washer
17. Rear bearing
18. Rotor
19. Pulley assembly

Fig. L.6 Details of alternator (Paris-Rhone) -
single phase.

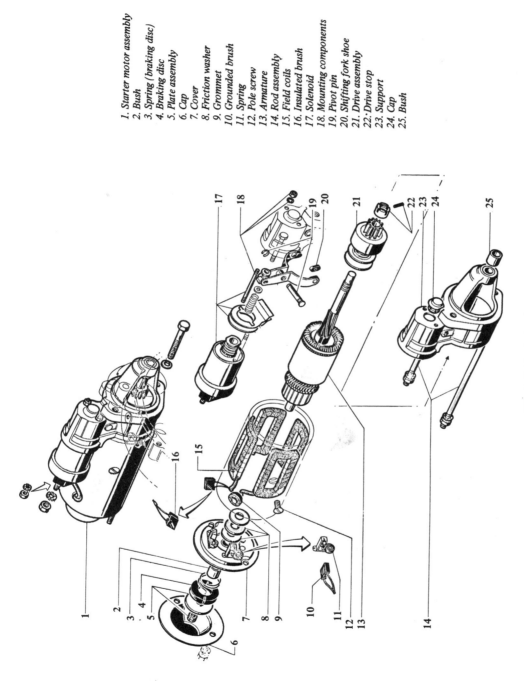

1. Starter motor assembly
2. Bush
3. Spring (braking disc)
4. Braking disc
5. Plate assembly
6. Cap
7. Cover
8. Friction washer
9. Grommet
10. Grounded brush
11. Spring
12. Pole screw
13. Armature
14. Rod assembly
15. Field coils
16. Insulated brush
17. Solenoid
18. Mounting components
19. Pivot pin
20. Shifting fork shoe
21. Drive assembly
22. Drive stop
23. Support
24. Cap
25. Bush

Fig. L.7 Exploded view of starter motor (Ducellier).

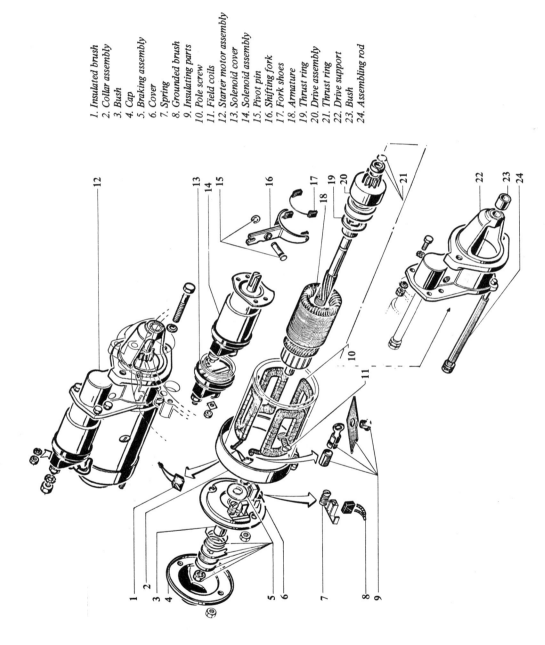

1. Insulated brush
2. Collar assembly
3. Bush
4. Cap
5. Braking assembly
6. Cover
7. Spring
8. Grounded brush
9. Insulating parts
10. Pole screw
11. Field coils
12. Starter motor assembly
13. Solenoid cover
14. Solenoid assembly
15. Pivot pin
16. Shifting fork
17. Fork shoes
18. Armature
19. Thrust ring
20. Drive assembly
21. Thrust ring
22. Drive support
23. Bush
24. Assembling rod

Fig. L.8 Exploded view of starter motor
(Paris - Rhone).

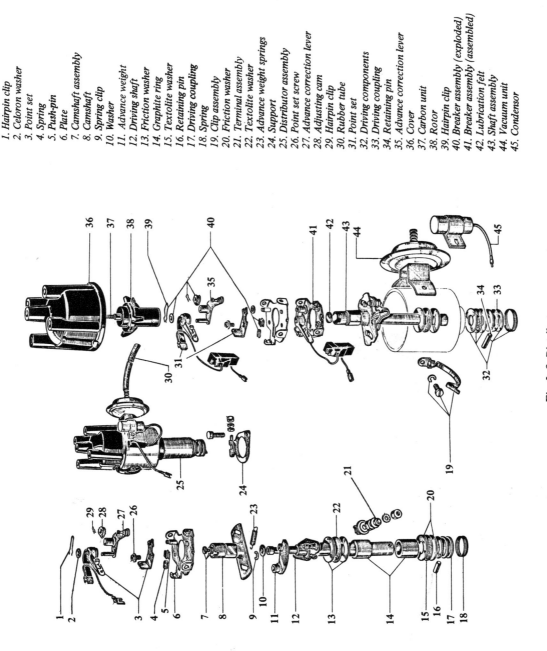

1. Hairpin clip
2. Celoron washer
3. Point set
4. Spring
5. Push-pin
6. Plate
7. Camshaft assembly
8. Camshaft
9. Spring clip
10. Washer
11. Advance weight
12. Driving shaft
13. Friction washer
14. Graphite ring
15. Textolite washer
16. Retaining pin
17. Driving coupling
18. Spring
19. Clip assembly
20. Friction washer
21. Terminal assembly
22. Textolite washer
23. Advance weight springs
24. Support
25. Distributor assembly
26. Point set screw
27. Advance correction lever
28. Adjusting cam
29. Hairpin clip
30. Rubber tube
31. Point set
32. Driving components
33. Driving coupling
34. Retaining pin
35. Advance correction lever
36. Cover
37. Carbon unit
38. Rotor
39. Hairpin clip
40. Breaker assembly (exploded)
41. Breaker assembly (assembled)
42. Lubrication felt
43. Shaft assembly
44. Vacuum unit
45. Condensor

Fig. L.9 Distributor components.

Technical Data

IGNITION SYSTEM

Distributor	Ducellier M 43	304

204 with XK motor 1st fitting up to Serial Nos.
204 Luxe 6 069 609
204 (GL) 8 640 660
204 B   6 745 316
204 C   6 414 818
204 Co   6 474 901
204 U4   6 501 867
204 with XK4 engine from Serial
Nos. 204 Luxe 6 074 501
204 (GL) 8 744 001
204 B   6 487 001
204 C   6 418 201
204 Co   6 486 901
204 U4   6 503 401

Ducellier M 68   204 with XK motor 2nd fitting up to Serial Nos.
204 Luxe 6 074 500
204 (GL) 8 074 500
204 B   6 787 000
204 C   6 418 200
204 Co   6 486 900
204 U4   6 503 400

Ducellier M 59   204 with low compression XK engine

Sparking plugs   AC 42 XL   304
Marchal 35 HS   204 with XK motor 1st fitting or low
or AC 44 XL   compression

Marchal GT   204 with XK motor 2nd fitting and
34 HD or   204 with XK4 engine
AC 42 XL or
Champion N6Y

Sparking plug gap   0.6 mm (0.023 in.)
Contactor breaker gap   0.4 mm (0.016 in.)
Centrifugal advance starts 400/600 rpm

Centrifugal advance max.   M 43 11°/13° at 2650 rpm
M 68 14°/16° at 2650 rpm
M 59 17°/19° at 2250 rpm

Vacuum advance starts-nominal   M 43 110 mm/Hg
M 68 110 mm/Hg
M 59 100 mm/Hg

Vacuum advance - max.   M 43 4°/6° at 220 mm/Hg
M 68 4°/6° at 220 mm/Hg
M 59 6.5°/8.5° at 220 mm/Hg

Wiring Diagram

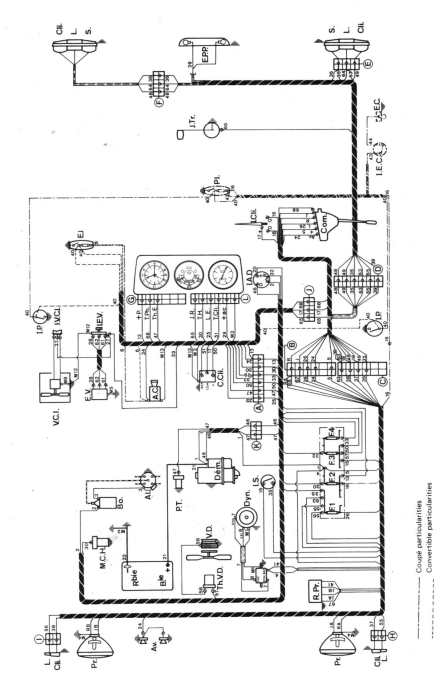

204 COUPES & CONVERTIBLES (GENERATOR)

From serial number : 204 Coupé 6 472 501 and 204 Convertible 6 414 001

Double curved headlights with Iodine lamps necessitating a relay.

——— Coupé particularities

- - - - Convertible particularities

Wiring Diagram

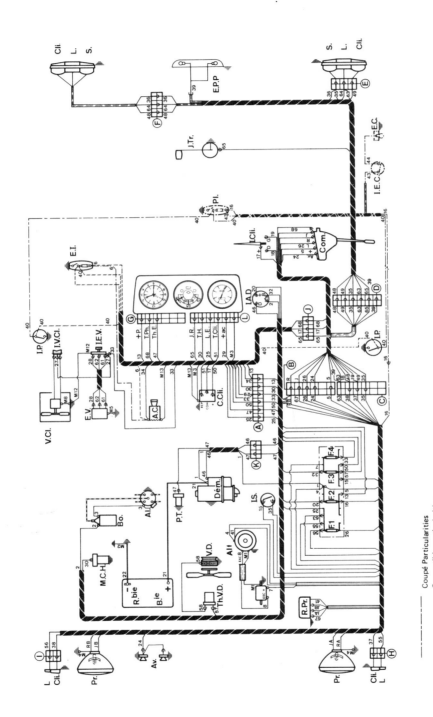

204 COUPES & CONVERTIBLES (ALTERNATOR)

——————— Coupé Particularities

- - - - - - - Convertible particularities

REMINDER :

The SEV Motorola alternator has been fitted to cars from the following serial numbers :

204 Coupé - *6 478 834*

204 Convertible - *6 415 528*

Wiring Diagram

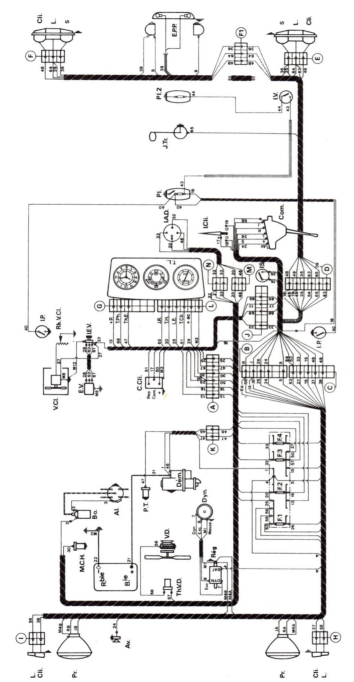

204 SALOONS & ESTATE CARS

...... Particularities Break GL

From serial numbers : 204 GL - 8 744 001 204 B - 6 787 001
- Side light warning light on instrument panel
- SOFICA heater and rheostat
- single trumpet horn
- 5 position horizontal bolt anti-theft lock under the steering wheel.

Wiring Diagram

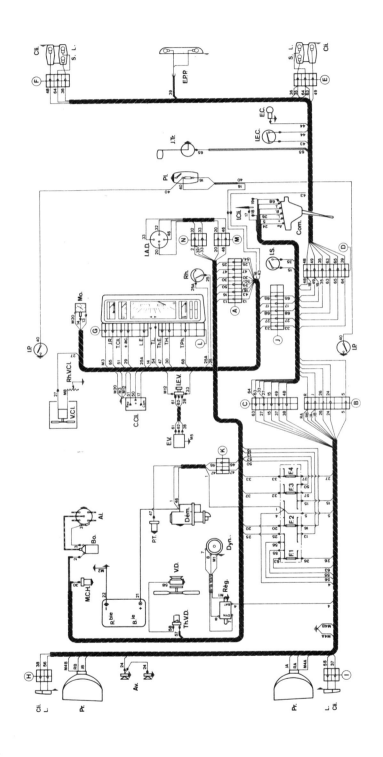

304 MODELS

KEY TO WIRING DIAGRAMS

SYMBOL	DEFINITION	SYMBOL	DEFINITION
A to Z	Connectors	J.R.	Fuel gauge
A.C.	Cigarette lighter	J.Tr.	Fuel transmitter gauge
Al.	Distributor with condensor	L.	Side light
Alt.	Alternator	L.E.	Instrument panel light
Av.	Horn	M.	Earthing
Bie	Battery	M.C.H.	Oil pressure switch
Bo.	Ignition coil	Mo.	Clock
Bo.P.	Pre-heater plug	Pl.	Roof light and switch
C. Cli.	Flasher unit	Pl.2	Rear roof light (break, light van)
Cli.	Direction indicators	Pr.	Headlight
Com.	Light and horn switch	P.T.	Water temperature socket (thermo switch with thermometer on the instrument panel) (thermo switch with indicator light on the instrument panel)
Dem.	Solenoid starter		
Dyn.	Generator		
E.C.	Luggage boot light	R.Bie.	Main battery switch
E.l.	Interior lighting	Reg.	Regulator
E.P.P.	Number plate light	Rh.	Instrument panel light Rheostat
E.V.	Windscreen wiper	Rh. V.Cl.	Heater Rheostat
F1 to F5	Fuses	R.Ph.	Headlight circuit
H.E.	Oil and water warning light	R.T.	Warning resistance
I.A.D.	Ignition and starter switch	T.Cli.	Direction indicator warning light
I.C.	Davauto switch or anti-theft lock	T.H.	Oil pressure warning light
I.Cli.	Indicator switch	Th.E	Water temperature warning light
I.E.C.	Luggage boot light switch	Th.V.D.	Self-disengaging fan thermo switch
I.E.V.	Windscreen wiper switch	T.L.	Side light warning light
I.P.	Door light switch	T.Ph.	Main beam warning light
I.P.Ch.D.	Pre-heating and starter switch	V.	Thermal voltmeter
I.S.	Stop light switch	V.Cl.	Heater fan
I.V.	Tail gate switch	V.D. + a.c. + P.	Self-disengaging fan Live after contact Live
I.V.Cl.	Heater fan switch		

133

Trouble Shooting

Engine

SYMPTOMS

	a	b	c	d	e	f	g	h	i	j	k	l	m	n	o	p	q	r	s	t	u	v
ENGINE WILL NOT CRANK	*	*	*	*																		
ENGINE CRANKS SLOWLY	*	*	*																			
ENGINE CRANKS BUT DOES NOT START					*	*	*	*				*										
ENGINE STARTS BUT RUNS FOR SHORT PERIODS ONLY					*	*		*	*													
ENGINE MISFIRES AT LOW SPEED					*	*		*		*												
ENGINE MISFIRES AT HIGH SPEED					*	*			*	*												*
ENGINE MISFIRES AT ALL SPEEDS					*	*	*		*	*	*	*	*							*	*	
ENGINE MISFIRES ON ACCELERATION AND FAILS TO REV.					*	*		*		*												*
ROUGH IDLE					*	*		*	*	*	*		*		*	*				*	*	
RUNS ROUGH AT HIGH SPEED					*	*	*	*	*	*	*	*	*	*	*					*	*	
LACK OF POWER			*		*	*	*	*	*	*			*	*	*					*		
POOR ACCELERATION					*	*	*	*				*		*	*	*				*		
LACK OF TOP SPEED					*	*	*	*		*		*		*	*	*				*		
EXCESSIVE FUEL CONSUMPTION			*		*	*									*	*						
EXCESSIVE OIL CONSUMPTION																*	*	*	*			
PINKING					*	*																
COMPRESSION LEAK								*			*	*	*			*				*	*	
	a	b	c	d	e	f	g	h	i	j	k	l	m	n	o	p	q	r	s	t	u	v

PROBABLE CAUSE

a. Fault in the starting system - Refer to the ELECTRICAL EQUIPMENT section for diagnosis.
b. Engine oil too thick.
c. Stiff engine.

d. Mechanical seizure.
e. Fault in the ignition system - Refer to the IGNITION SYSTEM section for diagnosis.
f. Fault in the fuel system - Refer to the FUEL SYSTEM section for diagnosis.
g. Incorrect valve timing.
h. Compression leak.
i. Air leak at inlet manifold.
j. Restriction in exhaust system.
k. Poor valve seating.
l. Sticking valves.
m. Leaking cylinder head gasket.
n. Worn camshaft lobes.
o. Incorrect tappet clearances.
p. Worn or damaged cylinder bores, pistons and/or piston rings.
q. Worn valve guides.
r. Damaged valve stem seals.
s. Leaking oil seal or gasket.
t. Incorrectly installed spark plug.
u. Cracked cylinder.
v. Broken or weak valve springs.

REMEDIES

b. Drain oil and replace with correct oil.
c. Add small quantity of oil to the fuel and run engine gently.
d. Strip engine and renew parts as necessary.

g. Retime engine.
h. Trace and seal.
i. Trace and seal.
j. Remove restriction.
k. Regrind seats.
l. Free and trace cause.
m. Renew gasket.
n. Fit new camshaft.
o. Adjust tappets.
p. Exchange engine.
q. Replace valve guides.
r. Replace seals.
s. Replace gasket.
t. Replace plug with correct one.
u. Renew cylinder block.
v. Replace springs.

Trouble Shooting

Lubrication System

SYMPTOMS

	a	b	c	d	e	f	g	h	i	j	k	l	m	n
EXCESSIVE OIL CONSUMPTION	*	*	*	*								*	*	
LOW OIL PRESSURE					*	*	*	*	*	*	*		*	

PROBABLE CAUSE

a. Worn or damaged cylinder bores, pistons and/or piston rings.

b. Worn valve guides.
c. Damaged valve stem seals.
d. Leaking oil seal or gasket.
e. Faulty oil pressure gauge, switch or wiring.
f. Relief valve defective.
g. Oil pick-up pipe strainer blocked.
h. Oil filter over-flow valve defective.
i. Worn oil pump.
j. Damaged or worn main and/or big-end bearings.
k. Incorrect grade of engine oil.
l. Oil level low.
m. Oil level too high.
n. Oil leak or the pressurised side of the lubrication system.

REMEDIES

a. Regrind cylinder bores and fit new oversize pistons and rings.
b. Replace valves and guides.
c. Replace seals.
d. Seal leak or replace gasket.
e. Trace and rectify.
f. Check and replace if necessary.
g. Remove blockage.
h. Check and replace if necessary.
i. Replace pump or parts.
j. Renew bearings.
k. Replace oil with correct grade.
l. Top up oil.
m. Drain off surplus oil.
n. Trace and remedy.

Cooling System

SYMPTOMS

	a	b	c	d	e	f	g	h	i	j	k	l	m	n	o
OVERHEATING	*	*	*	*	*	*		*	*	*	*	*	*		
ENGINE FAILS TO REACH NORMAL OPERATING TEMPERATURE							*							*	

PROBABLE CAUSE

a. Insufficient coolant.
b. Drive belt slipping or broken.
c. Radiator fins clogged.
d. Cooling fan defective.
e. Water pump defective.
f. Thermostat jammed shut.
g. Thermostat jammed open.
h. Ignition timing too far retarded.
i. Excessive vehicle load or dragging brakes.
j. Internal passage in the engine and/or radiator blocked.
k. Hoses blocked.
l. Carburettor mal-adjustment
m. Excessive carbon deposit in the cylinders.
n. Insufficient engine oil or use of inferior grade of oil.
o. Excessive radiator area.

REMEDIES

a. Top up radiator.
b. Tighten belt or renew.
c. Unclog fins.
d. Trace fault, rectify or renew.
e. Replace water pump.
f. Replace thermostat.
g. Replace thermostat.
h. Retime ignition.
i. Unload car, check brakes.
j. Trace and clear.
k. Trace and clear blockage.
l. Adjust correctly.
m. Decarbonise engine, top overhaul.
n. Top up with correct grade. Drain if necessary.
o. Partially blank off in winter only.

Trouble Shooting

Ignition System

SYMPTOMS

	a	b	c	d	e	f	g	h	i	j	k	l	m	n	o	p	q	r
ENGINE CRANKS BUT DOES NOT START	*	*	*			*	*		*	*	*	*	*	*				
ENGINE STARTS BUT RUNS FOR SHORT PERIODS ONLY	*	*	*			*	*		*	*	*	*	*					
ENGINE MISFIRES AT LOW SPEED	*						*	*	*									
ENGINE MISFIRES AT HIGH SPEED		*	*	*	*	*			*	*	*	*		*				
ENGINE MISFIRES AT ALL SPEEDS		*	*	*	*	*	*		*	*	*	*	*	*				
ENGINE MISFIRES ON ACCELERATION AND FAILS TO REV.		*	*	*	*	*			*	*	*	*		*				
ROUGH IDLE	*	*	*				*	*	*	*	*	*	*	*	*		*	
ENGINE RUNS ROUGH AT HIGH SPEED		*	*	*	*	*		*	*	*	*	*		*	*		*	
LACK OF POWER		*	*	*	*	*	*	*	*	*	*	*		*	*		*	
POOR ACCELERATION		*	*	*	*	*	*	*	*	*	*	*		*	*		*	
LACK OF TOP SPEED		*	*	*	*	*	*	*	*	*	*	*		*	*		*	
EXCESSIVE FUEL CONSUMPTION		*	*	*	*	*	*	*	*	*	*	*				*	*	*
PINKING	*	*		*	*		*			*	*				*	*		*
	a	b	c	d	e	f	g	h	i	j	k	l	m	n	o	p	q	r

PROBABLE CAUSE

a. Battery discharged or defective.
b. Contact breaker points need cleaning or renewing.
c. Incorrect contact breaker points.
d. Contact breaker spring weak.
e. Spark plugs need cleaning or renewing.
f. Incorrect spark plug gaps.
g. Wrong type of spark plug fitted.
h. Static ignition timing incorrect.
i. Coil or capacitor defective.
j. Open circuit or loose connection in the L.T. circuit.
k. Open circuit, short to earth or loose connection on the coil H.T. lead.
l. Open circuit, short to earth or loose connection on the spark. plug leads.
m. Plug leads incorrectly connected.
n. H.T. leak on coil distributor cap or rotor, due to oil, dirt, moisture or damage.
o. Centrifugal advance not functioning correctly.
p. Vacuum advance not functioning correctly.
q. Worn distributor cam or distributor shaft bush.
r. Using wrong grade of fuel.

REMEDIES

a. Recharge or replace battery.
b. Clean or renew.
c. Fit correct points.
d. Renew contact breaker set.
e. Clean or renew plugs.
f. Adjust gaps.
g. Fit correct plugs.
h. Retime ignition.
i. Replace as necessary.
j. Trace and rectify.
k. Trace and rectify.
l. Trace and rectify.
m. Connect correctly.
n. Clean with dry lint free rag.
o. Examine and oil sparingly.
p. Check and rectify.
q. Replace defective parts.
r. Change to correct grade of fuel.

Trouble Shooting

Fuel System

SYMPTOMS

	a	b	c	d	e	f	g	h	i	j	k	l	m	n	o	p	q	r	s	t	u	v
ENGINE CRANKS BUT DOES NOT START	*	*	*	*	*	*	*															
ENGINE STARTS BUT RUNS FOR SHORT PERIODS ONLY	*		*	*	*		*	*	*	*	*							*	*			
ENGINE MISFIRES AT LOW SPEED			*	*			*	*														
ENGINE MISFIRES AT HIGH SPEED	*		*	*			*	*						*								
ENGINE MISFIRES AT ALL SPEEDS	*	*	*	*	*		*	*			*	*	*									
ENGINE MISFIRES ON ACCELERATION AND FAILS TO REV.	*		*	*			*	*			*	*	*	*	*	*			*			
ROUGH IDLE			*				*	*	*	*	*	*				*	*			*	*	
ENGINE RUNS ROUGH AT HIGH SPEED			*				*	*			*	*	*	*				*			*	
LACK OF POWER			*				*				*	*	*	*				*		*	*	
POOR ACCELERATION			*				*				*	*	*	*	*	*		*		*	*	
LACK OF TOP SPEED			*				*				*	*	*	*	*		*	*		*	*	
EXCESSIVE FUEL CONSUMPTION			*	*				*	*							*	*	*	*		*	*
PINKING															*					*	*	
BACKFIRE			*					*		*		*	*									

| a | b | c | d | e | f | g | h | i | j | k | l | m | n | o | p | q | r | s | t | u | v |

PROBABLE CAUSE

a. Fuel tank empty.
b. Fuel line blocked.
c. Fuel pump defective.
d. Blockage in carburettor.
e. Air lock in fuel line.
f. Fuel filter blocked.
g. Carburettor needle valve jammed.
h. Water in carburettor.
i. Erratic fuel flow due to blockage.
j. Idling speed too low.
k. Incorrect setting of choke control.
l. Incorrect carburettor fuel/float level.
m. Carburettor icing.
n. Air leak at inlet manifold.
o. Incorrect grade of fuel.
p. Carburettor accelerator pump defective.
q. Throttle linkage mal-adjusted.
r. Incorrect adjustment of idling mixture.
s. Air filter clogged.
t. Incorrect ignition timing.
u. Carburettor piston sticking.
v. Wrong carburettor jets fitted.

REMEDIES

a. Fill tank.
b. Blow out obstruction with compressed air.
c. Replace pump.
d. Remove blockage.
e. Trace and bleed out.
f. Clean filter.
g. Free needle.
h. Drain out water, dry out.
i. Remove blockage.
j. Adjust throttle stop screw.
k. Reset control.
l. Adjust level.
m. Wait for ice to melt. If persistent, trace cause.
n. Trace leak and seal.
o. Dilute fuel with highest octane rating obtainable.
p. Trace fault and rectify.
q. Adjust correctly.
r. Adjust mixture control.
s. Clean filter.
t. Retime ignition.
u. Oil carburettor.
v. Replace with correct jets.

Clutch

SYMPTOMS

	a	b	c	d	e	f	g	h	i	j	k	l	m	n	o	p	q	r
CLUTCH SLIPPING (WILL NOT ENGAGE PROPERLY)	*	*	*	*	*	*												
CLUTCH DRAG (WILL NOT DISENGAGE PROPERLY)			*		*		*	*	*	*	*						*	*
CLUTCH JUDDER	*	*	*				*		*	*	*	*	*					
CLUTCH GRAB (ON ENGAGEMENT)	*	*	*	*			*	*		*	*		*	*				*
CLUTCH NOISE - SQUEAL WHEN DEPRESSING THE PEDAL																*		
CLUTCH NOISE - RATTLE WHEN IDLING			*							*				*				
CLUTCH NOISE - CHATTER ON ENGAGEMENT										*				*				
	a	b	c	d	e	f	g	h	i	j	k	l	m	n	o	p	q	r

PROBABLE CAUSE

a. Insufficient free-play in release linkage.
b. Clutch disc facing worn or hardened.
c. Grease or oil on clutch disc facing.
d. Weak or broken pressure plate coil springs or diaphragm spring.
e. Air in hydraulic system.
f. Insufficient free-travel at clutch pedal.
g. Excessive free-play in release linkage.
h. Misalignment of clutch housing.
i. Clutch disc hub binding on splines of gearbox input shaft.
j. Clutch disc facing loose or broken.
k. Pressure plate mating surface warped.
l. Clutch cover distorted.
m. Looseness in transmission or suspension.
n. Clutch disc distorted.
o. Loose drive plate hub.
p. Release bearing defective.
q. Release arm bent.
r. Low hydraulic fluid level.

REMEDIES

a. Adjust linkage.
b. Replace clutch disc.
c. Clean and remedy cause.
d. Renew springs.
e. Bleed system.
f. Adjust travel.
g. Adjust or renew worn parts.
h. Realign housing.
i. Remove cause of binding.
j. Replace clutch disc.
k. Fit new parts.
l. Replace cover.
m. Take up play.
n. Renew disc.
o. Replace hub.
p. Renew bearing.
q. Straighten or renew.
r. Top up hydraulic fluid.

Trouble Shooting

Steering

SYMPTOMS

	a	b	c	d	e	f	g	h	i	j	k	l	m	n	o	p	q	r	s
STEERING STIFFNESS	*	*	*	*	*	*													
STEERING SLACK				*			*	*	*		*	*	*						
STEERING WANDER	*	*	*	*			*	*	*	*	*	*	*	*	*				
WHEEL SHIMMY			*	*			*	*	*		*	*	*	*	*				
CAR PULLS TO ONE SIDE	*			*			*		*					*	*	*	*	*	
POOR RECOVERY OF STEERING WHEEL TO CENTRE	*	*	*	*	*													*	
EXCESSIVE OR ABNORMAL TYRE WEAR	*			*			*	*	*					*	*	*	*	*	*
	a	b	c	d	e	f	g	h	i	j	k	l	m	n	o	p	q	r	s

PROBABLE CAUSE

a. Tyre pressures incorrect or uneven.
b. Lack of lubricant in steering gear.
c. Lack of lubrication at steering linkage ball joints.
d. Incorrect wheel alignment.
e. Incorrectly adjusted steering gear.
f. Steering column bearings too tight or column bent or misaligned.
g. Steering linkage joints worn or loose.
h. Front wheel bearings worn or incorrectly adjusted.
i. Slackness in front suspension.
j. Road wheel nuts loose.
k. Steering wheel loose.
l. Steering gear mounting bolts loose.
m. Steering gear worn.
n. Shock absorbers defective or mountings loose.
o. Road wheels imbalanced or tyres unevenly worn.
p. Suspension springs weak or broken.
q. Brakes pulling on one side.
r. Chassis frame or suspension misaligned.
s. Improper driving.

REMEDIES

a. Inflate and balance tyres.
b. Inject lubricant.
c. Lubricate.
d. Check steering geometry.
e. Adjust correctly.
f. Adjust renew defective parts.
g. Tighten or replace joints.
h. Adjust or renew bearings.
i. Tighten to correct torque.
j. Tighten nuts to correct torque.
k. Tighten to correct torque.
l. Tighten to correct torque.
m. Replace worn parts.
n. Replace with new.
o. Balance wheels.
p. Renew springs.
q. Balance brakes.
r. Realign.
s. Arrange tuition on driving.

Trouble Shooting

Braking System

SYMPTOMS

	a	b	c	d	e	f	g	h	i	j	k	l	m	n	o	p	q	r	s	t	u	v	w
BRAKE FAILURE					*		*		*		*									*		*	
BRAKES INEFFECTIVE	*	*	*	*	*	*	*	*	*	*						*		*					
BRAKES GRAB OR PULL TO ONE SIDE	*	*	*	*					*		*	*	*	*		*						*	
BRAKES BIND						*								*		*	*	*		*		*	
PEDAL SPONGY					*	*	*	*												*		*	
PEDAL TRAVEL EXCESSIVE	*		*					*			*	*	*			*				*		*	
EXCESSIVE PEDAL PRESSURE REQUIRED	*	*	*		*			*	*											*		*	*
HYDRAULIC SYSTEM WILL NOT MAINTAIN PRESSURE							*	*												*		*	
BRAKE SQUEAL DEVELOPS	*	*	*	*												*		*					
BRAKE SHUDDER DEVELOPS	*	*	*	*							*	*	*			*		*				*	
HANDBRAKE INEFFECTIVE OR REQUIRES EXCESSIVE MOVEMENT	*	*	*	*												*							
	a	b	c	d	e	f	g	h	i	j	k	l	m	n	o	p	q	r	s	t	u	v	w

PROBABLE CAUSE

a. Brake shoe linings or friction pades excessively worn.
b. Incorrect brake shoe linings or friction pads.
c. Brake shoe linings or friction pads contaminated.
d. Brake drums or discs scored.
e. Incorrect brake fluid.
f. Insufficient brake fluid.
g. Air in the hydraulic system.
h. Fluid leak in the hydraulic system.
i. Fluid line blocked.
j. Mal-function in the brake pedal linkage.
k. Unequal tyre pressures.
l. Brake disc or drum distorted or cracked.
m. Brake back plate or calliper mounting bolts loose or looseness in the suspension.
n. Wheel bearings incorrectly adjusted.
o. Weak, broken or improperly installed shoe return springs.
p. Uneven brake lining contact.
q. Incorrect brake lining adjustment.
r. Pistons in wheel cylinder or calliper seized.
s. Weak or broken pedal return spring.
t. Master cylinder defective.
u. Fluid reservoir overfilled or reservoir air vent restricted.
v. Servo vacuum hose disconnected or restricted, or servo unit defective.
w. Wheel cylinder or calliper defective.

REMEDIES

a. Replace linings or pads.
b. Replace with correct linings or pads.
c. Clean thoroughly.
d. Renew drums or discs.
e. Bleed out old fluid and replace with correct type.
f. Top up reservoir.
g. Bleed brake system.
h. Trace and seal.
i. Trace and clear blockage.
j. Correct as necessary.
k. Adjust and balance tyre pressures.
l. Renew disc or drum.
m. Tighten as necessary to correct torque.
n. Adjust wheel bearings.
o. Renew or install correctly.
p. Trace cause and remedy.
q. Adjust correctly.
r. Free and clean.
s. Renew spring.
t. Replace master cylinder and seals.
u. Lower fluid level. Clear air vent.
v. Check and replace hose. Renew servo unit if defective.
w. Replace as necessary;

Trouble Shooting

Electrical Equipment

SYMPTOMS

	a	b	c	d	e	f	g	h	i	j	k	l	m	n	o	p	q	r
STARTER FAILS TO OPERATE	*	*	*	*				*	*									
STARTER OPERATES BUT DOES NOT CRANK ENGINE	*	*	*		*	*	*											
STARTER CRANKS ENGINE SLOWLY	*	*	*															
STARTER NOISY IN OPERATION				*		*	*											
IGNITION WARNING LIGHT REMAINS ILLUMINATED WITH ENGINE AT SPEED		*								*	*	*						
IGNITION WARNING LIGHT FAILS TO ILLUMINATE WHEN IGN. IS SWITCHED ON	*	*							*		*	*						
IGNITION WARNING LIGHT STAYS ON WHEN IGN. IS SWITCHED OFF									*		*	*						
LIGHTS DIM OR WILL NOT ILLUMINATE	*	*									*		*		*	*	*	
BULBS BLOW FREQUENTLY AND BATTERY REQUIRES FREQUENT TOPPING-UP											*							
DIRECTION INDICATORS NOT FUNCTIONING PROPERLY	*	*							*				*		*		*	

a b c d e f g h i j k l m n o p q r

PROBABLE CAUSE

a. Stiff engine.

b. Battery discharged or defective.
c. Broken or loose connection in circuit.
d. Starter pinion jammed in mesh with flywheel ring gear.
e. Starter motor defective.
f. Starter pinion does not engage with flywheel ring gear due to dirt on screwed pinion barrel.
g. Starter drive pinion defective or flywheel ring gear worn.
h. Starter solenoid switch defective.
i. Ignition/starter switch defective.
j. Broken or loose drive belt.
k. Regulator defective.
l. Generator/alternator defective.
m. Bulb burned out.
n. Mounting bolts loose.
o. Fuse blown
p. Light switch defective.
q. Short circuit.
r. Flasher unit defective.

REMEDIES

a. Add a small quantity of oil to the fuel and run the engine carefully.
b. Recharge or replace battery.
c. Trace and rectify.
d. Release pinion.
e. Rectify fault or replace starter motor.
f. Clean and spray with penetrating oil.

g. Replace defective parts.
h. Trace fault, renew if necessary.
i. Renew switch.
j. Replace belt.
k. Adjust or replace.
l. Adjust or replace.
m. Renew bulb,
n. Tighten bolts to correct torque.
o. Replace fuse after ascertaining cause of blowing.
p. Renew switch.
q. Trace and rectify.
r. Replace unit.

Tightening Torques

ENGINE

	m.kg.	lbs./ft.
Cylinder head attaching bolts (tallowed)	6	43.5
2-piece cylinder blocks	5.5	40
1-piece cylinder blocks	5.25	38
Main bearing cap nuts	4	29
Connecting rod bolts	0.75	5.5
Rocker gear cover attaching bolts	9	65
Pinion-to-crankshaft attaching nut	2	14.5
Camshaft chain-wheel attaching bolt	1.5	11
Timing gear housing attaching bolts	1.25	9
Oil passage cover attaching bolts	3.5	25
Oil filter bowl assembling bolt	1.5	11
Oil filter bracket attaching bolts	1.5	11
Generator support attaching bolts	1.3	9.4
Generator attaching collar nut	3.5	25
Water pump shaft nut	2.25	16
Water pump-to-support attaching bolt	1.5	11
Water pump support-to-cylinder block attaching bolt	6.5	47
Crankshaft pulley attaching nut	4	29
Belt tension roller attaching nut	1.75	13
Tension roller support lug attaching bolt	1.75	13
Tension roller adjusting lug attaching bolt		

POWER UNIT MOUNTING

3 POINT MOUNTING

	m.kg.	lbs./ft.
Tie link securing bolts	1.75	13
Engine mounting pad bolts	3.5	25

4 POINT MOUNTING
Upper mounting

		m.kg.	lbs./ft.
Upper intermediate L.H. support	on generator support cylinder	2	14.5
	head and block	3.25	23.5
Upper intermediate R.H. support on timing gear housing		2	14.5
Lower intermediate supports on the L.H and R.H. wing valances		2	14.5
Rubber block		3.25	23.5
Limiting stop		3.25	23.5

Lower mounting

		m.kg.	lbs./ft.
Yoke on front frame		1.25	9
Rubber block	on yoke	1.25	9
	on support	3.25	23.5
Limiting stop		3.25	23.5

CLUTCH

	m.kg	lbs./ft.
Clutch housing to-cylinder block assembling bolts	1.25	9
Clutch cover attaching bolts	1	7.25
Ring gear support-to-plate attaching bolts (180DP-bolt marked "100")	2.75	20
Mechanism assembling bolts (180DP)	1	7.25
Mechanism assembling bolts (200 DE or TS 190 clutch)	2.5	18

GEARBOX AND DIFFERENTIAL ASSEMBLY

		m.kg	lbs./ft.
Nut on lower gear change control rod (Nylstop)		1	7.25
Housing-to-cylinder block assembling bolt		1	7.25
Reverse sliding gear shaft stop bolt		0.75	5.5
Layshaft bearing cap nuts		2.25	16
Layshaft thrust plate bolts		1	7.25
Oil thrower attaching bolts (up to February, 1966)		1	7.25
Gearbox cover attaching bolts		1	7.25
Oil pump strainer attaching bolts		0.75	5.5
Differential assy. assembling bolts		5.75	42
Differential housing-to-gearbox housing			
Gearbox	8 mm dia.	2	14.5
	10 mm dia.	4	29
Differential housing cover attaching bolts		1.75	13
Oil sump securing bolts		1.5	13
Layshaft bearing oil passage union bolt		1.75	13

TRANSMISSION

		m.kg	lbs./ft.
Front axle drive nut		25	181.0
REAR AXLE			
Rear cross-bar support to body attaching bolts	with 8x1.25 dia. bolts	1.75	13
	with 10x1.50 nuts	2.75	20
Cross-bar attaching pin nuts		3.5	25
Rear suspension arm shaft nuts		11	79.7
Shock absorber lower attaching pins		5.5	40
Shock absorber rod nut		1.75	13
Shock absorber support-to-self attaching nuts		1	7.25
Brake plate attaching bolts		3.5	25
Hub nut	with ball bearings pre-torque	3	22
	final torque	1	7.25
	with taper roller bearings	See Class 5	
Anti-roll bar attachment nuts to rear cross bar		3.25	23.5

FRONT AXLE

	m.kg	lbs/ft.
Front cradle attaching bolts	3.25	23.5
Front triangle pivot pin nuts	2.75	20
Shock absorber support-to-wing valance attaching bolts	1	7.25
Hub bearing nut	18	130.1
Hub knuckle-to-steering knuckle attaching bolts	3.5	25
Steering knuckle 10 mm dia.	2.75	20
Ball-head nut 11 mm dia.	3.75	27
Ball joint nut socket cover	0.75	5.5
Shock-absorber cover nut	8	58
Shock-absorber rod nut	4.5	33
Anti-roll to tie link attachment	4.5	33
Anti-roll bar to front triangle, attachment	1.25	9
Anti-roll bar bearing attachment	1	7.25

STEERING GEAR

Steering column attachment nuts	1	7.25
Flector collar to column securing nut	1	7.25
Steering housing attaching screws	3.5	25
Rack coupling finger bolt	3.5	25
Connecting link ball joint nut	4.25	31
Flector assembling screw	1.75	13
Steering wheel attaching nut	4.5	33
Rack eye lock nut	3	22

Special torque for double rod steering gear

Rack link finger bolt	3.5	25

Special torques for single rod steering gear

Flector collar to pinion bolt	1	7.25
Cover bush to housing attachment bolt	1	7.25

BRAKES

Master cylinder-to-pedal support of Mastervac attaching nuts	1	7.25
Mastervac-to-pedal support attaching nuts	0.7	5.07
Brake fluid reservoir attaching screws	1.5	11
Compensator mounting parts	1.75	13
Brake calliper 3 piston callipers attaching screws	7	51
2 piston callipers	5	36
Swivelling union on 3-piston type calliper	2.25	16
Hose fitting on swivelling union	2.3	16.6

ROAD WHEELS

Front and rear road wheel nuts	6	43.5

1965 >   204   PEUGEOT

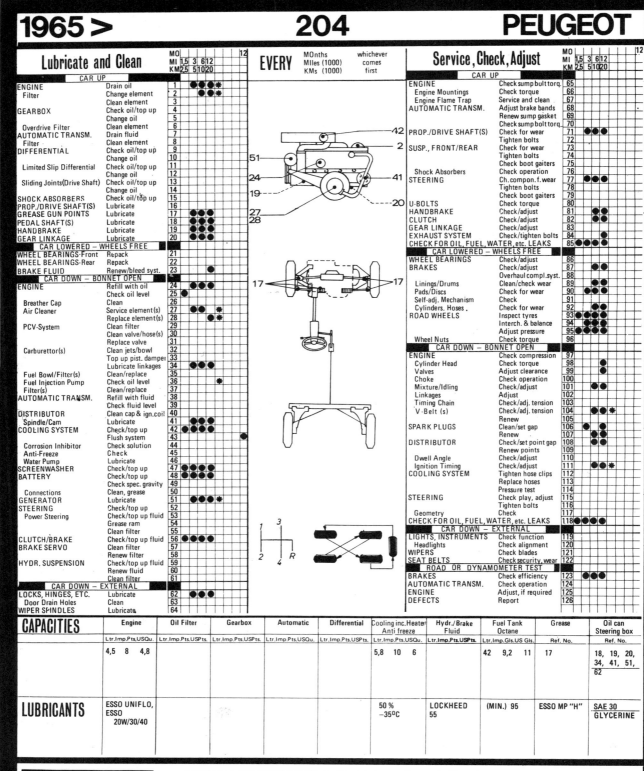

Lubricate and Clean

	Operation	No.	MO MI 1,5 / KM 2,5	3 / 5	6 / 10	12 / 20
CAR UP						
ENGINE	Drain oil	1	●	●	●	*
Filter	Change element	2		●	●	*
	Clean element	3				
GEARBOX	Check oil/top up	4				
	Change oil	5				
Overdrive Filter	Clean element	6				
AUTOMATIC TRANSM.	Drain fluid	7				
Filter	Clean element	8				
DIFFERENTIAL	Check oil/top up	9				
	Change oil	10				
Limited Slip Differential	Check oil/top up	11				
	Change oil	12				
Sliding Joints(Drive Shaft)	Check oil/top up	13				
	Change oil	14				
SHOCK ABSORBERS	Check oil/top up	15				
PROP./DRIVE SHAFT(S)	Lubricate	16				
GREASE GUN POINTS	Lubricate	17	●	●	●	
PEDAL SHAFT(S)	Lubricate	18	●	●	●	
HANDBRAKE	Lubricate	19	●	●	●	
GEAR LINKAGE	Lubricate	20	●	●	●	
CAR LOWERED – WHEELS FREE						
WHEEL BEARINGS-Front	Repack	21				
WHEEL BEARINGS-Rear	Repack	22				
BRAKE FLUID	Renew/bleed syst.	23				●
CAR DOWN – BONNET OPEN						
ENGINE	Refill with oil	24	●	●	●	
	Check oil level	25	●			
Breather Cap	Clean	26				
Air Cleaner	Service element(s)	27		●	●	*
	Replace element(s)	28			●	*
PCV-System	Clean filter	29				
	Clean valve/hose(s)	30				
	Replace valve	31				
Carburettor(s)	Clean jets/bowl	32				
	Top up pist. damper	33				
	Lubricate linkages	34				
Fuel Bowl/Filter(s)	Clean/replace	35				
Fuel Injection Pump	Check oil level	36				*
Filter(s)	Clean/replace	37				
AUTOMATIC TRANSM.	Refill with fluid	38				
	Check fluid level	39				
DISTRIBUTOR	Clean cap & ign.coil	40				
Spindle/Cam	Lubricate	41	●	●	●	
COOLING SYSTEM	Check/top up	42	●	●	●	●
	Flush system	43				●
Corrosion Inhibitor	Check solution	44				
Anti-Freeze	Check	45				
Water Pump	Lubricate	46				
SCREENWASHER	Check/top up	47	●	●	●	
BATTERY	Check/top up	48	●	●	●	
	Check spec. gravity	49				
Connections	Clean, grease	50				
GENERATOR	Lubricate	51	●	●	●	*
STEERING	Check/top up	52				
Power Steering	Check/top up fluid	53				
	Grease ram	54				
	Clean filter	55				
CLUTCH/BRAKE	Check/top up fluid	56	●	●	●	●
BRAKE SERVO	Clean filter	57				
	Renew filter	58				
HYDR. SUSPENSION	Check/top up fluid	59				
	Renew fluid	60				
	Clean filter	61				
CAR DOWN – EXTERNAL						
LOCKS, HINGES, ETC.	Lubricate	62	●	●	●	
Door Drain Holes	Clean	63				
WIPER SPINDLES	Lubricate	64				

EVERY

MOnths / MIles (1000) / KMs (1000) — whichever comes first

Service, Check, Adjust

	Operation	No.	MO MI 1,5 / KM 2,5	3 / 5	6 / 10	12 / 20
CAR UP						
ENGINE	Check sump bolt torq.	65				
Engine Mountings	Check torque	66				
Engine Flame Trap	Service and clean	67				
AUTOMATIC TRANSM.	Adjust brake bands	68				
	Renew sump gasket	69				
	Check sump bolt torq.	70				
PROP./DRIVE SHAFT(S)	Check for wear	71	●	●	●	
	Tighten bolts	72				
SUSP., FRONT/REAR	Check for wear	73				
	Tighten bolts	74				
	Check boot gaiters	75				
Shock Absorbers	Check operation	76				
STEERING	Ch. compon. f. wear	77	●	●	●	
	Tighten bolts	78				
	Check boot gaiters	79				
U-BOLTS	Check torque	80				
HANDBRAKE	Check/adjust	81			●	●
CLUTCH	Check/adjust	82				●
GEAR LINKAGE	Check/adjust	83				
EXHAUST SYSTEM	Check/tighten bolts	84				●
CHECK FOR OIL, FUEL, WATER, etc. LEAKS		85	●	●	●	●
CAR LOWERED – WHEELS FREE						
WHEEL BEARINGS	Check/adjust	86				
BRAKES	Check/adjust	87				
	Overhaul compl.syst.	88				
Linings/Drums	Clean/check wear	89			●	●
Pads/Discs	Check for wear	90	●	●	●	
Self-adj. Mechanism	Check	91				
Cylinders, Hoses.	Check for wear	92			●	●
ROAD WHEELS	Inspect tyres	93	●	●	●	●
	Interch. & balance	94			●	
	Adjust pressure	95	●	●	●	●
Wheel Nuts	Check torque	96				
CAR DOWN – BONNET OPEN						
ENGINE	Check compression	97				
Cylinder Head	Check torque	98				●
Valves	Adjust clearance	99				●
Choke	Check operation	100				
Mixture/Idling	Check/adjust	101			●	●
Linkages	Adjust	102				
Timing Chain	Check/adj. tension	103				
V-Belt(s)	Check/adj. tension	104			●	● *
	Renew	105				
SPARK PLUGS	Clean/set gap	106			●	●
	Renew	107				● ●
DISTRIBUTOR	Check/set point gap	108			●	●
	Renew points	109				
Dwell Angle	Check/adjust	110				
Ignition Timing	Check/adjust	111			●	● *
COOLING SYSTEM	Tighten hose clips	112				
	Replace hoses	113				
	Pressure test	114				
STEERING	Check play, adjust	115				
	Tighten bolts	116				
Geometry	Check	117				
CHECK FOR OIL, FUEL, WATER, etc. LEAKS		118	●	●	●	●
CAR DOWN – EXTERNAL						
LIGHTS, INSTRUMENTS	Check function	119				
Headlights	Check alignment	120				
WIPERS	Check blades	121				
SEAT BELTS	Check security, wear	122				
ROAD OR DYNAMOMETER TEST						
BRAKES	Check efficiency	123	●	●	●	
AUTOMATIC TRANSM.	Check operation	124				
ENGINE	Adjust, if required	125				
DEFECTS	Report	126				

CAPACITIES

	Engine	Oil Filter	Gearbox	Automatic	Differential	Cooling inc.Heater Anti freeze	Hydr./Brake Fluid	Fuel Tank Octane	Grease	Oil can Steering box
	Ltr.Imp.Pts.USQu.	Ltr.Imp.Pts.USPts.	Ltr.Imp.Pts.USPts.	Ltr.Imp.Pts.USPts.	Ltr.Imp.Pts.USPts.	Ltr.Imp.Pts.USQu.	Ltr.Imp.Pts.USPts.	Ltr.Imp.Gls.US Gls.	Ref. No.	Ref. No.
	4,5 8 4,8					5,8 10 6		42 9,2 11	17	18, 19, 20, 34, 41, 51, 62

LUBRICANTS

	Engine	Cooling inc.Heater Anti freeze	Hydr./Brake Fluid	Fuel Tank Octane	Grease	Oil can Steering box
	ESSO UNIFLO, ESSO 20W/30/40	50 % −35°C	LOCKHEED 55	(MIN.) 95	ESSO MP "H"	SAE 30 GLYCERINE

AUTOSERVICE DATA CHART

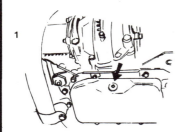
1

2

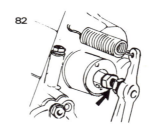
82

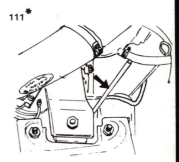
111 *

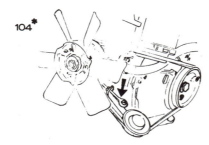
104 *

1-3-4-2

TECHNICAL NOTES

1 — IN THE CASE off intensive driving with frequent stops and starts. ENGINE OIL should be changed every 2,500 KM/1,500 MI.

2 — DIESEL ENGINES - Change OIL FILTER at 15,000 KM/9,000 MI and subsequently every 10,000 KM/6,000 MI.
Bleed the FUEL TANK every 20,000 KM/12,000 MI.
CHECK TIGHTENESS of the bolts and crews of the injection and feed devices, dynamo and starter.

27 — CLEAN ELEMENT by plunging it several times into a mixture of 80 % Diesel oil & 20 % Engine oil. Refit after drip drying.
IF AN OIL BATH AIR CLEANER is fitted-remove the filter and rinse it in diesel oil. Refit after drip drying-Clean the bowl after removing the lower plate. Refit the plate and pour ENGINE OIL into the bowl, covering the MINIMUM LEVEL.

28 — MORE frequently if driving in very dusty roads.

36 — DIESEL ENGINE - Drain water trapped - every 5,000 KM/3,000 MI.

51 — PARIS RHONE only.

104 — SELF - DISENGAGING FAN
The normal gap between the electromagnet and the fan plate is 0,30 and 0,40 mm/,012 and 0,16 in.
Reset the above value by means of the three adjusting screws if required.
FAN BELT TENSION
Fan belt tension should be adjusted only if the belt is loose. The engine should be cold. Belt tension must be adjusted when the engine is cold by moving the lower pulle after having unscrewed the sector screw to obtain an elongation of 2 % - 3 %.

111 — CONCORDANCE between the 8 mm/,31 dig. hole in the clutch housing and the notch on the clutch plate indicates the exact sparking point.

ENGINE DATA

COMPRESSION kg/cm²/psi	VALVE CLEARANCE INLET mm/in.hot(h)/cold(c) OUTLET	IDLING SPEED rpm.	SPARK PLUG GAP mm/inches	DISTR. POINT GAP mm/inches	DWELL ANGLE degrees	STATIC – IGN.-TIMING – STROB. degr.-BTDC degr.-BTDC/rpm.
	0,10 / ,004 (c) 0,25 / ,010	750	0,6 / ,024	0,4 /,016		12

TYRES
Pressure kg/cm²/psi

STANDARD SIZE	FRONT PRESSURE normal/full	REAR PRESSURE normal/full	OPTIONAL SIZE	FRONT PRESSURE normal/full	REAR PRESSURE normal/full	BRAKES	MINIMUM THICKNESS SHOE mm/in. PAD
145 x 14	—	—					2 / ,08
MICHELIN X	1,5 / 22,5	1,9/28,5 2,5/35					
DUNLOP SPEC.	1,6 / 23	2,1/30,5 2,5/35					
KLEBER-COLOMBES V 10	1,7 / 24	2,2/31,5 2,5/35					

STEERING GEOMETRY

TEST LOAD kg/lbs.	TOE-IN(i)/OUT(o) front-mm/in.	CAMBER degrees/min.	CASTOR degrees/min.	KING PIN INCLN. degrees/min.	TOE-IN(i)/OUT(o) rear-mm/in.	CAMBER degrees/min.	TOE-ON TURNS degr.at degr. LOCK	
NIL	(o) 2 ± 1/,08 ± ,04	1/2	1/2	9 1/2				

TORQUE VALUES
mkg/lb.ft.

65	80	84	86	96	98	V-BELT TENSION mm/inches	RAD. CAP. PRESS. kg/cm²/psi	CLUTCH PLAY mm/inches
					5 - 6 / 36,2 - 43,4	*		2,7 / 10

TBA

MICHELIN X KLEBER-COLOMB. DUNLOP SPECIAL 145 x 14	12 V / 40 Ah	MARCHAL GT 34 D AC 42 XL CHAMPION N6Y		PD 1109, 08			

AUTOSERVICE DATA CHART

Lubricate and Clean

Intervals — MO / MI: 1,5 3 6 12   KM: 2,5 5 10 20   / 12

CAR UP

Item	Operation	No.
ENGINE	Drain oil	1
Filter	Change element	2
	Clean element	3
GEARBOX	Check oil/top up	4
	Change oil	5
Overdrive Filter	Clean element	6
AUTOMATIC TRANSM.	Drain fluid	7
Filter	Change element	8
DIFFERENTIAL	Check oil/top up	9
	Change oil	10
Limited Slip Differential	Check oil/top up	11
	Change oil	12
Sliding Joints(Drive Shaft)	Check oil/top up	13
	Change oil	14
SHOCK ABSORBERS	Check oil/top up	15
PROP./DRIVE SHAFT(S)	Lubricate	16
GREASE GUN POINTS	Lubricate	17
PEDAL SHAFT(S)	Lubricate	18
HANDBRAKE	Lubricate	19
GEAR LINKAGE	Lubricate	20

CAR LOWERED – WHEELS FREE

Item	Operation	No.
WHEEL BEARINGS-Front	Repack	21
WHEEL BEARINGS-Rear	Repack	22
BRAKE FLUID	Renew/bleed syst.	23

CAR DOWN – BONNET OPEN

Item	Operation	No.
ENGINE	Refill with oil	24
	Check oil level	25
Breather Cap	Clean	26
Air Cleaner	Service element(s)	27
	Replace element(s)	28
PCV-System	Clean filter	29
	Clean valve/hose(s)	30
	Replace valve	31
Carburettor(s)	Clean jets/bowl	32
	Top up pist. damper	33
	Lubricate linkages	34
Fuel Bowl/Filter(s)	Clean/replace	35
Fuel Injection Pump	Check oil level	36
Filter(s)	Clean/replace	37
AUTOMATIC TRANSM.	Refill with fluid	38
	Check fluid level	39
DISTRIBUTOR	Clean cap & ign.coil	40
Spindle/Cam	Lubricate	41
COOLING SYSTEM	Check/top up	42
	Flush system	43
Corrosion Inhibitor	Check solution	44
Anti-Freeze	Check	45
Water Pump	Lubricate	46
SCREENWASHER	Check/top up	47
BATTERY	Check/top up	48
	Check spec. gravity	49
Connections	Clean, grease	50
GENERATOR	Lubricate	51
STEERING	Check/top up	52
Power Steering	Check/top up fluid	53
	Grease ram	54
	Clean filter	55
CLUTCH/BRAKE	Check/top up fluid	56
BRAKE SERVO	Clean filter	57
	Renew filter	58
HYDR. SUSPENSION	Check/top up fluid	59
	Renew fluid	60
	Clean filter	61

CAR DOWN – EXTERNAL

Item	Operation	No.
LOCKS, HINGES, ETC.	Lubricate	62
Door Drain Holes	Clean	63
WIPER SPINDLES	Lubricate	64

EVERY

MOnths / MIles (1000) / KMs (1000) — whichever comes first

(Central diagrams — engine lubrication points 42, 2, 51, 24, 41, 19, 20, 27, 28; underbody points 17 – 17; gearshift pattern 1 2 3 4 R; wheel rotation diagram)

Service, Check, Adjust

Intervals — MO / MI: 1,5 3 6 12   KM: 2,5 5 10 20   / 12

CAR UP

Item	Operation	No.
ENGINE	Check sump bolt torq.	65
Engine Mountings	Check torque	66
Engine Flame Trap	Service and clean	67
AUTOMATIC TRANSM.	Adjust brake bands	68
	Renew sump gasket	69
	Check sump bolt torq.	70
PROP./DRIVE SHAFT(S)	Check for wear	71
	Tighten bolts	72
SUSP., FRONT/REAR	Check for wear	73
	Tighten bolts	74
	Check boot gaiters	75
Shock Absorbers	Check operation	76
STEERING	Ch.compon.f.wear	77
	Tighten bolts	78
	Check boot gaiters	79
U-BOLTS	Check torque	80
HANDBRAKE	Check/adjust	81
CLUTCH	Check/adjust	82
GEAR LINKAGE	Check/adjust	83
EXHAUST SYSTEM	Check/tighten bolts	84
CHECK FOR OIL, FUEL, WATER, etc. LEAKS		85

CAR LOWERED – WHEELS FREE

Item	Operation	No.
WHEEL BEARINGS	Check/adjust	86
BRAKES	Check/adjust	87
	Overhaul compl. syst	88
Linings/Drums	Clean/check wear	89
Pads/Discs	Check for wear	90
Self-adj. Mechanism	Check	91
Cylinders. Hoses	Check for wear	92
ROAD WHEELS	Inspect tyres	93
	Interch. & balance	94
	Adjust pressure	95
Wheel Nuts	Check torque	96

CAR DOWN – BONNET OPEN

Item	Operation	No.
ENGINE	Check compression	97
Cylinder Head	Check torque	98
Valves	Adjust clearance	99
Choke	Check operation	100
Mixture/Idling	Check/adjust	101
Linkages	Adjust	102
Timing Chain	Check/adj. tension	103
V-Belt(s)	Check/adj. tension	104
	Renew	105
SPARK PLUGS	Clean/set gap	106
	Renew	107
DISTRIBUTOR	Check/set point gap	108
	Renew points	109
Dwell Angle	Check/adjust	110
Ignition Timing	Check/adjust	111
COOLING SYSTEM	Tighten hose clips	112
	Replace hoses	113
	Pressure test	114
STEERING	Check play, adjust	115
	Tighten bolts	116
Geometry	Check	117
CHECK FOR OIL, FUEL, WATER, etc. LEAKS		118

CAR DOWN – EXTERNAL

Item	Operation	No.
LIGHTS, INSTRUMENTS	Check function	119
Headlights	Check alignment	120
WIPERS	Check blades	121
SEAT BELTS	Check security, wear	122

ROAD OR DYNAMOMETER TEST

Item	Operation	No.
BRAKES	Check efficiency	123
AUTOMATIC TRANSM.	Check operation	124
ENGINE	Adjust, if required	125
DEFECTS	Report	126

CAPACITIES

	Engine	Oil Filter	Gearbox	Automatic	Differential	Cooling inc.Heater Anti freeze	Hydr./Brake Fluid	Fuel Tank Octane	Grease	Oil can Steering box
	Ltr.Imp.Pts.USQu.	Ltr.Imp.Pts.USPts.	Ltr.Imp.Pts.USPts.	Ltr.Imp.Pts.USQu.	Ltr.Imp.Pts.USPts.	Ltr.Imp.Pts.USQu.	Ltr.Imp.Pts.USPts.	Ltr.Imp.Gls.US Gls.	Ref. No.	Ref. No.
	4 7 4,2					5,8 10 6		42 9,2 11	17	18, 19, 20, 34, 41, 51, 62

LUBRICANTS

	Engine	Cooling	Hydr./Brake	Fuel Tank	Grease	Oil can / Steering box
	ESSO UNIFLO. ESSO 20W/30/40	50% −35°C	LOCKHEED 55	95	ESSO MP "H"	SAE 30 GLYCERINE

AUTOSERVICE DATA CHART

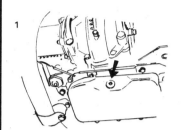
1

2

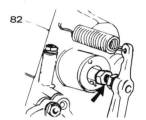
82

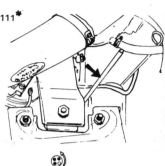
111*

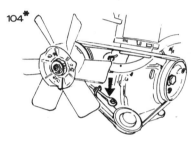
104*

1-3-4-2

TECHNICAL NOTES

1 – IN THE CASE off intensive driving with frequent stops and starts. ENGINE OIL should be changed every 2,500 KM/1,500 MI.

27 – CLEAN ELEMENT by plunging it several times into a mixture of 80 % Diesel oil & 20 % Engine oil. Refit after drip drying.
IF AN OIL BATH AIR CLEANER is fitted-remove the filter and rinse it in diesel oil.
Refit after drip drying-Clean the bowl after removing the lower plate.
Refit the plate and pour ENGINE OIL into the bowl, covering the MINIMUM LEVEL.

28 – MORE frequently if driving in very dusty roads.

51 – PARIS PHONE only.

104 – SELF-DISENGAGING FAN
The normal gap between the electromagnet and the fan plate is 0,30 and 0,40 mm/,012 and ,016 in.
Reset the above value by means of the three adjusting screws if required.
FAN BELT TENSION
Fan belt tension should be adjusted only if the belt is loose. The engine should be cold.
Belt tension must be adjusted when the engine is cold by moving the lower idler pulley after having unscrewed the sector screw, to obtain an elongation of 2 % - 3 %.

111 – CONCORDANCE between the 8 mm/,31 in dig. hole in the clutch housing and the notch on the clutch plate indicates the exact sparking point.

ENGINE DATA

COMPRESSION kg/cm²/psi	VALVE CLEARANCE INLET mm/in.hot(h)/cold(c) OUTLET	IDLING SPEED rpm.	SPARK PLUG GAP mm/inches	DISTR. POINT GAP mm/inches	DWELL ANGLE degrees	STATIC – IGN.-TIMING – STROB. degr.-BTDC degr.-BTDC/rpm.
	0,10 / ,004 (c) 0,25 / ,010	750	0,6 / ,024	0,4 / ,016		12

TYRES
Pressure kg/cm²/psi

STANDARD SIZE	FRONT PRESSURE normal/full	REAR PRESSURE normal/full	OPTIONAL SIZE	FRONT PRESSURE normal/full	REAR PRESSURE normal/full	BRAKES	MINIMUM THICKNESS SHOE mm/in. PAD	
145 x 355								2 / ,08
MICHELIN X DUNLOP SPEC.	1,6 / 23 1,8 / 26	1,9 / 27 2,1 / 29						

STEERING GEOMETRY

TEST LOAD kg/lbs.	TOE-IN(i)/OUT(o) front-mm/in.	CAMBER degrees/min.	CASTOR degrees/min.	KING PIN INCLN. degrees/min.	TOE-IN(i)/OUT(o) rear-mm/in.	CAMBER degrees/min.	TOE-ON TURNS degr.at degr. LOCK	
NIL	(o) 2 ± 1/,08 ± ,04	1/2	· 1/2	9 1/2				

TORQUE VALUES
mkg/lb.ft.

65	80	84	86	96	98	V-BELT TENSION mm/inches	RAD. CAP. PRESS. kg/cm²/psi	CLUTCH PLAY mm/inches
					4 - 5,5 / 29 - 39,5	*		2,7 / ,10

TBA

145 x 355	12 V / 40 Ah	AC 42 XL CHAMPION N7Y		PD 1109, 11				

AUTOSERVICE DATA CHART

Part Names and Alternatives

Certain parts of motor cars are known by other names in different
areas and countries. A list of the common alternatives is given below.

ENGINE

Gudgeon pin	Piston pin, small end pin, Wrist pin
Inlet valve	Intake valve
Piston oil control ring	Piston scraper ring
Induction manifold	Inlet manifold, intake manifold
Oil sump	Oil pan, Oil reservoir, Sump tray
Core Plug	Expansion plug, Welch plug, Sealing disc
Dipstick	Oil dipper rod, Oil level gauge rod, Oil level indicator
Silencer	Muffler, expansion box, diffuser
Tappets	Valve lifter, push rods

FUEL

Carburettor choke	Carburettor venturi
Slow running jet	Low speed jet, Idler jet
Volume control screw	Idling mixture screw
Fuel pump	Petrol pump, Fuel lift pump
Air cleaner	Air silencer, Muffler
Fuel tank	Petrol Tank
Accelerator	Throttle

CLUTCH

Clutch release bearing	Throwout bearing, Thrust bearing
Clutch lining	Disc facing, Friction ring
Spigot bearing	Clutch pilot bearing
Clutch housing	Bell housing

GEARBOX

Gearbox	Transmission
Gear lever	Change speed lever, Gearshift lever
Selector fork	Change speed fork, Shift fork
Input shaft	Constant motion shaft, First motion shaft, drive gear, First reduction pinion. Main drive pinion, Clutch shaft, Clutch gear
Countershaft	Layshaft
Synchro cone	Synchronizing ring
Reverse Idler gear	Reverse pinion

REAR AXLE

Rear Axle	Final drive unit
Crown wheel	Ring gear, Final drive gear, Spiral drive gear
Bevel pinion	Small pinion, spiral drive pinion
"U" bolts	Spring clips
Axle shaft	Half shaft, Hub driving shaft, Jack driving shaft
Differential gear	Sun wheel
Differential pinion	Planet wheel

ELECTRICAL

Generator	Dynamo
Control box	Cut out, Voltage regulator, Voltage control, Circuit breaker
Capacitor	Condenser
Interior light	Dome lamp
Lens	Glass
Head lamp ring	Headlamp surround, Headlamp moulding
Direction indicators	Signal lamps, Flashers
Micrometer adjustment	Octane selector
Rear lamps	Tail lamps
Reversing light	Back-up light

STEERING

Drop arm	Pitman arm
Rocker shaft	Pitman shaft, Drop arm shaft
Swivel pin	Pivot pin, King pin, Steering pin
Stub axle	Swivel axle
Track rod	Cross tube, Tie rod
Drag link	Side tube, Steering connecting rod
Steering column	Steering gear shaft
Steering column bearing	Mast jacket bearing
Steering arm	Steering knuckle arm
Stator tube	Control tube
Steering joints	Steering knuckles

BRAKES

Master cylinder	Main cylinder
Brake shoe lining	Brake shoe facing

BODY

Bonnet	Hood
Luggage locker	Boot, Luggage compartment
Luggage locker lid	Boot lid, Rear deck
Mudguards	Quarter panels, Fenders, Mud wings
Roof	Canopy
Nave plate	Wheel disc, Hub cap
Finishing strip	Moulding, Chrome strip
Windscreen	Windshield
Rear window	Rear windscreen, Rear windshield Backlight
Quarter vent	(N.D.V.) No draught ventilator
Bumpers	Fenders
Loom	Harness
Odometer	Trip recorder
Bonnet catch	Hood latch
Kerosene	Paraffin
Boot	Trunk